JEWISH

COMMUNITIES

OF THE WORLD

EDITED BY DR. AVI BEKER

LERNER PUBLICATIONS COMPANY

INSTITUTE OF THE WORLD JEWISH CONGRESS

This edition first published in the United States in 1998 by Lerner Publications Company
241 First Avenue North, Minneapolis, Minnesota 55401, U.S.A.
Website address: www.lernerbooks.com

This book is available in two editions:
ISBN: 0–8225–1934–8 (hardcover)
ISBN: 0–8225–9822–1 (paperback)

LIBRARY OF CONGRESS CATALOGING-IN-PUBLICATION DATA

Jewish communities of the world / edited by Dr. Avi Beker.
      Previously published: Institute of the World Jewish Congress, 1996.
      Includes index.
      ISBN 0–8225–1934–8
      1. Jews—Politics and government—1948–   I. Beker, Avi.
DS143.J455 1997
909.82—dc21   97–19189

Cover images (top to bottom):
Torah shield, Poland, mid-18th century
The menorah, symbol of the State of Israel
Jewish amulet, Persia, mid-18th century

Manufactured in the United States of America
1 2 3 4 5 6 – JR – 03 02 01 00 99 98

TABLE OF CONTENTS

PREFACE

For Jews, to paraphrase Dickens, this is "the best of times and the worst of times." Never has Israel been as strong or enjoyed greater recognition among the family of nations. Nor has North American Jewry been so comfortable and confident. Most of the Jews of Latin America live in democracies, and those in western Europe enjoy freedoms comparable to their brethren in North America. There is a Jewish reawakening in eastern Europe and the former Soviet Union, and Jews who elect to leave for Israel or elsewhere can do so freely. However, the figures on Jewish demography in this volume show the bad news. Many Jews are choosing not to be Jewish.

Today the most insidious threat to Jews and Judaism is not from traditional anti-Semitism in its many varieties, but rather that posed by Jews who opt out of Judaism. Instead of harping on "Jewish continuity" we have to look for a daring new approach, both innovative and imaginative. We cannot simply continue "business as usual." Jewish dispersion, as this guide demonstrates, encompasses more than 100 countries around the globe. However, modern communication technology can help us to create our own global Jewish village—but only if we join forces to implement a new strategy.

Keeping Diaspora Jewry alive (and growing) means personally reviving the traditions of learning which have sustained our communities for two millennia. We must find out how to imbue succeeding generations with the beauty of our traditions, and teach the fulfillment that can only come from leading a Jewish life.

The motto of the World Jewish Congress was taken from the Talmudic proverb "All Jews are responsible for each other" (כל ישראל ערבים זה בזה). *Today Jewish responsibility takes on new dimensions, a new meaning that remains critical to our survival as a people.*

Edgar M. Bronfman
President of the World Jewish Congress
New York, January 1998

Chief Editor:	Dr. Avi Beker
Associate Editor:	Dr. Laurence Weinbaum
Managing Editor:	Ziva Fox
Senior Contributing Editor:	Arieh Doobov
Contributing Editors:	Mordechai Arbell (on the Caribbean)
	Simona Kedmi
	Robin Kolodny
Editorial Advisor:	Dr. Geoffrey Wigoder
Copy Editors:	Rachel P. Cohen, Hella Moritz
Administrative Assistant:	Hana Kimche
Design and Production:	Kesem, Kibbutz Saad

ACKNOWLEDGMENTS

The Institute of the World Jewish Congress gratefully acknowledges the help of the following individuals (and Jewish communities) throughout the world in reviewing entries and providing information:

Yvan Ceresnjes (Bosnia and Herzegovina), Dr. Mikhail Chlenov (C.I.S.), David Cohen-Paraira (Netherlands), Gela and Charlie Danziger (Guatemala), Helena Datner and Leszek Piszewski (Poland), Keren Durant-Jacobs (Indonesia), Eileen Franklin (Asia and Oceania), Charles Hoffman (Ukraine), Sami Kahan (Finland), Rabbi James Lebau (Japan), Ilja Lempertas (Lithuania), Sam Levy (Portugal), Maureen Malkinson (Ireland), Isabella Nespoli (Belgium, Italy, Portugal, and Spain), Renee Neuman-Fenton (Sweden), Dr. Serruya Oro (Brazil), Marcia and Maurice Ostroff (Zimbabwe), Marlena Schmol (U.K.), Dina Segal (Mexico), Dr. Shlomo Shafir (Germany), Paula Siler (South Africa), Josef Zissels (Ukraine), Naomi Zubkova (C.I.S.).

Jewish communities that replied to WJC Institute questionnaire:
Argentina, Austria, Bolivia, Canada, Chile, Colombia, Croatia, Czech Republic, Ecuador, England, Estonia, Fiji, Greece, Hong Kong, Hungary, India, Japan, South Korea, Lithuania, Mexico, New Caledonia, Paraguay, the Philippines, Poland, Portugal, Russia, Singapore, Sweden, Taiwan, Thailand, Turkey, Yugoslavia.

Other sources:
U.O. Schmelz and Sergio Della Pergola, the Division of Jewish Demography and Statistics of the Hebrew University of Jerusalem, Israel Central Bureau of Statistics, Jewish Agency, Encyclopaedia Judaica, periodic reports from communities, WJC publications and documents, and others.

INTRODUCTION:
THE QUESTION OF JUDAISM

Theodor Herzl's immortal words, written after the first Zionist Congress in Basel in September 1897, stand as pillars in Jewish consciousness: "At Basel I founded the Jewish state... Perhaps in five years, but certainly in fifty, everyone will know it." Indeed, it took 50 years and a few months for the State of Israel to come into being. After 2,000 years of exile, the Diaspora faced a sovereign Jewish state.

A lesser known aspect of Herzl's vision dealt with the future of the Jewish Diaspora after the creation of the Jewish state. In November 1899, he wrote to Czar Nicholas II:

> We do not intend to bring about the emigration of all Jews... We know that those who live in comfort will not leave... Zionism solves the Jewish question on the one hand by letting out those elements who cannot integrate and on the other hand it accelerates the full assimilation of those left behind. These will be integrated with the majority population, perhaps with their religion and through intermarriages. In the next generation they will disappear and with them all the ugly burden for both Christians and Jews.

Similarly in *Altneuland,* Herzl wrote that 20 years after the establishment of the Jewish state the emancipation would be an established fact, and Jews would be able to assimilate openly without fear.

Almost 50 years after the establishment of the state and 100 years after the first Zionist Congress, Herzl's statement on the future of the Diaspora seems prophetic, providing a realistic assessment of the state of world Jewry today.

The trends, as reflected in this volume, demonstrate how the demographic map of world Jewry has been drastically altered. With the continuing *aliya* and its natural growth, Israel is expected in the coming decade to overtake the United States as the world's largest Jewish community and to become home to the majority of world Jewry. In the Diaspora the number of Jews is dwindling. Demographically the Jewish people has never recovered from the Holocaust and is far from attaining its pre-war numerical strength of 18 million, to say nothing of the lost reproductive potential of that segment of the population which perished at the hands of the Nazis.

The loss was qualitative as well as quantitative because the Jews of eastern Europe were both the demographic reservoir of the Jewish people and the heart and soul of Judaism. Eastern Europe was the incubator for new ideas, movements, and culture for world Jewry.

The estimated strength of world Jewry today is little more than 13 million. We say "estimated" not just because of the traditional Jewish reluctance to count its people, but also because of the impossible task of reaching out to so many unaffiliated Jews in the Diaspora. When the children of Israel wandered in the desert, having escaped from Egyptian bondage, they were instructed by God in the Book of Exodus to count their rank and file by indirect means (through the half shekel coin which everyone deposited) so as to avoid the evil eye and the plague. However, at the beginning of the Book of Numbers, the great commentator Rashi explains that God's love for his people was reflected in his continuous desire to count them.

The compilation of the Jewish communities of the world, and the statistical information which it contains, has also been produced out of love and concern for the Jewish people. This approach explains why such an encyclopedic type of work on the history and life of Jewish communities carries an alarmist tone concerning the threat of assimilation.

We collected our data from demographic and other academic studies, community reports, and updates in the general media. We also consulted with experts to verify our findings before reaching our assessments and estimates. We would welcome comments, suggestions, and corrections.

Even the figure of 13 million Jews is optimistic and will be dismissed by some experts. It is not just a matter of defining "who is a Jew?" but rather identifying what American demographers call the "core" Jewish population. According to the definition of the survey on American Jewry (see p. 30), core Jews include those who report adherence to Judaism, Jews by choice, and born Jews without a current religion ("secular Jews"). While the overall figure in America is 5.6 million Jews, there are 4.1 million core Jews of whom only 3.5 million belong to families in which both parents are Jews. The shocking news on intermarriage only reconfirmed what was already felt: more than 50% of the Jews in the United States who married during the 1980s chose a non-Jewish partner (of which only 1 in 20 has become Jewish). Add to this the low birth rate and the growing phenomenon of Jewish singles, and the future seems ominous. The decline in American Jewry is even sharper in relation to the general American population, which doubled from its post-war figure to 270 million. During the same period, the percentage of Jews in America dropped from 4% to 2% today (with no discernible impact on their social and political influence). Some Jewish observers dismiss these worries, claiming that the Jewish people was never in competition with the Chinese. Although Jews were never great in numbers, they have always made a qualitative contribution to society. Some of those contributions are enumerated here. However, despite our pride and satisfaction, we cannot reject the feeling that our book deals with an endangered species.

The European and Latin American scenes are not more encouraging. In Argentina over the past two decades, like in Britain and New York City over four decades, the actual number of Jews has declined by about one-third. There is a revival in tradition and observance in some Diaspora pockets in the United States, France, and elsewhere, but it mainly affects those segments who were already active and affiliated. For about 80% to 90% of the Diaspora Jews, this phenomenon is irrelevant. Even worse, the strengthening of Orthodoxy and ultra-Orthodoxy has often led to growing polarization, schism, and ghettoization in many communities.

In reviewing Jewish communities of the world, our estimates are that there are about 500,000 ultra-Orthodox Jews in Israel and 350,000 in the Diaspora, most of them in the United States. All in all, Orthodox Jewry in the Diaspora, including the modern Orthodox (or religious-Zionists as they are called in Israel), accounts for about 1 million (the majority are in the United States). Our estimates indicate that there are almost twice as many Orthodox in America as the 6% of the American federations survey. In the major concentrations of Jewish ultra-Orthodoxy, there is very little interaction with the rest of the community (e.g., in New York, Los Angeles, Miami, Toronto, Montreal, London, or Antwerp). In Paris the Sephardi ultra-Orthodox are relatively more involved in the Jewish community at large, essentially because the latter is traditional and respects Orthodox religious practices. This polarization between Orthodox and non-Orthodox (including secular Jews) is perhaps the major division and source of internal conflict in Jewish life today in Israel and in the Diaspora, and to some extent it has created two different peoples. The crisis in Israel (see pp. 22–24) is projected to the Diaspora, for there is much interdependence among the Orthodox communities around the world. The basic difference is that in Israel the conflict affects the democratic process, coalition-building in the Knesset, and allocation of national resources, and it frequently requires the intervention of the Supreme Court. In the Diaspora, the divisions are sometimes total, with no interaction between parts of the organized Jewish community, each operating on its own vis-a-vis the non-Jewish environment.

Although there are no Jewish communities outside Israel with a positive balance of natural growth (a phenomenon which exists only in Orthodox communities), there are a few places that, due to Jewish immigration, have increased their population at the expense of other Jewish communities. The most impressive and consistent growth occurred in Canada, which in about three decades increased its Jewish population by 50%. In Germany the pace of growth has been even higher. Within about two decades, it doubled its Jewish population to 60,000 (although immigrants from the former Soviet Union or from Israel are, for the most part, not yet integrated into the community). Some growth was recorded in Brazil (130,000), and among small communities, the most outstanding have been Panama (7,000) and Hong Kong (2,500), which tripled their numbers in two decades.

There are different sources of contemporary Jewish mobility and immigration that shape the size and distribution of world Jewry. The Jews of the former Soviet Union, most of whom settled in Israel, represent the greatest source of mobility. However, tens of thousands chose to settle in the United States, Canada, Germany, and Austria. Jews who left South Africa went to the United States, Canada, Australia, and Israel. About 500,000 Israelis have left the state since its establishment. Many of them have children and grandchildren born abroad. They live primarily in the United States (350,000–400,000), Canada (40,000), France (40,000), the United Kingdom (30,000), South Africa (10,000), Germany (8,000), Australia (5,000), and in many other smaller Jewish communities. In some cases, particularly in smaller Jewish communities, the Israelis help to foster ties between Israel and the Diaspora, and they also serve as teachers of Judaic studies. However, the majority live outside the framework of the local Jewish community and are not integrated into its activities.

There is continuing uncertainty concerning the future of Jews in the former Soviet Union. In our research, it was difficult to determine their numbers. While academic demographers tend to present conservative figures in Russia (300,000) and Ukraine (180,000), the records of those who deal with *aliya* to Israel are different. We need to have broader definitions of Jewish identity (sometimes just the potential of identity), since experience has shown that many who are uncounted by the demographers may end up as immigrants and Israeli citizens in accordance with the Law of Return. However, our figures for Russia (450,000) and Ukraine (310,000) in 1997 do not say much about the intensity of Jewish life there. Fewer than 20% of the Jews in the former Soviet Union are currently involved in Jewish communal activity of any kind (in Ukraine the figures are more encouraging than in Russia). If we elect to use the criteria of active Jewish affiliation, we end up with fewer than 5 million Jews in the entire Diaspora, and, together with Israel, fewer than 10 million in the world today.

Still one cannot dismiss the revival and reawakening of Jewish life in the former Soviet Union and eastern Europe. The flurry of Jewish activity in these countries is impressive. It has taken a rather different direction from that planned by *aliya* authorities in Israel. Under assumptions from the days of Communist oppression, Israeli emissaries did not encourage the local self-organization of Jewish communities in the former Soviet Union. The irony is that although many of the activities there were organized by Israel-oriented bodies, some of them helped to develop local Jewish identity, which laid the foundation for the beginning of Jewish communal life in the post-totalitarian era.

The growing gap between Israel and the Diaspora should be another cause for concern. As the concern for Israel's survival eases, Jews in Israel and in the Diaspora have began to turn inward. Although many Jews in the Diaspora still subscribe to the centrality of Israel as a pillar of faith, in practice the priorities and resources of most communities are being diverted to the local needs of Jewish education and social welfare. Opposing trends in Israel and the Diaspora reinforce the alienation. In the Diaspora, the return to tradition and religion (in a pluralistic sense) is regarded as important for the preservation of Jewish identity by Jews of all religious strands. In Israel, however, and especially in the wake of the domestic debate on the peace process, the dominant non-religious society is moving in the opposite direction. In this book we focused mainly on the Jewish character of Israel and less on its economy and foreign policy.

Israelis can rightly take pride in the fact that in their society intermarriage barely exists and that the Jewish state is the home of 40% of the Jewish school-age population in the world and two-thirds of the enrollment in Jewish schools. There is no doubt that Israel has become the dominant force in contemporary Jewish identity and culture worldwide, but this cannot be guaranteed forever. The question which is looming over Israel's future has to do with the post-Zionist debate, which has already left the academic ivory towers and is reflected in the mass media and social discourse. It is still too early to determine whether post-Zionism is just a passing mood or a historic trend ushering in an era that, according to some of its voices, aims to establish an Israeli republic free of Jewish content.

The strong desire of many Israelis to return to "normalcy" after so many years of tensions and threats comes precisely at a time when there is a need for greater Israeli involvement in Diaspora life. Naturally the relationship between Israel and the Jews abroad presents a unique and abnormal phenomenon. The words of our sages in the Talmud tractate of *Pesahim* are perplexing but reflect the realities of the Jewish condition: "God did a favor for the Jews in dispersing them among the nations," ‏"צדקה עשה הקב"ה עם ישראל שפזרן לבין האומות"‏. This can be interpreted as a Diasporist point of view of Jewish existence, as a reflection on Jewish survivalism through dispersion, or as a vision about the mission of light unto the nations. In any case, it is a realistic statement on Jewish dispersion that Israelis and Zionists must accept in order to reassess the dictum of "negating the Diaspora."

The changing times call for the revival of the concepts of Ahad Ha'am, the Zionist thinker who, at the beginning of the century, envisaged Israel as the spiritual center for the Diaspora. Ahad Ha'am was troubled by the estrangement of the leaders of the Zionist movement, particularly Herzl and Max Nordau, from Jewish values and culture. He accused them of neglecting cultural work that was critical to protect Jews against cultural sterility and assimilation. This particular "crossroads" in Jewish history, to use his term, has arrived. The overall impression from the sum total of entries on more than 120 Jewish communities worldwide is that of a people in a crisis of spirit and identity. With the shifting agenda of Jewish communities, there is a need to devote more attention to the Jewish soul. In the words of Ahad Ha'am, the "Jewish Question" has been superseded by the "Judaism Question."

Avi Beker

Jerusalem, January 1998

WORLD JEWRY

Country	Population	Country	Population	Country	Population
United States	5,600,000	Georgia	13,000	Ecuador	1,000
Israel	4,700,000	Kazakhstan	12,000	Ethiopia	1,000
France	600,000	Austria	10,000	Monaco	1,000
Russia	450,000	Denmark	8,000	Portugal	900
Canada	360,000	Poland	8,000	Zimbabwe	900
Ukraine	310,000	Panama	7,000	Cuba	800
United Kingdom	300,000	Morocco	6,500	Turkmenistan	700
Argentina	230,000	Lithuania	6,000	Luxembourg	600
Brazil	130,000	Slovakia	6,000	Bolivia	500
Australia	95,000	Colombia	5,650	Bosnia and Herzegovina	500
South Africa	92,000	Czech Republic	5,000	Gibraltar	500
Hungary	70,000	Greece	5,000	Yemen	500
Germany	60,000	India	5,000	Kenya	400
Belarus	45,000	New Zealand	5,000	Netherlands Antilles	400
Mexico	40,700	Kyrgystan	3,500	Congo (Zaire)	320
Belgium	40,000	Bulgaria	3,000	Curacao	300
Italy	30,000	Peru	3,000	Jamaica	300
Netherlands	30,000	Puerto Rico	2,500	Singapore	300
Uruguay	30,000	Costa Rica	2,500	U.S. Virgin Islands	300
Venezuela	30,000	Estonia	2,500	Dominican	
Iran	25,000	Hong Kong	2,500	Republic	250
Chile	21,000	Yugoslavia	2,500	Philippines	250
Azerbaijan	20,000	Croatia	2,000	Thailand	250
Turkey	20,000	Japan	2,000	Bahamas	200
Uzbekistan	20,000	Tunisia	1,900	Suriname	200
Moldova	18,000	Tajikistan	1,800	South Korea	150
Sweden	18,000	Norway	1,500	El Salvador	120
Switzerland	18,000	Ireland	1,300	Iraq	120
Latvia	15,000	Guatemala	1,200	Syria	120
Romania	14,000	Finland	1,200	Tahiti	120
Spain	14,000	Paraguay	1,000	Armenia	110

COMMUNITIES WITH FEWER THAN 100 PERSONS

Afghanistan	Cayman Islands	Honduras	Namibia
Albania	China	Indonesia	New Caledonia
Algeria	Cyprus	Lebanon	Nicaragua
Aruba	Egypt	Macedonia	Reunion
Bahrain	Fiji	Malta	Slovenia
Barbados	French Guyana	Martinique	Taiwan
Bermuda	Guadeloupe	Mozambique	Zambia
Botswana	Haiti	Myanmar (Burma)	

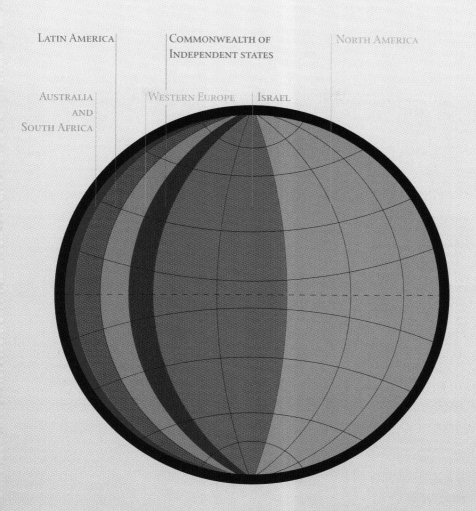

LATIN AMERICA

COMMONWEALTH OF
INDEPENDENT STATES

NORTH AMERICA

AUSTRALIA
AND
SOUTH AFRICA

WESTERN EUROPE

ISRAEL

CITIES WITH LARGEST JEWISH POPULATION IN THE DIASPORA*

New York, U.S.A.	1,900,000		Moscow, Russia	200,000
Los Angeles, U.S.A.	585,000		Buenos Aires, Argentina	180,000
Miami, U.S.A.	535,000		Toronto, Canada	175,000
Paris, France	350,000		Washington, D.C., U.S.A.	165,000
Philadelphia, U.S.A.	315,000		Kiev, Ukraine	110,000
Chicago, U.S.A.	250,000		Baltimore, U.S.A.	100,000
Boston, U.S.A.	225,000		Montreal, Canada	100,000
San Francisco, U.S.A.	210,000		St. Petersburg, Russia	100,000
London, U.K.	200,000			

* Greater metropolitan areas

A 19th-century drawing of holy sites in Jerusalem and other parts of the Land of Israel

ISRAEL

General population (GP) 5,800,000 ♦ Jewish population (JP) 4,700,000

♦ DEMOGRAPHY ♦

Israel's absorption of hundreds of thousands of immigrants twice set world records. In its first two years of existence (1948–1950), the fledgling Jewish state doubled its population by absorbing 687,000 immigrants. From 1989 to 1995, Israel absorbed a similar number (700,000)—primarily from the former Soviet Union and its successor states—increasing the population by 15%. The first great wave of *aliya* was almost evenly divided between Holocaust survivors and refugees from Arab lands. In the subsequent years, an additional 300,000 Jews came from the Arab world. This visionary process of the "ingathering of the exiles" has brought 2.5 million Jews to Israel since the establishment of the state: 59% of the immigrants came from Europe (including the former Soviet Union), 19% from Africa, 15% from Asia, and 7% from the Americas and Oceania. A breakdown of the *aliya* reveals that 900,000 came from the former Soviet Union, 380,000 from North Africa (Algeria, Morocco, Tunisia), 274,000 from Romania, 172,000 from Poland, 130,000 from Iraq, 77,000 from Iran, 73,000 from the United States, 61,000 from Turkey, 52,000 from Yemen, 50,000 from Ethiopia, 45,000 from Argentina, and 43,000 from Bulgaria. Thousands more came from countries as diverse as Afghanistan and Zimbabwe. The absorption of the immigrants was a staggering task for the newly established Jewish state, and it created enormous socioeconomic problems. In the 1950s, the immigration necessitated austerity and produced recession. Thus the benefits of this tremendous immigration were slow to reveal themselves. The *aliya* of the 1990s, however, led to spectacular economic growth that helped to raise Israel's economic indices to Western levels.

Within Jewish society in Israel, there are two major sources of social tensions: the ethnic division between Ashkenazim and Sephardim, and the rift between the religious and non-religious. Sephardim only accounted for 23% of the state's initial population. By the 1980s, they had become a majority (approximately 55%). In the 1990s, as a result of the *aliya* from the former Soviet Union, the proportions were reversed. Despite some social and political crises, the forces of integration prevailed: about 30% of marriages are between Ashkenazim and Sephardim, and the young generation of Israeli-born Sabras is a product of the Israeli melting pot. Although social and ethnic problems still exist, they are overshadowed by the growing divisions between religious and non-religious in Israel (see below). It is hard to quantify the religious–secular divide, since many Israelis, particularly Sephardim, consider themselves "traditionalists," and they

LARGEST CITIES (1997)
(in thousands)

Jerusalem 603 *(Jews 422)*
Tel Aviv–Jaffa 355.8 *(Jews 341.0)*
Haifa 252.3 *(Jews 225.6)*
Rishon-le-Ziyon 165.9
Holon 163.8
Petach Tikvah 153.1
Be'er Sheva 152.6
Netanya 146.4
Bat Yam 142.3
Bene Beraq 128.6
Ashdod 126.4
Ramat Gan 121.7

help to moderate the conflict. It seems that about 20% of the Jewish population of Israel is modern religious Zionist (and serve in the armed forces and study in universities and other secular institutions). About 10% of the Jewish population is ultra-Orthodox, and 30% to 50% are traditionalists of varying degrees. The balance is secular.

There are also two communities that regard themselves as representative of ancient Jewish sects: the Karaites (about 15,000) and the Samaritans (300 in both Holon and Shechem [Nablus]), who profess strict adherence to the Torah.

More than 90% of Israelis are city dwellers, but Israel is famous for its unique cooperative settlements in rural areas: the *kibbutz* and the *moshav*. A little more than 2% of Israelis live in some 270 *kibbutzim,* which are self-contained socioeconomic units, the members of which collectively own their property and means of production. The early settlers in the *kibbutzim* and *moshavim* (in which each family owns its own farm, but where purchasing and marketing is cooperative) were Zionist pioneers who committed themselves to a remarkable social experiment. Today *kibbutzim* strive to maintain their original framework and adjust to the more individualistic, technological, and consumer-oriented Israeli society.

Israel's population, unlike that of Diaspora communities, has a high rate of natural increase (average of 2.9 children—and among ultra-Orthodox Jews, much higher). Both *aliya* and this birth rate are drastically altering the demographic map of world Jewry. It is expected that in the coming decade Israel will overtake the United States as the world's

The 80-year old, German-born proprietor of a nursery in Moshav Bet Yitzhak

largest Jewish community. Israel is also fast becoming one of the most densely populated countries in the world, particularly its central coastal area.

✦ H I S T O R Y ✦

Zionism, the Jewish national liberation movement, transformed centuries of Jewish religious, cultural, and national yearning for Zion into a feasible political platform. Unremitting anti-Semitism and persecution of the Jews in exile contributed to this phenomenon. The Land of Israel is the birthplace of the Jewish people and its early history is recorded in the Bible. Jewish history began 4,000 years ago with the three patriarchs Abraham, Isaac, and Jacob and continued with the return of the children of Israel from Egyptian bondage, the conquest of the land, and the establishment of the Jewish monarchy of Israel. King David (ca.1004–965 B.C.E.) made Jerusalem his capital, and his son, King Solomon, constructed the temple that became the center of the people's national and religious life. The kingdom later split into Judah and Israel. The temple was destroyed by the Babylonians (586 B.C.E.), marking the beginning of the First Exile and the Jewish Diaspora. The Biblical prophets of Israel continued to preach in the Judean hills for a century after the destruction of the First Temple, while in Babylon the Jews began to develop their own unique lifestyle and adapt Jewish ideas to the reality of life outside the Land of Israel.

Jews returned from Babylon as early as 538 B.C.E. led by Zerubbabel and a century later by Ezra the Scribe. They built the Second Temple and established the Knesset Hagedolah (Great Assembly), the supreme religious and judicial body (today "Knesset" is the name of Israel's parliament). After a series of occupations and invasions (by the Persians, Greeks, and Romans), Judea was brought under direct Roman administration (63 C.E.). The Jewish Revolt resulted in the total destruction of Jerusalem (70 C.E.) and the defeat of the last Jewish fortress, Masada. Another revolt, led by Bar Kokhba, was crushed in 135, after which the Romans renamed the country Palestine.

Even during exile, through long years of dispersion, there was always a physical presence of Jews in the Land of Israel. Those outside it continued to remember and pledge their loyalty to Zion and Jerusalem.

Jews and Judaism in Palestine survived these tragic encounters and gradually recovered. The Jews located the Sanhedrin in Yavneh, where the Mishnah (body of Jewish law) was compiled. Other communities were established across the

"O Jerusalem, let my right hand forget its cunning, let my tongue cleave to the roof of my mouth, if I remember you not, if I set not Jerusalem above my chiefest joy."
(Psalms 137: 5–6)

land, notably in Tiberias on the Sea of Galilee. Centuries later the Mishnah was codified in the *Shulchan Aruch* by Joseph Caro who lived in Safed, which was the center of Jewish mysticism—the Kabbala.

The Jewish community was to witness successive rulers and persecutors: the Christian Byzantines; the Arabs, who entered in the 7th century; the Crusaders, who arrived in 1099; and the Egyptian Mamluks, who ruled from Damascus until the Ottoman Conquest in 1516. There were small Jewish communities in the Galilee, and also in Acre and Caesarea. In Jerusalem the community was refounded by Nahmanides between 1267 and 1270.

During all these periods of foreign rule, the Land of Israel was never treated as an independent entity, and, with the brief exception in the Crusader period, no conqueror made Jerusalem his capital. During the Ottoman era, Jews resided in Shechem and Gaza

The Citadel, popularly known as the Tower of David, looms over Jerusalem.

and continued to dwell in the four "Holy Cities" of Safed, Tiberias, Hebron, and Jerusalem. But the land was desolate.

At the beginning of the 19th century, there were 2,000 Jews in Jerusalem, and in 1845, 7,120 (together with 5,000 Muslims and 3,390 Christians). From that time, the Jews were to remain the largest single religious community. They became a majority of the population in the city from 1854. In 1860 the first Jewish suburb outside the walls was built. With the arrival of more Jews, new rural villages were established, including Mikve Israel (1870) and Petach Tikvah (1878).

The First Aliya was composed of immigrants from two very different communities: Russia and Yemen. This was symbolic of the ingathering of exiles that was to come. Many of the Russian Jews were members of Hovevei Zion (Lovers of Zion), an organization that preceded the political Zionist movement.

When Theodor Herzl convened the first Zionist Congress in Basel (1897), the total Jewish population in Palestine was 50,000. By the outbreak of World War I (1914), it had reached 100,000 (the Arab population was 500,000). Many of the Jews settled on wasteland, on sand dunes, and in malarial marshes. They also had to contend with the hostile attitude of the Ottoman administration.

Following the British conquest of Palestine in 1917, and the declaration by the British foreign secretary, Arthur James Balfour, recognizing Jewish Zionist aspirations, the League of Nations entrusted Great Britain with the Mandate for Palestine (1922). The League reaffirmed "the historical connection of the Jewish People with Palestine" and called upon Great Britain to facilitate "the establishment of a Jewish national home" there. A few months later the League and Great Britain agreed that these provisions should not apply to Transjordan, which later became the Hashemite Kingdom of Jordan and constituted three-quarters of the territory of the mandate.

The British mandate authorities granted the Jewish and Arab communities the right to run their own internal affairs. During this time, the development of the country gained momentum. Dramatic strides were made in raising the level of education, health, and culture, and the standard of living. Despite the British "White Paper," restrictions on *aliya* enacted in response to Arab protests, the Jewish community continued its efforts aimed at a national revival. Arab resentment erupted in periods of intense violence and unprovoked attacks against the Jewish population. The Jewish underground movements, meanwhile, endeavored to bring Jewish refugees out of Europe in defiance of British restrictions. British limitations on *aliya* continued during and after the Shoah, the Nazi Holocaust that claimed the lives of one-third of the Jewish people.

About 85,000 displaced persons (Holocaust survivors) were transported to Israel by the Jewish underground networks between 1945 and 1948. At the same time, an active struggle was being waged against the British. When in November 1947 the United Nations voted to approve the Palestine partition resolution, the Jewish community accepted the plan, while the Arabs rejected it outright.

Following the U.N. vote, Arabs from inside and outside Palestine launched violent attacks on Jews. When the British mandate ended

> *"Palestine sits in sackcloth and ashes. Over it broods the spell of a curse that has withered its fields and fettered its energies. Palestine is desolate and unlovely Palestine is no more of this workday world. It is sacred to poetry and tradition, it is dreamland."*
> Mark Twain, 1867

IDF soldiers pause to pray.

and the state of Israel was proclaimed on May 14, 1948, the regular armies of Egypt, Jordan, Syria, Lebanon, and Iraq invaded the country. The War of Independence lasted 15 months, claiming over 6,000 Israeli lives, until the newly formed Israel Defense Forces (IDF) succeeded in repulsing the invaders. In 1949 armistice agreements were signed on the Greek island of Rhodes.

The fight for independence and security continued while Israeli society was engaged in building the state. The Arab states refused to recognize Israel, and following the incursion of terrorist squads, Israel launched the successful Sinai Campaign (1956). After international assurances, it agreed to withdraw from the Sinai peninsula. Following a decade of relative tranquility, the situation on the borders deteriorated. Terrorist raids intensified, as did the Syrian bombardment of settlements in the north. This was accompanied by a massive Arab military buildup and constant threats of a war of extermination. It culminated in Egypt's closure of the Straits of Tiran

and the expulsion of the U.N. Sinai/Gaza forces. The 1967 Six-Day War was an outstanding Israeli victory that changed the previous cease-fire lines. Judea, Samaria, Gaza, the Sinai, and the Golan Heights came under Israel's control, and Jerusalem was reunified. The 1973 Yom Kippur War, when Egypt and Syria launched a surprise assault against Israel, cost the lives of 2,700 Israeli soldiers.

The Yom Kippur War also started the peace process, resulting in Israeli withdrawal from certain territories and disengagement-of-forces agreements with Egypt and Syria. The Arab rejectionist cycle was broken with the visit of Egyptian President Anwar Sadat to Jerusalem in 1977, the Camp David Accords in 1978, and the subsequent withdrawal of Israel from the Sinai. The 1982 Operation Peace for the Galilee did not end Israeli security problems in the north, and the situation in Lebanon remains tied to developments on the Syrian front. The Madrid peace conference of 1991, following the end of the Gulf War, brought together Israel and all its Arab neighbors and led to bilateral and multilateral talks. A significant breakthrough occurred in 1993 when Israel and the PLO, after talks in Oslo, exchanged letters and signed agreements of peace and mutual recognition. This was followed by the Gaza-Jericho accords, the establishment of the Palestinian Authority, and the redeployment of Israeli forces from Palestinian population centers.

The peace treaty between Israel and Jordan was signed at the Arava border in October 1994, and Israel has since exchanged ambassadors with Jordan. The peace process in its various stages led to the award of Nobel Peace Prizes to three Israelis: Prime Minister Menachem Begin (who shared the prize with President Sadat), Prime Minister Yitzhak Rabin, and Foreign Minister Shimon Peres (who both shared the award with PLO Chairman Yasir Arafat). Intense debate on the peace process led to the use of harsh rhetoric by both detractors and proponents. In November 1995, a Jewish extremist assassinated Prime Minister Rabin at a peace rally in Tel Aviv. The Israeli public responded with an unprecedented, spontaneous outpouring of grief and national mourning. Rabin's funeral was attended by world leaders, including several Arab heads of state.

The funeral was dramatic evidence of Israel's place among the nations and the fact that the Jewish state has achieved an outstanding level of recognition. At the beginning of 1997, Israel maintained relations with 153 countries and had 107 diplomatic missions abroad.

◆ FROM COMMUNITY TO JEWISH SOVEREIGNTY ◆

Independence created the need to adjust the pre-state institutions to a democratic political system. Israel was to become a Western-style parliamentary democracy, and as such, a secular entity. From a narrow legal point of view, the State of Israel is not a Jewish state in

the sense of "the State of Judaism." However, it is clear from Israel's declaration of independence and some of its laws, including the basic laws which are viewed as Israel's constitution, that there is an important legal dimension to the "Jewishness" of Israel. As explained by Moshe Landau, a former chief justice of Israel's Supreme Court,

> [Is it not obvious] to mention the Declaration of Independence, which starts by describing the "historic and conditional link" of the Jewish people to the Land of Israel, where its spiritual, religious, and political character was formed, and states that it did not cease to pray and hope to return to its land and regain its political freedom? Within this spirit the Law of Return was passed, which is the law about the people who return to their land. We cannot disregard the historic sources and context of the law in which nationality and religion are two parts of the same.

The Jewish religion is also reflected in the state symbols: the flag, the emblem (the menorah), and the anthem (Hatikva), as well as its working week and national holidays. In some legislative acts, there is a clear input from and reference to Jewish values as, for example, in the compulsory education law that calls for the teaching of Jewish values, or in the Broadcasting Authority Law. The Knesset elections law disqualifies parties that deny the existence of Israel as the state of the Jewish people.

Already before the establishment of the state, its prime minister-to-be, David Ben-Gurion, committed himself to solving the more problematic aspect of Israeli Jewishness, the so-called status quo on religion. In his letter to the leaders of the ultra-Orthodox movement Agudath Israel, Ben-Gurion pledged that in four areas—education, *kashrut, shabbat,* and family law—Halacha would prevail. Therefore the state enabled the existence of a religious stream in the national school system, as well as an expanded ultra-religious system. *Kashrut* and *shabbat* are observed in public institutions, including at military bases. All marital matters were placed in the hands of the Rabbinate, the highest Halachic authorities.

In recent years, some segments of the Israeli public have challenged the basic tenets of Israel's Jewishness. Some point out that there is a contradiction between democracy and religious law, and others, so-called 'post-Zionist' thinkers, bring into question the traditional interpretation of Israeli history and much of the Zionist ethos in which national identity has been rooted. Some of these writers have advocated jettisoning the Law of Return or making an amendment to those paragraphs in the Declaration of Independence that express commitment to the Jewish essence of the state and to the task of the "ingathering of the exiles." They also point out that with a non-Jewish minority accounting for almost 20% of the population, the Jewish character of the state should be replaced by a "civil society." Although this group represents a small minority, even among Israeli intellectuals, it enjoys broad access to the media. Moreover it capitalizes on the general crisis of Jewish identity in an Israel fast becoming a modern, liberal, consumer-oriented society.

◆ STATE AND RELIGION ◆
Maintaining the balance between the Jewishness of the state and its democratic essence is a complex task. Moreover it is not easy to find a consensus formula on the role

"The central mystery of Zionism, it seems to me, is the relation within it of religion to nationalism with the suspicion, within the mystery, that religion and nationalism may ultimately be two words for the same thing. The early Zionists were mostly avowed secularists, but their enterprise derived most of its power and all of its territorial orientation from a religious book and the ancient longing it inspired."
—Conor Cruise O'Brien,
Irish author

of Jewish religion in a society whose members have various degrees of religious observance and in which a large segment regards itself as secular. It seems that the polarization between religious and secular may be exaggerated by the Israeli media. According to several academic studies, the Israeli Jewish population has a strong traditional bent. It is often said that the conflict with the Arabs and security problems have prevented changes in religious legislation in Israel. The structure of the Knesset enabled the religious political parties to hold the balance of power for many years—thereby ensuring the preservation of the status quo. There were, however, public rifts on the issue, and as a result, the status quo was gradually weakened. In a large number of towns, cinemas were opened on the sabbath, and the local authorities did not act vigorously to enforce the law. The fate of the laws prohibiting the sale of pork was similar.

It became apparent that in a democratic, pluralistic society, in which a minority of the population are Orthodox observers of Halacha, it is impossible to enforce laws that are not accepted by the majority. As a result of what is termed the "constitutional revolution" in Israel, the growing emphasis on human rights and individual freedoms could only strengthen this trend. The Israeli Supreme Court, in its capacity as the High Court of Justice, has in recent years increased its involvement in the rift between state and synagogue.

According to Israeli law, religious authorities (Jewish, Christian, Muslim, and Druze) have a formal monopoly on marriages and divorces performed in Israel, but actual practice is something of a muddle. The Interior Ministry records marriages and divorces that were registered abroad (sometimes even by mail), even if they contradict the religious principles of Israeli family law. While the Israeli Supreme Court grants *de facto* recognition to Reform and Conservative conversions, Israeli Orthodox rabbis will not perform marriages for such converts. Changes in the area of marriage and divorce may create one schism amongst Jews in Israel and another between Israeli and Diaspora Jews.

⋆Who is a Jew?⋆

The question of "who is a Jew?" was the cause of considerable controversy in the history of the State of Israel and caused a political crisis between Israel and the Diaspora, the American Jewish community in particular. As part of the Law of Return, the definition of "who is a Jew?" touches the very heart of Zionist ideology, the Jewish character of Israel, and its relations with the Diaspora. The law, passed by the Knesset in 1950, explicitly states that "every Jew has the right to come to the country as an *oleh.*" However, it excludes those who endanger the public and state security.

The Law of Return is basically a national secular law, but as a result of a Supreme Court ruling, political pressure led to an amendment which introduced a Halachic concept, defining a Jew as a person who was born of a Jewish mother or who has converted to Judaism. At the same time, the law did not specify what kind of conversion is allowed (Orthodox, Conservative, or Reform), and it also opened the door for intermarried couples and their children and grandchildren. Religious pressure aimed at granting exclusive legitimacy to Orthodox conversions has failed in several legislative and political battles. On a number of occasions, delegations from the Diaspora came to Israel in order to object to the amendment of the Law, and this helped the government to resist religious pressure. Diaspora intervention reflected a feeling that a legislative act by the Knesset can be interpreted as an attempt to excommunicate a large segment of Jews in the Diaspora. In this particular instance, it seems that religious legislation in the Knesset has a price, and it creates, sometimes, a certain subordination of the religious establishment to the secular institutions in Israel.

⋆Israel–Diaspora⋆

The relationship between Israel and the Jews abroad is unique and differs from other homeland–diaspora relationships. On the one hand, as a young country surrounded by enemies, immediately after the Holocaust Israel signified for the Jewish world a major change in the Jewish condition. It was an object of pride and identity and was worthy of active support. On the other hand, there was the Zionist dogma that implied the "negation of the Diaspora" and fed tensions and feelings of guilt abroad. The Diaspora, especially American Jewry, provided financial, moral, and political support while Israel became a haven for oppressed Jews in the world. The Jewish Agency for Israel (JAFI) and the World Zionist Organization (WZO) provided the institutional bridge in this partnership between Jews in the Diaspora and the Israeli government and establishment. Every year hundreds of millions of dollars are collected by world Jewry to finance *aliya*, settlement, and renewal projects in Israel. The JAFI also deals with Jewish education around the world.

In addition to the Law of Return, Israeli–Diaspora relations were formalized through the Laws of Status in 1952 and the covenant of 1954 between Israel and the WZO–JAFI. These laws designated these bodies as responsible for the "ingathering of the exiles" and for their absorption in Israel and expressed the expectation that all Jews would help in the

⋆

building of the state and would be united by it. The Six-Day War of 1967, with the early sense of emergency and the later victory, strengthened Diaspora identity with Israel and was a source of pride and honor. For many otherwise assimilated Jews, whose way of life and culture reflected that of their Gentile neighbors, Israel has become a way in which they express their Judaism—a kind of secular religion and social gospel.

The Jewish dimension of Israel's foreign policy has been reflected in several instances, and sometimes this has led to conflict between state interests and the interests of local Jewish communities. Moreover, political debates in Israel on the peace process and on the country's future borders are often reflected in Diaspora communities and particularly in the United States. In some cases of anti-Semitism, Israeli leaders intervened on behalf of Jewish communities and approached governments on the subject. This role is formalized in the governmental committee that monitors anti-Semitism in the world and publishes a yearly report and in the existence of a department of Diaspora affairs in the Foreign Ministry.

In 1960, Israel acted as a legal successor of the Jewish people in the Diaspora by abducting Adolf Eichmann, one of the principal organizers of the Nazi Final Solution, and by bringing him to justice in Jerusalem. Eichmann was found guilty of crimes against humanity and against the Jewish people and was sentenced to death (the only time this penalty has been applied under Israeli law).

In recent years, it has became apparent that Israel–Diaspora relations have been too narrowly based on the machinery of fundraising and political lobbying for Israel. Israel's feeling of self-reliance, the improvement in its international standing and economic condition, and its emulation of a consumer society are now widening the gulf in its "abnormal" ties with the Diaspora.

There is an increasing number of plans to reform these institutions and make them more relevant to a new agenda. This agenda

Lubavitcher Chassidim at Kfar Chabad upon hearing the news of the death of the Lubavitcher Rebbe, June 1994

The Small Town (Tel Aviv) *by Nahum Guttman.*
Collage, ink, gouache

will have to reconcile the Diaspora inclination to look inward (including the struggle against assimilation) and trends in Israel toward alienation from Jewish peoplehood.

✦ RELIGIOUS LIFE ✦

The officially recognized institutions in Israel are Orthodox, but in recent years, the Conservative and Reform movements, which cater to a very small minority, received more recognition in the Israeli courts and also some state subsidies.

The chief rabbinate is a continuation of the British mandatory institution as well as of the Ottoman institution of the *Haham Bashi.* The authority is divided between an Ashkenazi and a Sephardi chief rabbinate, as in the presidency of the Supreme Rabbinical Court. The ultra-Orthodox community does not accept the authority of the chief rabbinate and it has its own rabbis and religious courts. The Ministry of Religious Affairs maintains the holy places and, through the local religious councils, provides religious services (synagogues and *yeshivot*). The local religious councils and the rabbis are state employees, and in this sense, the Jewish communities in Israel have not developed the type of volunteer activities and lay leadership that characterize the Diaspora.

✦ EDUCATION ✦

Israel is clearly the world's largest center of Jewish education. There are about 1 million Jewish children in thousands of schools, with close to 100,000 teachers, in Israel. The state education system has a general stream (non-religious) with about 70% of the children, a religious stream (23%), and schools run by the ultra-religious (including a few in Yiddish). There are seven institutions of higher learning: the Technion in Haifa (founded in 1924), the Hebrew University of Jerusalem (1925), the Weizmann Institute of Science in Rehovot (1934), Bar-Ilan University in Ramat Gan (1955), Tel Aviv University (1956), Haifa University (1963), and Ben-Gurion University of the Negev in Be'er Sheva (1969). There is also an open university and more than 200 *yeshivot.*

Jewish studies in Israeli institutions deal, by definition, with a living and dynamic organism in a Jewish state and society where even digging at archeological sites is a field of Jewish creativity. Israeli institutions offer independent departments for each of the central areas of Jewish civilization, and Israel has greatly influenced the worldwide expansion of Jewish studies in more than 1,300 universities.

✦

Israeli society is currently confronting a serious decline in Judaic studies in the secular schools and universities, which some attribute to the broader crisis of Israel's Jewish identity. A commission convened by the Ministry of Education called for a major overhaul in the Jewish studies curriculum.

Israel is the world center for Holocaust study and documentation. Every university in the country has at least one chair devoted to research and instruction on the subject. Yad Vashem, the Martyrs' and Heroes' Remembrance Authority, is the most important institution of its kind in the country. The Yad Vashem Hall of Remembrance is an important stop for most official and unofficial visitors to the state. Kibbutz Lochamei HaGettaot, near Acre, also houses a Holocaust museum.

+CULTURE+

The renaissance of Hebrew and Jewish studies is coupled with staggering cultural growth. Jewish dimensions are reflected in all fields: literature, music, dance, theater, plastic arts, and even sports. In every artistic medium, original Jewish and Israeli motifs have been employed. The works of Israeli writers in the reborn Hebrew language have been translated into numerous foreign languages, and one author, Shmuel Yosef Agnon, received the 1966 Nobel Prize for literature for his work.

The Israel Museum offers an outstanding collection of Judaica (several entire synagogues are specially reconstructed on its grounds), archeological artifacts (including the Dead Sea Scrolls, housed in the Shrine of the Book), as well as paintings, sculpture, and numismatics.

Other important museums in Jerusalem are the Bible Lands Museum, the Rockefeller Museum, and the Tower of David.

In Tel Aviv, the Nahum Goldmann Museum of the Jewish Diaspora—Beth Hatefutsoth—chronicles the story of the exile of the Jewish people from ancient times until the modern day. The museum contains practically no original artifacts but features recreations of Jewish life as it was lived throughout the world. It has departments devoted to Jewish youth activities, genealogy, photography, and musicology. The Tel Aviv Museum and the Ha'aretz Museum are also among the country's outstanding institutions.

Important theaters include the Habima (Israel's National Theater) and Cameri in Tel Aviv, Khan in Jerusalem, and the Haifa Theater. Bat-Sheva, Inbal, and Bat-Dor, all in Tel Aviv, are the leading dance companies. The Israel Philharmonic Orchestra, with its home in Tel Aviv's Mann Auditorium, is the country's leading symphony. There is also a symphony orchestra in Jerusalem.

The Israel Philharmonic Orchestra

Israel is the most important center of Jewish journalism. In addition to the major dailies that appear in Hebrew, there are also daily newspapers in Russian, English, Arabic, Romanian, Hungarian, German, and Yiddish and weeklies in a number of other languages. Hebrew

Aerial view of the Tefen Industrial Park in the Galilee

journals cater to every field of interest and espouse a broad range of political, religious, and social viewpoints. The Israel Broadcasting Authority is not only heard in Israel but is also beamed all over the world on shortwave. Israel's two television channels often focus on Jewish programming, including information on the communities in the Diaspora, the Holocaust, and other facets of Jewish history.

Israeli teams participate in most major international sporting competitions, including the Olympics. Every four years, Jewish athletes from around the world come to Israel to participate in the Maccabi Games—a kind of all-Jewish Olympics.

◆SITES◆

Israel, the Jewish state and the Holy Land, is by definition a cornucopia of Jewish and non-Jewish sites. The major Jewish holy sites are in Jerusalem or in close proximity to it. Foremost are the Temple Mount (Mt. Moriah) and the Western Wall in the Old City of Jerusalem. Since 1967 Israel has ensured worshippers of all three faiths unrestricted access to their holy places throughout the city. There are many other holy and historic places in the rest of the country, especially in the Galilee, and along the shores of the Dead Sea (Masada).

For more information on sites and tours, visitors should consult the Israeli Government Tourist Information Centers.

The Tel Aviv Promenade looking toward Jaffa

The Menorah, symbol of the State of Israel,
in front of the Knesset

NORTH AMERICA
AND
THE CARIBBEAN

The Touro Synagogue in Newport, Rhode Island, inaugurated in 1763.
The building, the oldest Jewish house of worship in the United States,
has been declared a national landmark.

Hudson Bay

CANADA

Newfoundland

LAURENTIAN UPLAND

Great Lakes

C. Race

APPALACHIAN MTS.

Missouri

Mississippi

BERMUDA

UNITED STATES

Coastal Plain

Great Plains

BAHAMAS

CUBA

CAYMAN ISLANDS

DOMINICAN REPUBLIC

PUERTO RICO

JAMAICA HAITI

U.S. VIRGIN ISLANDS

Popocatepetl 17,996

GUADELOUPE

MARTINIQUE

CURAÇAO AND ARUBA

BARBADOS

Tehuantepec

Orinoco

SURINAME

Guiana Massif

FRENCH GUYANA

Isthmus of Panama

Orinoco

GALAPAGOS IS.

Chimborazo 20,702

Amazonas

Selvas

Pta. de Aguja

ANDES

Madeira

São Fran

Illampu 21,489

Planalto do Brasil

Gran Chaco

Aconc...

UNITED STATES

GP 270,000,000 ♦ JP 5,600,000

♦ DEMOGRAPHY ♦

The demographic survey of American Jewry published in 1991 is viewed as a major watershed. The shocking revelations on the current rate of intermarriage (more than 50%) and assimilation aroused a feeling of pessimism in the public life of the largest Jewish community in the world. The study, which was commissioned by the Council of Jewish Federations, estimated at 4.1 million the "core" Jewish population (or 5.8 million based on local community counts). Only 3.5 million belong to families in which both parents are Jews. The survey also revealed an aging population with a birth rate that is steadily falling behind the rest of the society. Fewer Jews are getting married and fewer are getting a Jewish education. Moreover, only a small percentage of the non-Jewish partners in intermarriages has converted.

America's position in world Jewry is in decline. In 1948 it was nearly ten times the population of Israel, in 1960 three times, and in 1990 the ratio was 3 to 2 and fast approaching parity. Coupled with the assimilation process, there were significant geographic shifts among the Jewish population of the United States. In the last two to three decades, there has been a double movement of Jews away from the Northeast (and to some extent from the Midwest) to the South and West, and away from the big cities to the suburbs and even to the exurbs. These demo-geographic changes have served to dissolve established Jewish communities and have increased distances between Jewish centers, creating smaller and more dispersed communities. At the same time, many of the Jewish communities in smaller cities and towns are disappearing as Jews are drawn by the opportunities in the large urban agglomerations.

CITIES WITH LARGEST JEWISH POPULATIONS*

New York 1,900,000
Los Angeles, California 585,000
Miami, Florida 535,000
Philadelphia, Pennsylvania 315,000
Chicago, Illinois 250,000
Boston, Massachusetts 228,000
San Francisco, California 210,000
Washington, DC 165,000
Baltimore, Maryland 100,000
Detroit, Michigan 95,000
Rockland County, New York 83,000
Orange Country, California 75,000
San Diego, California 70,000
Atlanta, Georgia 67,000
Cleveland, Ohio 65,000
St. Louis, Missouri 53,000
Phoenix, Arizona 50,000
Denver, Colorado 46,000
Houston, Texas 42,000
Dallas, Texas 35,000
Seattle, Washington 29,000
Milwaukee, Wisconsin 28,000
Hartford, Connecticut 26,000

* Greater metropolitan areas

♦ HISTORY ♦

At the time of the Declaration of Independence (1776), there were already 1,500 to 2,500 Jews in the United States. The first Jews arrived in New Amsterdam in 1654. They were 23 Sephardi refugees who had fled Brazil in the wake of its conquest by the Portuguese. By the time the British occupied the city and changed its name to New York in 1664, there was already a developing Jewish community. Even before the Revolutionary War, it had become

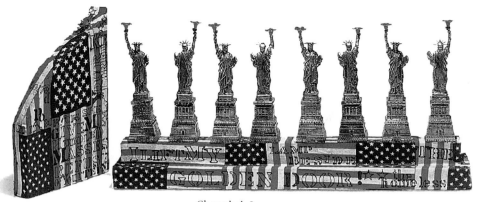

Chanukah Lamp
by Mae Schafter Rockland, 1974.
Wood covered in fabric with molded plastic figures

the largest in North America. At that time, there were Jewish communities in New York, Newport, Philadelphia, Charleston, and Savannah.

With independence American Jews received equal rights as an integral part of the immigrant society. In the fledgling republic, emancipation was implicit and did not necessitate a political struggle. This was expressed in a letter by the country's first president, George Washington, to the Jewish community in Newport, Rhode Island, in 1790: "May the children of the stock of Abraham, who dwell in this land, continue to merit and enjoy the good will of the other inhabitants, while everyone shall sit in safety under his own vine and fig tree, and there shall be none to make him afraid. May the father of all mercies scatter light and not darkness in our paths, and make us all in our several vocations useful here, and in his own due time and way everlastingly happy."

The cultural hegemony of Spanish-Portuguese Jews was slowly reduced in the wake of immigration from Germany. The new arrivals bolstered the Jewish population from 6,000 in 1826 to 15,000 in 1840 and 280,000 in 1880. Beginning in 1881, a wave of immigration from the Russian Empire and other parts of eastern Europe commenced, and by the turn of the century, the Jewish population

had already reached 1.1 million. That immigration continued until the imposition, in 1924, of strict quotas designed to restrict the entry of new immigrants from eastern and southern Europe. Until that time, the United States absorbed about two-thirds of the total number of Jewish emigrants leaving eastern Europe. By 1918 the country had already become the largest Jewish community in the world.

In the 1930s, only a small fraction of the Jewish refugees clamoring to escape the threat of Nazism was admitted. Still, by 1940, the Jewish population had risen to 4,500,000, and that number increased after the war when many Holocaust survivors arrived on American shores. In the last 30 years, some 250,000 Israelis have immigrated to the United States, as have 150,000 Soviet Jews, 30,000 Jews from Iran, and thousands of others from Latin America, South Africa, and elsewhere. This immigration offset the community's low birth rate and strong tendency toward assimilation.

Jewish immigrants dreamed of the United States as a promised land, a *goldene medina*, but the reality was harsh. Most newcomers worked at manual labor in appalling conditions. The largest concentration was in New York's Lower East Side, which at one time was home to over 350,000 Jews crammed into a single square mile. The dominant Russian and eastern European element spoke Yiddish and established a rich cultural and religious life. They also banded together with other *landsmann* (immigrants from the same localities in Europe), and at one point there were 1,200 such *landsmannschaft* associations in New York.

With the passage of time, the patterns of education and occupation changed. Ever greater numbers of Jews entered the free professions, and Jews distinguished themselves constituting a distinct sub culture. Moreover, many Yiddish words have crept into the general idiom *(chutzpa, schlep, schlemiel, yenta, meshuga, megilla)*. Certain Jewish communities form groups that preserve special customs and traditions. These include the Bukharan and Syrian Jews in Queens, New York; Soviet Jews in Brighton Beach, Brooklyn, New York; and Iranian Jews in Los Angeles. The United States, particularly Brooklyn, is also the home of many Chassidic groups.

Model of the Beth Shalom Synagogue in Elkins Park, Pennsylvania, designed by Frank Lloyd Wright and consecrated in 1954, displayed at Bet Hatefusoth

in commerce, industry, and science. Jews play an especially active role in art, communication, and entertainment (including Hollywood films and Broadway theater). The proportion of Jewish university graduates is higher than that of the general population, and Jews hold high positions in government. The number of senators (10) and congressmen (33) reached a peak after the November 1992 elections. Many of the country's outstanding universities are headed by Jews, and all include disproportionately large Jewish student and faculty populations.

Jewish cuisine (particularly the bagel) is also enjoyed by non-Jews, and Jewish motifs are an integral part of American culture,

✦ C O M M U N I T Y ✦

A Forest of Organizations: It is easy to locate more than 2,000 organizations and 700 federations in many cities, towns, and neighborhoods, and of course, thousands of synagogues. The Jewish community finds expression and fulfillment in a tremendous range of associations and institutions. Many of these inevitably overlap, so there is a considerable degree of duplication.

The Council of Jewish Federations (CJF) is the strongest roof organization in terms of allocation of funds and national planning. Various education and welfare boards are connected to the CJF, which also embraces Canadian Jewry.

✦

Among the leading voluntary Jewish organizations in the United States are two Jewish advocacy groups: the American Jewish Committee, established by Jews of German origin in 1906, and the American Jewish Congress, which was founded in 1918 by Rabbi Stephen Wise, who later co-founded the World Jewish Congress with Nahum Goldmann. The B'nai B'rith Jewish Brotherhood was founded in 1843 by German immigrants and today focuses on social and welfare activities. These include the lively Hillel chapters on university campuses and several Jewish hospitals. The Anti-Defamation League (ADL) was founded in 1913 as a B'nai B'rith committee to combat anti-Semitism, and today operates as an independent organization. In terms of membership, the largest organization is Hadassah, the women's Zionist group, with 385,000 members. The community's main fundraising instrument is the United Jewish Appeal (UJA). Today the majority of money that is collected is used to meet the domestic needs of American Jewry. About 30% is donated to Israel through the Jewish Agency and the World Zionist Organization. The UJA also finances the American Jewish Joint Distribution Committee (JDC), which alleviates the hardships of many communities around the world.

Jewish Lobby: The term "Jewish lobby" actually denotes a number of organizations which seek to promote Jewish interests in American political life. The leading body of this type is the American–Israel Public Affairs Committee (AIPAC), which was established

Yiddish license plates, Los Angeles, 1986

in 1950 and is a registered political lobby.

The Presidents' Conference, founded in 1954 by WJC President Nahum Goldmann, serves as an instrument to coordinate the activities of the heads of the leading Jewish organizations on international issues and primarily with regard to the State of Israel.

Anti-Semitism: The atmosphere of the melting pot meant that the United States was, for the most part, free of the anti-Semitic prejudices that existed in Europe. That bigotry compelled many Jews to seek a new home in America. Anti-Semitism was never, at least ostensibly, official U.S. policy. Jews were never forced to live in ghettos or to accept an inferior position. Nevertheless there were always expressions of anti-Semitism, and Jews have confronted them as best they could.

In spite of the official commitment to equality of rights, Jews often encountered discrimination (including restrictions) at private and sometimes even public schools and universities (many of which maintained strict quotas on the admission of Jews). At certain hotels, firms, residential quarters, and country and social clubs, Jews were not admitted. This type of anti-Semitism persisted until very recently, and manifestations of it still occur from time to time.

In recent years, anti-Semitism has become a serious problem among certain segments of the African-American population. There are also occasional incidents of neo-Nazism or manifestations of Holocaust denial. The U.S. Holocaust Memorial Museum, located on the

Mall in Washington, DC, alongside some of the nation's most outstanding museums, is an important tool in the struggle against Holocaust revisionism.

⋆ RELIGIOUS LIFE ⋆

Each of the three main religious trends —Orthodox, Conservative, and Reform— has its own national association of synagogues and rabbis.

The Union of Orthodox Jewish Congregations also manages the supervision of much of the kosher food produced in the United States. The union has its own rabbinical organization, the Rabbinical Council of America (RCA), and a youth movement. The RCA is ideologically close to the religious Zionist stream. There is also a Union of Orthodox Rabbis, which is close to the Agudath Israel party, as well as other Orthodox rabbinical

The United States, especially its founding fathers, drew upon the Bible for inspiration in nation building, and many of its cities and towns were named after places in the Hebrew scriptures. Half of the states in the Union contain a town named Bethel. There are 30 Jerusalems and 20 Hebrons, and one can even find such places as Pisgah, Canaan, Zion, Moriah, Gilead, and Sodom. Mormons, who settled in Utah, believed that the American Indians were Jews, and other early European settlers thought that they could hear Hebrew in the various Indian dialects.

groups identified with the Satmar, Lubavitch (Chabad), and other Chassidic groups.

The Conservative establishment is the United Synagogue Council with its own Rabbinical Assembly.

The Reform movement is represented by the Union of American Hebrew Congregations. The Reform rabbinical union is called the Central Conference of American Rabbis.

The small Reconstructionist stream has its own college of rabbis in Philadelphia.

In 1926 a roof organization called the Synagogue Council of America was established to coordinate synagogues of all the different Jewish streams and especially the interreligious contacts with Christian churches. In the 1990s, however, the council was dissolved. Only 47% of American Jews are affiliated with

A street in New York's Lower East Side at the beginning of the 20th century

Jewish New Year Greetings.
Attributed to Happy Jack (Inuit, ca. 1870–1918), Nome, Alaska, 1910.
Engraved walrus tusk with gold insert

synagogues (of which only one-third attend on a regular basis). According to the 1990 survey, 38% of the total population defined themselves as Reform, 35% Conservative, and 6% Orthodox.

The United States is the second largest producer of kosher food in the world, and it exports a wide variety of such products, including matzot, meat, and wine, all over the world. In New York City in particular, there are kosher restaurants to suit every palate, including "classic" deli food, Chinese, Indian, Italian, and French (sometimes with names like Shang-Chai or Luigi Goldstein).

In certain neighborhoods of Brooklyn, and also in a number of towns in the Catskill Mountains in New York State, vibrant Chassidic communities have been established, and something of the atmosphere of the east European *shtetl* has been recreated.

✦ CULTURE AND EDUCATION ✦

Only about 15% of Jewish children attend Jewish day schools. There are more than 300 Orthodox day schools and more than 50 Conservative ones. Most of the schools of the Reform movement are affiliated with synagogues and only have classes on Sunday. There are two major institutions of higher learning under Jewish auspices: Yeshiva University in New York City and Brandeis University in Waltham, Massachusetts. There are also several smaller Jewish colleges and specialized institutes. Many non-sectarian and Christian universities also have programs of Jewish studies. Moreover, there are a number of rabbinical seminaries and teacher-training institutions. Of the former, the most noteworthy are the Isaac Elchanan Seminary connected to Yeshiva University (Orthodox), the Jewish Theological Seminary (Conservative), and the Hebrew Union College–Jewish Institute of Religion (Reform). Some of the most outstanding Jewish libraries in the world are located in the United States.

✦ MEDIA ✦

The American Jewish press is characterized by its great diversity. Virtually every organization has its own organ or bulletin. The Jewish Telegraphic Agency (JTA) distributes its *Daily News Bulletin* in the United States and throughout the world. Many Jewish papers depend on this wire service to provide them with coverage of events outside of their immediate communities. There are about 80 Jewish weeklies and several dozen monthlies and quarterlies. Of the once-great Yiddish press, only a scant number of publications remains. A number of publishers specialize in Jewish works, and many of the non-Jewish publishing houses also print books on Jewish themes. In almost all large Jewish communities, there are Jewish radio and television programs. However, the leading source of Jewish and Israeli news is the general American media and its major newspapers.

✦ ISRAEL ✦

The American–Israeli relationship has been characterized as "special." Washington's relations with Jerusalem have had an important strategic significance for Israel and have prevented its total isolation during critical periods of political pressure, especially during economic and political boycotts. Since 1985 American aid to Israel has amounted to $3 billion per annum, of which $1.8 billion represents military assistance and $1.2 billion is used for the repayment of Israel's debts to Washington.

Apart from the embassy in Washington, Israel has a consulate general in New York and consulates in Atlanta, Boston, Chicago, Houston, Los Angeles, Miami, Philadelphia, and San Francisco.

Aliya: Since 1948, 73,000 American Jews have emigrated to Israel.

✦ S I T E S ✦

Among the leading sites are the U.S. Holocaust Memorial Museum in Washington, D.C., and the Bet HaShoah–Museum of Tolerance in Los Angeles. In New York City, the Jewish Museum, the Lower East Side, and the Chassidic

neighborhoods such as Boro Park, Williamsburg, and Crown Heights are leading stops on any Jewish visitor's itinerary. The story of the immigrants, Jewish and non-Jewish, is chronicled at Ellis Island, which once served as a reception center for new arrivals. There are also many historic synagogues—first and foremost that of Newport, Rhode Island—a fine example of American colonial architecture. In distinct contrast is the ultra-modern synagogue of Elkins Park, Pennsylvania, which was designed by the famous American architect Frank Lloyd Wright. Nearly all of the large communities have a Jewish museum.

Consulate General
800 Second Avenue
New York, NY 10017
Tel. 212 499 5400, Fax 212 499 5455

Embassy
3514 International Drive N.W.
Washington, D.C. 20008
Tel. 202 364 5500, Fax 202 364 5607

✦

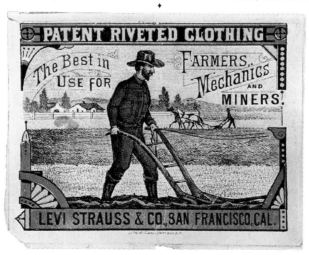

Advertisement for overalls, manufactured by Levi Strauss & Co.,
San Francisco, after 1875

Levi Strauss (1829–1902) came to the United States from Bavaria at the tender age of 19. In 1850, during the gold rush, he moved to California and opened a dry goods business. Three years later he began to manufacture trousers from blue denim reinforced with copper rivets. "Levis" jeans revolutionized the world of fashion. Close to 150 years later, they are the most widely coveted name-brand garment in every country from Afghanistan to Zimbabwe.

CANADA

GP 29,680,000 ◆ JP 360,000

◆ DEMOGRAPHY ◆

Canada's largest communities are Toronto (175,000) and Montreal (100,000), followed by Vancouver (30,000), Winnipeg (15,000), Ottawa (12,000), Calgary (7,500), Hamilton (5,000), and Edmonton (5,000). The level of intermarriage has increased over the last ten years, but remains significantly lower than in the United States. Most of the community is Ashkenazi, but there is a large population of French-speaking Moroccan Jews in Montreal. In the last decade, primarily due to immigration, Canadian Jewry grew by 14%, making it one of the fastest-growing communities in the Diaspora. Twenty-five percent of all Jews who immigrated to Canada in the past ten years were born in the Soviet Union or its successor states and 20% in Israel (an estimated 30,000 Israelis live in Canada).

◆ HISTORY ◆

After their exclusion during the period of French rule, Jews arrived together with the British soldiers who made their homes in Montreal. The first synagogue, Shaarei Israel, was consecrated there in 1768. The census of 1831 recorded 107 Jews (but there were probably others who did not declare their religion). In 1832 Canadian Jews were granted full civil rights. However, until the 1850s, aside from a few Jews scattered throughout the country, nearly all of Canadian Jewry lived in Montreal. In the 1850s, Jewish immigrants arrived from Lithuania and began to settle in Toronto and Hamilton, raising the number of Jews to 2,500 by the early 1880s.

The 1880s were watershed years for Canadian Jewry. Russian oppression brought a new influx of Jewish refugees that increased the

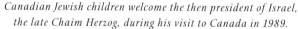

Canadian Jewish children welcome the then president of Israel,
the late Chaim Herzog, during his visit to Canada in 1989.

Jewish population to 16,000 in 1900 and to 126,000 in 1921. In the face of the Nazi onslaught against European Jews, Canada slammed its doors shut. In the years preceding the war, and during the Holocaust itself, only a few thousand Jews managed to find sanctuary there (2,000 in 1940).

The energetic campaign of the Canadian Jewish Congress after the war helped to open the gates to Holocaust survivors and refugees from North Africa. This immigration significantly increased the size of Canadian Jewry from 170,000 (1941) to 260,000 (1961). Twenty years ago, the communities of Montreal and Toronto were similar in size (i.e., 100,000), but over the years many Jews moved from Montreal to Toronto out of concern for the consequences of a possible Quebec breakaway. In the past 20 years, Toronto's Jewish community has grown by 70%.

Samuel Bronfman House, national headquarters of the Canadian Jewish Congress in Montreal

✦COMMUNITY✦

The community is well organized on both local and national levels, with programs in many different fields. The main national organization is the Canadian Jewish Congress with six regional subdivisions and headquarters at Samuel Bronfman House in Montreal. The Zionist Federation, B'nai B'rith, WIZO, and other organizations are also active, as are all the major international Jewish youth groups. The community operates a number of nursing homes and hospitals, and the latter serve both the Jewish and non-Jewish communities.

The ongoing secessionist struggle of French-speaking Quebec, in which fully one-third of the community resides, is a cause of worry to Canadian Jewry. The Montreal community is about 20% Sephardi, and many of these people are native French speakers.

The Canadian Jewish community has been especially active in several international Jewish campaigns (Soviet and Ethiopian Jewry, Israel, and Jews in Arab lands) and in some domestic legal and public struggles against anti-Semitism, Holocaust denial, and the presence of Nazi war criminals. The Canadian communities are part of the American-based Council of Jewish Federations and attend its meetings regularly.

✦

The rivalry between Montreal and Toronto Jewry is sometimes played out in discussions on the quality of the bagels produced by each community. The consensus, however, is that Montreal is the leader—a fact borne out by the vending of "Montreal bagels" in certain Toronto stores. To date there are no shops in Montreal that sell Toronto bagels.

✦ Religious Life ✦

Canadian Jews tend to be more traditional than their American co-religionists, and in 1990 some 40% of the affiliated Jews identified themselves as Orthodox, 40% Conservative, and 20% Reform. There are synagogues in nearly all the communities. In Montreal and Toronto, Chassidic Jews worship in a number of *shtiebelach*. Kosher food is widely available, and kosher restaurants are to be found in Toronto, Montreal, Winnipeg, and Ottawa. Kosher food produced in Canada is also exported to other countries.

✦ Culture and Education ✦

Toronto and Montreal have 12 Jewish schools and several *yeshivot*. There are also Jewish schools in Calgary, Vancouver, Winnipeg, and Ottawa. In Montreal some 60% of the Jewish children attend Jewish primary schools and 30% Jewish high schools. In Toronto the figures are 40% and 12% respectively.

Some of the universities offer programs in Jewish studies, notably McGill in Montreal, which also offers courses in Yiddish.

There are about 20 Jewish periodicals and newspapers, of which the most widely read is the weekly *Canadian Jewish News*, based in Toronto. Jewish publications also appear in French, Hungarian, and Yiddish. The Montreal Jewish Public Library is the only institution of its kind in North America.

✦ Israel ✦

Israel and Canada have full diplomatic relations. In addition to the embassy in Ottawa, there are consulates general in Toronto and Montreal.

Aliya: Since 1948, 7,900 Canadian Jews have emigrated to Israel.

✦ Sites ✦

Canada boasts several impressive synagogues, notably in Montreal and Toronto. The synagogue in Victoria, British Columbia, the oldest in Canada, dates back to 1862 and is registered as a national landmark. Montreal's old Jewish neighborhood, the Main, looms large in Canadian Jewish consciousness and draws many visitors. The Beth Tzedec Synagogue in Toronto houses the Canadian branch of the New York Jewish Museum that features the Cecil Roth collection of Judaica. There are also small Holocaust museums in Toronto, Winnipeg, and Ottawa.

Canadian Jewish Congress
Samuel Bronfman House
1590 Avenue Dr. Penfield
Montreal Que H3G 1C5
Tel. 514 931 7531, Fax 514 931 0548

Embassy
50 O'Connor Street, Suite 1005
Ottawa, K1P 6L2
Tel. 613 567 6450, Fax 613 237 8865

✦

Canadian postage stamp commemorating
the victims of the Shoah, 1995

BAHAMAS

GP 284,000 ◆ JP 200

◆**HISTORY AND COMMUNITY**◆
The Bahamas were first settled by the British in 1620, but at that time, relatively few Jews came to the islands. Still, a Jew, Moses Franks, served as attorney general and chief justice of the islands in the 18th century. After World War I, a few Jewish families from Poland, Russia, and the United Kingdom settled in Nassau, the capital. Later Jews came to Freeport on Grand Bahamas Island. In Nassau there is a Conservative synagogue named for Luis de Torres, the Converso who served as Columbus's interpreter and who was the first European to set foot on the soil of the New World. In Freeport there is a Reform congregation. The two congregations are joined together in the United Bahamas Hebrew Congregation. There are some ancient Jewish graves in Nassau.

◆**ISRAEL**◆
Israel is represented by its ambassador in Santo Domingo and by an honorary consul in Nassau.

United Bahamas Hebrew Congregation
P.O. Box F1761
Freeport, Grand Bahama Island
Tel. 242 373 2008

BERMUDA

GP 64,000 ◆ JP 70

◆**HISTORY AND COMMUNITY**◆
Jews have lived on the island since the 17th century, but a congregation was formed only in the 20th century. The permanent Jewish population is often outnumbered by many Jewish tourists from Britain, the United States, and Canada, and Jewish personnel attached to the U.S. military base on the island. Religious services, conducted by a lay reader, are held once or twice a month, and also on the High Holy Days, in different locations.

Jewish Community of Bermuda
P.O. Box HM1793
Hamilton HMO5

CAYMAN ISLANDS

GP 32,000 ◆ JP 15

In addition to the permanent Jewish residents, there are also Jews from abroad who spend part of the year there.

Jewish Community
P.O.Box 72, Grand Cayman Island
Tel. 345 949 4670

GP 261,000 • JP 40

• HISTORY •

Spanish and Portuguese Jews from Dutch Brazil, Cayenne, Suriname, England, Hamburg, and Leghorn came to Barbados a year after its settlement by the British in 1627. In 1654 the Jewish community of Bridgetown, the capital, was formed and a synagogue established. Another synagogue was established in Speightown, the second largest city, but it was eventually burned down by a British mob in 1739. In 1678 the Jewish population numbered 300. They cultivated sugar and coffee and engaged in general commerce. However, Jews received full civil rights only in 1820. A series of disastrous hurricanes destroyed many of the plantations and caused a general decline in the Jewish population. By 1848 only 70 Jews remained. Most of the Jewish emigrants moved to London, Newport, and the Island of Nevis. In 1925 the last professing Jew died. With the rise of Nazism in Europe, 30 Jewish families of eastern European origin settled in Barbados, and these were joined by Jews from Trinidad.

• COMMUNAL AND RELIGIOUS LIFE •

In 1987 the Nidhei Israel synagogue was rededicated and the old Jewish cemetery, containing some of the oldest Jewish graves on the American continent, was restored for use.

A group of Barbadan Jews initiated the formation of the Caribbean Jewish Congress.

• ISRAEL •

Israel is represented by its ambassador in Santo Domingo, Dominican Republic, and by an honorary consul in Bridgetown.

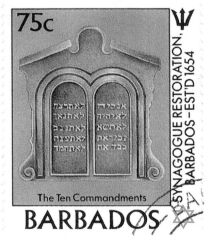

Barbadan postage stamp commemorating the 1987 rededication of the Bridgetown synagogue, built in 1654

Caribbean Jewish Congress
P.O.Box 1331, Bridgetown, Tel. 809 436 8163

Jewish Community Council
P.O.Box 256, Bridgetown, Tel. 809 432 0840

One of the most illustrious members of the Barbadan Jewish community was Haham (rabbi) Rafael Hayim Carigal, a Sephardi Jew born in Hebron. At the end of the 18th century, Carigal came to the New World to teach Judaism and Hebrew in isolated Jewish communities and also to mobilize support for the Jews in the Holy Land. He preached in Newport, Jamaica, Curacao, and Suriname, and eventually settled in Barbados, from where he tended to the needs of Caribbean Jewry. In his will, he requested that, after his death, his books and clothing be returned to Hebron.

Young members of the Conservative Patronato Synagogue in Havana, 1994

CUBA

GP 11,018,000 ♦ JP 800

♦HISTORY♦

During the Spanish colonial rule that lasted until 1898, very few Jews lived in Cuba, and nearly all of them were apostates or Jews from the Dutch Antilles holding Dutch citizenship. Jose Marti, the liberator of Cuba, enjoyed the support of the Jews of Jamaica, Texas, and Florida, and American Jewish veterans of the Spanish American War settled in Cuba. In 1904 they founded a congregation. These Jews were later joined by Sephardim from Turkey, who founded their own synagogue.

Cuba was a popular transit point for east European immigrants awaiting admission to the United States. Some of these Jews remained in Cuba. In the 1930s, a central Jewish committee was created to represent all Jewish groups. The plight of the Havana-bound passengers stranded on the German liner *St. Louis* dramatized the tragedy of Jewish refugees fleeing Nazi Germany, yet they were also denied admission to Cuba. In 1952

there were more than 12,000 Jews in Cuba; 75% lived in Havana and the rest in the rural provinces. At that time, Ashkenazim accounted for some three-quarters of the community. Cuban Jews participated in an active communal life, and they published a number of newspapers in Yiddish and Spanish with diverse religious and political orientations. Although the Cuban revolution was not directed against Jews, it destroyed the economic stability of Cuban Jewry, which was primarily middle class. The great majority of Cuban Jews, together with many of their non-Jewish countrymen, found sanctuary in Miami, Florida. Most of the remaining Jews in Cuba live in Havana.

♦COMMUNAL AND RELIGIOUS LIFE♦

The Casa de la Communidad Hebrea de Cuba is the Jewish communal organization. Four synagogues, two Sephardi and two Ashkenazi, still function. The Patronato Synagogue

---

Luis de Torres, the Converso who served as an interpreter on Columbus's first expedition (he specialized in Asian languages—Columbus was trying to reach the Far East), settled in Cuba and initiated the commercial exploitation of tobacco and its export to Europe. Five hundred years later, it remains Cuba's most famous export.

also keeps a kosher kitchen. The Jewish school closed in 1975, but the community maintains a Sunday school. Kosher food and ritual items are imported, primarily from Canada.

The Santiago de Cuba synagogue was re-dedicated in 1995 to serve the city's 80 Jews.

✦ISRAEL✦

Communist Cuba maintained normal relations with Israel until 1973, when it joined the Third World in severing diplomatic ties.

Aliya: Since 1948, 661 Cuban Jews have emigrated to Israel.

Comision Coordinadora de las Sociedades Religiosas Hebreas de Cuba, Calle I Esq.13 Vedado–Ciudad de la Habana 10400 Tel. 53 7 328 953, Fax 53 7 333 778

DOMINICAN REPUBLIC

GP 7,961,000 ✦ JP 250

✦HISTORY AND DEMOGRAPHY✦

The majority of Jews in the Dominican Republic live in Santo Domingo, the capital. There is also a community in Sosua. The great majority are of central European origin.

Jews from Curacao settled in Hispaniola in the 19th century but did not form a community. However, they did have a cantor and *mohel*. The oldest Jewish grave is dated 1826. The Jewish group became prominent in Dominican life, but over the years, intermarried with the local population, and most of them converted to Christianity. Among their descendants were President Francisco Henriquez y Carvajal (1916) and his son Pedro Henriques Urena, who became the leading Dominican man of letters.

The Dominican Republic was one of the very few countries prepared to accept mass Jewish immigration in the 1930s when Jews were imperiled by the rise of Nazism. At the Evian Conference, it offered to accept up to 100,000 Jewish refugees. The Dominican Republic Settlement Association (DORSA) was formed with the assistance of the JDC and helped settle Jews in Sosua, on the northern coast. About 700 European Jews reached the settlement, where they were assigned land and cattle. Other refugees settled in the capital, Santo Domingo. In 1943 the number of Jews in the republic peaked at 1,000. Since that time, it has been in constant decline due to emigration and assimilation. A very high percentage of the Jews has intermarried, but many non-Jewish spouses and the children of mixed marriages participate in Jewish communal life.

✦COMMUNAL LIFE✦

Jewish life is organized by the Parroquia Israelita de la Republica Dominicana. There are two synagogues, one in Santo Domingo and the other in Sosua. A rabbi divides his time between the two communities. A Sunday school in Santo Domingo is attended by 15–20 children. A chapter of the International Council of Jewish Women is active. The community publishes *Shalom*, a bimonthly magazine. In Sosua there is a small Jewish museum.

✦ISRAEL✦

Israel and the Dominican Republic enjoy full diplomatic relations.

Centro Israelita de la Republica Dominicana P.O.Box 2189 (Avenida Saraaota) Santo Domingo Tel. 809 535 6042, Fax 809 542 1908

Embassy Pedro Henriquez Urena 80 Apartado Postal 1404, Santo Domingo Tel. 809 541 8974, Fax 809 562 3555

FRENCH GUYANA

GP 153,000 ♦ JP 80

♦HISTORY AND COMMUNITY♦

In 1659 the Dutch West India Company nominated a refugee from Brazil, David Nassy, as a patron of an exclusive Jewish settlement on the island of Cayenne named Remire. There Jews were granted equal rights, freedom of conscience, public worship, and the right to establish a synagogue and a Jewish school. The Portuguese Jewish refugees from Brazil were joined by Sephardi Jews from Leghorn, Italy. The Jewish settlement of Remire enjoyed a short period of prosperity cultivating sugar cane and indigo. However, when the Dutch ceded Cayenne to the French in 1664, the Jews trekked to nearby Suriname and settled in "the Jewish Savannah." In 1992 a group of about 20 Jewish families from North Africa and Suriname refounded a community in Cayenne. Jews are aided in maintaining Jewish life by the Chabad organization. Israel is represented by its ambassador in Caracas, Venezuela.

Jewish Community
Pilo Sav 19, Av D'estrees
Cayenne 97300, BP 655 Cayenne
Guyane Francaise CEDEX 97335
Tel. 594 30 39 34, Fax 594 31 78 93

GUADELOUPE

GP 431,000 ♦ JP 50

♦HISTORY AND COMMUNITY♦

The first Jewish group to settle the island consisted of three shiploads of refugees from Brazil in 1654 who were cordially received by the French owner of the island. The Jews initiated sugarcane plantations, and refineries accounted for the island's main exports. Civil unrest, and ultimately British occupation, caused an exodus of Jews to other Caribbean islands. Finally "The Black Code" of Louis XIV in 1685 ordered the expulsion of Jews. In the second half of the 20th century, Jews from North Africa and France settled on the island. In 1988 the synagogue Or Sameah was founded together with a community center, Talmud Torah, kosher store, and cemetery.

Communaute Culturelle Israelite
1 Bas du Fort
97190 Gosier, Pointe-a-Pitre
Tel. 590 90 99 08

> *A Jewish refugee from Brazil called Pietre started a fish processing plant on the coast of Guadeloupe. Gradually that place was called Pietre's Point, and it ultimately became the town of Pointe-a-Pitre.*

HAITI

GP 7,259,000 ♦ JP 25

♦HISTORY AND COMMUNITY♦

Luis de Torres, Columbus's Converso interpreter, was the first Jew to set foot in Haiti. The first Jewish immigrants came from Brazil in the 17th century, after Haiti was conquered by the French. They were joined by Jews from Curaçao, Bayonne, and Bordeaux, and owned large plantations all over the island. However, as a result of the revolt of Toussaint L'Ouverture in 1804 their numbers, together with the rest of the white population, dwindled. In the beginning of the 20th century, Jews from Lebanon, Syria, and Egypt settled in Haiti, followed by Jews from eastern Europe in the 1930s. There has been steady emigration during the second half of the century. Most of the remaining Jews live in Port-au-Prince.

The Jews of Haiti have never been able to establish a communal organization. Religious services are organized in a private home.

♦ISRAEL♦

Israel and Haiti enjoy full diplomatic relations. Israel maintains an honorary consulate in Port-au-Prince and is represented by its ambassador in Panama.

Contact:
P.O. Box 687
Port-au-Prince
Tel. 509 1 20 638

MARTINIQUE

GP 384,000 ♦ JP 90

♦HISTORY♦

The first Jews settled in Martinique at the start of the 17th century, establishing themselves in Dutch commercial outposts. In 1654 the noble owner of Martinique, M. de Parquet, overcame the fierce opposition of the Catholic religious orders and admitted 300–400 Portuguese Jewish refugees from Brazil. These experienced farmers founded plantations and sugar refineries and also processed cacao and vanilla. In 1667 a synagogue was founded. However, the Jesuit opposition to Jewish settlement produced an order by Louis XIV expelling the Jews from the French islands in 1685. Most of the 96 remaining Jews in Martinique left for Curaçao. In the 1960s and 1970s, Jews from North Africa and France settled in Fort de France.

♦COMMUNAL LIFE♦

The community maintains a synagogue and community center. The latter includes a Talmud Torah, youth club, and *chevra kaddisha*. Kosher food is available, and there is a store that sells only kosher products.

> *The president of the first Jewish community of refugees from Brazil, Benjamin da Costa d'Andrade, learned cacao processing from the local Indians. He produced cacao pills and exported them to France under the name of "chocolate."*

Association Culturelle Israelite de la Martinique
Maison Grambin
Platean Fofo–Voie Principale
97233 Schoelcher, Martinique
Tel. 596 61 51 31

✦HISTORY✦

Jamaica was a Spanish colony from 1494 to 1655. During that period, there was a constant stream of Conversos from the Iberian peninsula, mainly from Portugal. The British occupation enabled these covert Jews to return to Judaism. They were joined by Jewish refugees from Brazil in 1662, from England in 1663, from Essequibo (Guyana) in 1666, and from Suriname, Barbados, and the European cities of Bordeaux, Bayonne, and Amsterdam. Although permitted to profess their religion openly and to own land, they did not obtain full equality until 1831. In the 17th and 18th centuries, the Jews controlled the sugar and vanilla industries and played a leading role in foreign trade and shipping. In the 19th century, they were prominent in the political, social, and cultural life of the country. In 1849, for example, 8 of the 47 members of the House of Assembly were Jews, and the House adjourned for Yom Kippur. In 1881 the Jewish population reached 2,535 out of 13,800 white citizens. In the 20th century, Jews from Syria and

Cemetery adjacent to the
Shaare Shalom Synagogue, Kingston

Germany joined the community. However, the Jewish population diminished due to economic decline, emigration, and intermarriage.

✦COMMUNAL LIFE✦

The various communities amalgamated to form the United Congregation of Israelites, which is mixed Sephardi–Ashkenazi. There is only one functioning synagogue, but the community also maintains a school called the Hillel Academy and a home for the aged. Chapters of WIZO and B'nai B'rith also exist.

✦ISRAEL✦

Israel and Jamaica enjoy full diplomatic relations. Israel is represented by its ambassador in Santo Domingo (Dominican Republic).

✦SITES✦

Jews settled all over Jamaica, and there were synagogues in Kingston, Spanish Town, Port Royal, and Montego Bay. The ruins of many of these can be visited, as can 14 Jewish cemeteries.

United Congregation of Israelites
Shaare Shalom Synagogue
P.O. Box 540, Kingston 6
Tel. 809 927 7948, Fax 809 978 6240

✦

CURACAO AND ARUBA

GP 197,000 in Curacao, 71,000 in Aruba
♦JP 300 in Curacao, 100 in Aruba

♦HISTORY♦

The first group of Jews arrived in the Netherlands Antilles from Amsterdam in 1651. They were later joined by Jews fleeing from Brazil, whom the Portuguese had captured from the Dutch. The Jewish community was founded in 1659, and in 1732 the synagogue Mikve Israel was consecrated in Willemstad, Curacao. In the last quarter of the 17th century, Jews established plantations growing sugarcane, tobacco, cotton, indigo, and citrus. They also played an important role in the country's commerce, especially in the import of supplies from Europe and the export of tropical produce. With the expulsion of Jews from the French islands of Martinique and Guadeloupe, the number of Jews in Curacao increased and by 1780 reached 2,000, constituting more than half of the white population. The Curacao community became the "mother community" of the Americas and assisted other communities in the area, mainly in Suriname and St. Eustatius. It also financed the construction of the first synagogues in New York and Newport.

By 1946 Jews in Aruba were sufficiently numerous to organize for worship and to plan Hebrew classes, a social center, and, in 1962, a synagogue.

In the 20th century, a number of Ashkenazi Jews settled in the Antilles, and today they account for a majority of the Jewish population. However, by the mid-20th century, the number of Jews started to decline, primarily due to emigration and intermarriage.

♦COMMUNAL LIFE♦

There are two synagogues in Willemstad, Mikve Israel–Emanuel, which is Sephardi–Reconstructionist, and an Orthodox Ashkenazi congregation. There is a community Hebrew school, and kosher food is available. There is also a synagogue in Oranjestad in Aruba. The community publishes a monthly journal called *Mikve Israel*.

A popular dish among Curacao Sephardim are sponge cookies. These are baked for the holidays and especially for brit mila *ceremonies.*
3 well-beaten eggs
3 1/2 ounces sugar
Pinch of salt
1/4 tsp. cinnamon
1/2 tsp. vanilla
5 1/2 ounces flour
1/2 tsp. baking powder
Beat eggs, sugar, salt, and cinnamon well. Blend in the vanilla. Fold in flour and baking powder by hand. Drop the batter by tablespoons on a greased sheet that has been lightly floured. Cookies should be about two inches apart. Bake at 350°F for 10 minutes, then lower the oven to 265°F for 5 minutes or until the cookies are brown. Take out and loosen from the sheet. Place them back in the "off" oven to crisp. The recipe is sufficient for two dozen cookies. The use of sugar, vanilla, and cinnamon highlights the importance of these products, traditionally produced by the Jews of the Caribbean.

Curacao's Mikve Israel–Emanuel Synagogue, built in 1732

✦ISRAEL✦

Israel is represented by its ambassador in Caracas and by an honorary consul in Willemstad.

✦SITES✦

A Jewish museum exists in the old Portuguese synagogue in Willemstad. The present Mikve Israel–Emanuel Synagogue, with its sand-covered floors, is a noted example of Western Sephardi synagogal architecture of the 18th century. The 17th-century Jewish cemetery in Blenheim is one of the oldest in the New World.

United Netherlands Portuguese Congregation
Mikve Israel–Emanuel
Kerk Strat 29, P.O. Box 322
Willemstad, Curacao, N.A.,Tel. 599 9 611067

Israelitische Gemeente
Beth Israel Synagogue, P.O.Box 50
Oranjestad, Aruba
Tel. 297 823 272, Fax 297 836 032

P U E R T O   R I C O

GP 3,736,000 ✦ JP 2,500

✦HISTORY✦

When the island passed from Spanish to American rule at the end of the Spanish-American War in 1898, there were practically no Jews there. However, with the rise of Nazism in Europe, Jewish refugees made their way to Puerto Rico. The Jewish Community Center was founded in 1942. In the 1950s and 1960s, the community was bolstered by the arrival of Jews from the United States and Cuba. Most of the Jews live in the capital, San Juan. There are a few families in Ponce and Mayaguez.

✦COMMUNAL LIFE✦

In San Juan, there are two synagogues, one Conservative and the other Reform. Chapters of Hadassah, B'nai B'rith, and Young Judea are active. Hebrew school classes are held in the building of the community center. Kosher food is available.

Shaare Zedek Synagogue–Community Center
903 Avenida Ponce de Leon
Santurca 00907
Tel. 809 724 4157

> *Leonard Bernstein, the Jewish conductor and composer, wrote the music for* West Side Story. *The classic American musical, which was adapted for Hollywood, focuses on a love story amidst the street battles between Puerto Rican and white ethnic gangs in New York's Hell's Kitchen. But the Jewish connection did not stop there. Stephen Sondheim wrote the lyrics and Arthur Laurents the original play. Ernest Lehman created the film script and Jerome Robbins was the choreographer. In the movie, the part of Maria, the love-struck Puerto Rican heroine, was played by Jewish actress Natalie Wood.*

U . S .   V I R G I N   I S L A N D S

GP 106,000 ✦ JP 300

✦HISTORY✦

Jewish settlement was initiated in 1655 when the islands were still under Danish rule. At that time Spanish and Portuguese Jews came as ship owners, planters of sugarcane, and producers of rum and molasses. They arrived from Recife, Brazil; Suriname; Barbados; Holland; and France. The real growth of the Jewish population in the islands of St. Thomas and St. Croix came as a direct result of the destruction in 1781 of the Jewish community on the nearby Dutch island of St. Eustatius, which was attacked by the British for having aided the American Revolution. In 1796 the synagogue Berakha v'Shalom v'Gmilut Hassadim in St. Thomas was founded, and that congregation exists to the present day. By 1850 Jews accounted for half the island's white population, or about 400 people.

The Danish authorities, and later the American ones, sometimes nominated Jews as governors of the islands. With the opening of the Panama Canal, the Jewish population diminished, and most of the islands' Jews emigrated to Panama. By 1942 the Jewish population numbered no more than 50. Today the number of Jews is increasing due to an influx of Jews from the North American mainland.

✦COMMUNAL LIFE✦

The synagogue in St. Thomas was reconstructed after a fire in 1833. The community enjoys the services of a rabbi.

Hebrew Congregation of St. Thomas
P.O. Box 266
St. Thomas 00804
Tel. 1 809 774 4312

SURINAME

GP 432,000 ♦ JP 200

♦ HISTORY ♦

The Jewish community of Suriname, concentrated in Paramaribo, is one of the oldest in the Americas. The first Jews settled between the years 1635 and 1639. They were joined by Jews from England during the British ownership of the island in 1660. The most important group arrived in 1664. The newcomers were refugees who had fled from the Jewish colony of Remire on the island of Cayenne when it was occupied by the French. With the Dutch occupation of Suriname in 1668, Spanish and Portuguese Jews came from Amsterdam. By the first half of the 18th century, they were joined by Ashkenazi Jews from Rotterdam, and the Jewish population reached 2,000, half of the white population of the territory. With special privileges they had received from the British, and later Dutch, authorities, the Jews settled in the "Jodensavanne" or "the Jewish Savannah" in which they owned more than 115 plantations specializing in sugar growing and refining. By the end of the 18th century, Jews began to settle in Paramaribo, where they founded two synagogues. However, in the 19th century, with the economic decline of the area, the number of Jews declined.

♦ COMMUNAL AND RELIGIOUS LIFE ♦

The communal organization is the Kerkeraad der Nederlands Portugees Israelitische Gemeente in Suriname. The two synagogues in the capital, dating back to the 18th century, have been restored by the Suriname government, together with private contributors, and today serve the needs of the Jewish community. There is a community newspaper called *Sim Shalom* that appears in Dutch.

♦ ISRAEL ♦

Israel and Suriname have enjoyed full diplomatic relations since the country attained independence in 1975. Israel is represented by its ambassador in Caracas and by an honorary consul in Paramaribo.

♦ SITES ♦

In Jerusalem on the Riverside, the capital of the abandoned semi-autonomous Jewish area known as "the Jewish Savannah," remain the ruins of one of the oldest synagogues in the Americas, Berakha ve' Shalom, founded in 1685.

Kerkeraad der Nederlands Portugees Israelitische Gemeente in Suriname
P.O. Box 1834, (Klipsenstr. 2–10), Paramaribo
Tel. 597 471 313, Fax 597 471 154

♦

The Jewish settlers saw "the Jewish Savannah" as a second holy land. They gave many of their plantations or settlements Hebrew biblical names. Therefore, in Suriname one could find Beersheba, Carmel, Mahanaim, Dothan, Succoth, Moriah, Nahamou, and many others.

Interior of the Ashkenazi synagogue in Suriname.
It is said that the sand-covered floor reminded the Jews of their
wandering in the desert and was also symbolic
of the Conversos' need to muffle footsteps in their clandestine synagogues.

LATIN AMERICA

ﺃﺭﺟﻨﺘﻴﻦ ﻣﻦ ﺑﻼﺩ ﺍﻣﺮﻳﻜﺎ

Jewish gauchos in a Jewish agricultural colony, 1920s

ARGENTINA
BOLIVIA
BRAZIL
CHILE
COLOMBIA
COSTA RICA
ECUADOR
EL SALVADOR
GUATEMALA
HONDURAS
MEXICO
NICARAGUA
PANAMA
PARAGUAY
PERU
URUGUAY
VENEZUELA

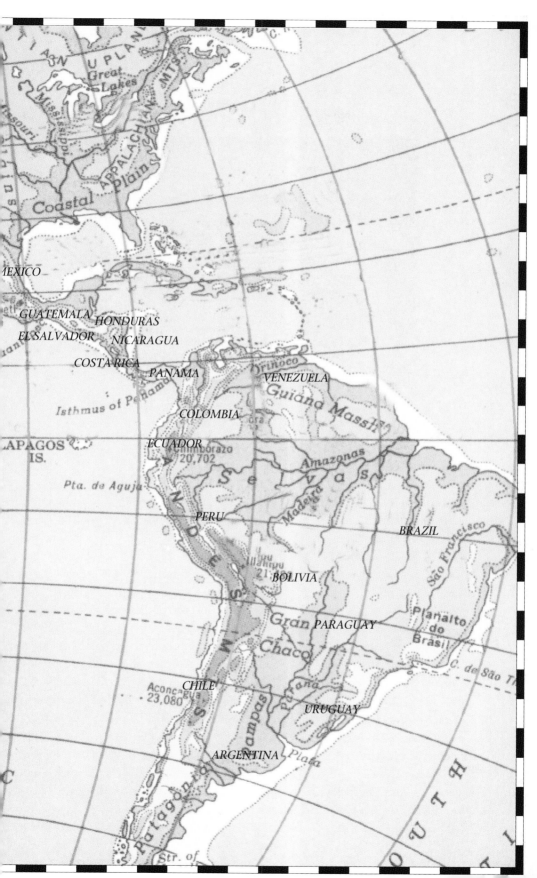

GP 35,219,000 ✦ JP 230,000

*Poster celebrating the 50th anniversary of the
Jewish agricultural colonies, 1939*

✦DEMOGRAPHY✦

The Argentine Jewish community is the largest in Latin America. There are 180,000 Jews in Buenos Aires, 20,000 in Rosario, and smaller communities in Cordoba (9,000) and in Santa Fe (4,000). The towns of La Plata, Bahia Blanca, Mendoza, and Mar del Plata each have a Jewish population of 4,000. Jews also reside in rural areas.

The majority of Argentine Jewry is Ashkenazi, with roots in central and eastern Europe. About 15% are Sephardim, descendants of immigrants from Syria, Turkey, and North Africa. Jews of east European stock are called "Rusos," whereas those with Middle Eastern roots are called "Turcos." Today most Jews are native Spanish speakers, and both Yiddish and Ladino are on the wane.

Argentine Jewry plays a prominent role in industry, commerce, politics, the free professions, and the arts. The democratic regime is seen as a catalyst accelerating the integration, and consequently the assimilation, of Jews in Argentina.

✦HISTORY✦

The first Jews to settle in Argentina were Conversos who came from Portugal and Spain in the 16th and 17th centuries. They quickly assimilated and disappeared. In the mid-19th century, immigrants from western Europe, especially from France, arrived. They were followed by those fleeing from the poverty and pogroms in Russia at the end of the same century. This vast immigration was prompted by Argentina's open-door policy towards immigrants. Aside from the small number of purely Jewish agricultural colonies which they established, Jews entered a basically heterogeneous society. Between 1918 and 1930, following the Russian Revolution, anti-revolutionary fervor developed into anti-Semitism directed against the Rusos. There was a prevailing atmosphere of antagonism toward Jews. Nevertheless limited Jewish

✦

immigration continued. During the years from 1930 to 1946, political unrest also manifested itself in the form of anti-Semitism.

The ascent to power in 1946 of President Juan Peron, a known Nazi sympathizer, was a source of concern for the community. Jewish immigration was halted, and Argentina became a haven for Nazi criminals on the run. Despite Peron's declarations of sympathy for the Jews and for Israel, Buenos Aires became an international center for anti-Semitic activity. After the overthrow of Peron in 1955, there was another wave of anti-Semitism, which was further aroused by the capture and abduction of Adolf Eichmann in 1960.

During the military regime of 1976 to 1983, 1,000 of the 9,000 known victims of state terrorism were Jews. Under the rule of President Raul Alfonsin and the introduction of democracy, Jewish civil and political status improved. The election of President Carlos Menem of the Peronist party in 1989 caused great apprehension within the community. However, Menem has sought to strengthen his ties with both the Argentine Jewish community and world Jewry.

·COMMUNITY·

The major political Jewish organization is the Delegation of Argentine Jewish Associations (DAIA), which represents all communities and organizations before the authorities and is responsible for safeguarding the rights of its members. The largest organization representing the Ashkenazi majority is the Argentina Jewish Mutual Aid Association (AMIA). The organization deals with the religious and cultural activities of the Ashkenazi commu-

nity. It is also responsible for social welfare, and the operation of several old-age homes, a Jewish hospital, and a community restaurant for the needy. The Sephardi community has three organizations of its own. The Vaad ha-Kehillot is the umbrella organization of all the communities in the provinces. The Zionist Federation (OSA) and its women's organizations are very active. The headquarters of the Latin American Jewish Congress is situated in Buenos Aires.

The bomb that devastated the Buenos Aires Jewish community center (the seat of DAIA and AMIA) in July 1994 was a physical and emotional blow to Argentine Jewry. The explosion cost 100 lives, Jews and non-Jews, and injured many more. It also destroyed the archives of the 100-year-old community. This attack followed the bombing of the Israeli Embassy in Buenos Aires in 1992. Much criticism has been directed against the government and the president for not doing enough to apprehend the perpetrators of these terrorist attacks.

In an effort to improve Argentina's public image, tainted as it was by anti-Semitism and the presence of Nazi criminals, and due to pressure by the World Jewish Congress, President Menem ordered the release of files concerning Nazis in Argentina. In 1988 the parliament also passed a law against racism and anti-Semitism. Nevertheless, there are still some 30 small neo-Nazi groups. In general Menem has developed a pro-Israeli, pro-Jewish, and pro-American line and has made a commitment to combating anti-Semitism and xenophobia.

Argentina's first Jewish gauchos (cowboys) arrived from Russia in 1889 aboard the S.S. Weser. These 824 Jews bought land and established the first Jewish agricultural colony, named Moisesville. Faced with many hardships, they turned to the Jewish philanthropist Baron Maurice de Hirsch. Baron Hirsch became the first Jewish benefactor to plan large-scale resettlement of Jews from Russia and founded the Jewish Colonization Association. At the peak of its activities, it owned some 600,000 hectares of land populated by more than 20,000 Jews. Although many of the cooperatives are now largely non-Jewish, they are still run by Jews.

♦ R E L I G I O U S L I F E ♦

Traditionally the Ashkenazim and Sephardim have their own separate synagogues and religious institutions. The majority of the synagogues are Orthodox, but in practice many are closer to the Conservative movement. Buenos Aires has 50 Orthodox synagogues, five Conservative, and one Reform. In 1962 the Conservative movement established the Argentine branch of the New York–based Jewish Theological Seminary, which prepares students for the rabbinate. Kosher food is readily available. There are many kosher butcher shops and markets, as well as several kosher restaurants.

♦ CULTURE AND EDUCATION ♦

There are some 70 Jewish educational institutions in Argentina, including elementary and secondary day schools and kindergartens, with some 22,000 Jewish pupils. About 17,000 Jewish children (20%)

Extricating the dead and wounded from the ruins of the AMIA-DAIA building, July 1994

study in the Jewish educational system of Buenos Aires. Most of the schools have a Zionist bent.

The nature of Jewish cultural life is greatly influenced by the presence of east European immigrants. Until recently many cultural activities, publications, and plays have been in Yiddish. The past few years have seen the appearance of publications in Hebrew *(Darom, Habima Haivrit)* and in Spanish *(El Israelita Argentino, Vida Nuestra, Comentario, La Luz)*. The Latin American Jewish Congress publishes the monthly, *Oji*, and the journal, *Cologio*. Buenos Aires is home to an independent branch of the YIVO Institute for Jewish Research, which was first founded in Vilna in the 1920s.

In Buenos Aires, there are also a Jewish museum, three libraries, and four Jewish book-stores. Each community has its own social club: Sociedad Hebraica (Ashkenazi) and Casa Sephardi. Cordoba has an impressive community center. The Maccabi Sport Federation is also very active in Argentina.

♦ I S R A E L ♦

Israel and Argentina established diplomatic relations in 1949.

Aliya: Since 1948 45,000 Argentine Jews have emigrated to Israel.

♦ S I T E S ♦

The country's oldest synagogue is in Buenos Aires. The attached Jewish Museum features photographs and artifacts from the early Jewish agricultural colonies. The major colonies are in Moisesville, Rivera, and General Roca, and these contain traces of the Jewish *gauchos.*

Delegacion de Asociaciones Israelitas Argentinas (DAIA)
Ayacucho 632, 6 Piso, 1026 Buenos Aires
Tel. 54 1 375 4747/ 375 4730/ 375 4742
Fax 54 1 375 4742

Latin American Jewish Congress
Casilla de Correo 20, Suc.53
(Larrea 744), 1453 Buenos Aires
Tel. 54 1 962 5028/ 961 4534
Fax 54 1 963 7056

Embassy
Avenida de Mayo 701 10 Piso
1007 Buenos Aires
Tel. 54 1 342 1465, Fax 54 1 342 5307

♦

B O L I V I A

GP 7,593,000 ✦ JP 500

✦DEMOGRAPHY✦

Bolivia's Jews mostly live in La Paz, the capital, but there are smaller communities in Santa Cruz and in Cochabamba. The majority of Bolivian Jews are Ashkenazim of central and eastern European descent. The Jewish community of Bolivia has decreased significantly since its peak of 10,000 in the late 1940s.

✦HISTORY✦

Spanish Conversos immigrated to Bolivia as early as the colonial period. They worked in silver mines and even participated in the founding of Santa Cruz. Established families in the area still maintain certain Jewish customs and are possibly descendants of these Conversos.

Courtyard of the Colegio Boliviano Israelita in La Paz

The modern Jewish community dates back to the arrival of immigrants from Europe in 1905. Still, by early 1933, only 30 Jewish families lived in Bolivia. Large-scale immigration began in the early 1930s, consisting mainly of refugees from eastern Europe. In addition some German and Austrian Jews immigrated to Bolivia at the beginning of World War II. Despite the government's decision in 1940 to grant Jews entry permits, Jewish immigration was on a small scale. Beginning in the 1950s, there was a continuous stream of Jewish emigration, resulting from the political and economic instability of the country, the severe climate, and the lack of educational opportunities.

✦ C O M M U N I T Y ✦

The Circulo Israelita de Bolivia is the central Jewish communal organization and is recognized by the Bolivian government. This organization is a union of its predecessors, the Circulo Israelita de La Paz, established by east European Jews, and the German Comunidad Israelita de Bolivia. The Circulo maintains a cemetery, the *bikur cholim,* two synagogues, and a home for the aged. There are branches of WIZO in La Paz and Santa Cruz and Maccabi sports clubs in La Paz and Cochabamba. Santa Cruz also has several other social organizations.

✦ R E L I G I O U S   L I F E ✦

In La Paz there are three synagogues but only one rabbi. Kosher food, including meat, is available. There is also a synagogue in Santa Cruz and another in Cochabamba.

✦ C U L T U R E   A N D   E D U C A T I O N ✦

The Colegio Boliviano Israelita has a kindergarten, a primary school, and a secondary school. Though it was founded in 1940 to serve Jewish children, the majority of its pupils are now non-Jewish. There is also a supplementary Jewish college and a Talmud Torah for bar and bat mitzvah preparation. The Bolivia–Israel Cultural Institute organizes activities to promote cultural understanding.

✦ I S R A E L ✦

Israel and Bolivia maintain full diplomatic relations.

Aliya: Since 1948, 396 Bolivian Jews have immigrated to Israel.

Circulo Israelita de La Paz
P.O. Box 1545, La Paz
Tel. 591 2 325 925, Fax 591 2 342 728

Embassy
Avenida Mariscal Santa Cruz No. 21
Edificio Esperanza, 10 Piso
Casilla 1309.1320, La Paz
Tel. 591 2 391 126, Fax 591 2 391 712

Moritz (Don Maurcio) Hochschild (1881–1965) was a German-born mining engineer who lived in Chile. In 1923 he moved to Bolivia, where he pioneered the development of tin mining. Hochschild's innovative methods for extracting tin provided employment for tens of thousands of Bolivians. With the rise of Hitler, Hochschild returned to his native Germany to recruit people to work in his mining enterprises. He also attempted to establish an agricultural colony for Jewish refugees and spent almost $1 million on the project, which was ultimately abandoned. Although he remained aloof from institutionalized Jewish life, thousands of Jews in Latin America owe their escape from Nazi-dominated Europe to Hochschild.

BRAZIL

GP 161,087,000 ✦ JP 130,000

✦DEMOGRAPHY✦

The great majority of Brazilian Jews are Ashkenazim and live in the two largest cities—Sao Paulo (60,000) and Rio de Janeiro (40,000). Smaller communities exist in Bahia, Belem, Manaus, Porto Alegre, Recife, and also in more remote areas.

✦HISTORY✦

Conversos arrived with the first settlers in 1500 when Brazil was proclaimed a Portuguese colony. From 1548 and throughout subsequent centuries, the persecution of Conversos in Portugal resulted in a steady stream of new arrivals who secretly continued Jewish traditions. Their major occupation was in the development of sugar plantations. Jews were also very active in Brazilian cultural life. The first Brazilian song was written by a Converso by the name of Bento Pinto (1601).

When the Dutch conquered several areas in Brazil in the mid-17th century, they were welcomed by the Conversos, who were again able to openly practice Judaism. During these years, they were joined by hundreds of Jews from Amsterdam, including Rabbi Isaac Aboab da Fonseca and the cantor Raphael Moses de Aguilar, both of whom settled in Recife. However, when the Dutch were ousted by the Portuguese in 1654, the Jews suffered tremendous persecution, and large numbers lost their lives as a result. Many Jews returned to Amsterdam or settled in the Caribbean. Twenty-three arrived in New Amsterdam (New York), where they laid the foundations for a new community. Others who continued to live in Brazil as Catholics were absorbed by the general population.

The overt Jewish presence in Brazil was renewed after the abolition of the Inquisition investigation in 1773 and again after Brazil's

✦

Prayers on Tisha b'Av in a synagogue in Belem, 1981

declaration of independence from Portugal in 1822. Moroccan Jews immigrated and formed small communities in northern Brazil, establishing the first synagogue in Belem in 1824 and later a synagogue in Manaus. There were also some west European Jews in Rio de Janeiro and Sao Paulo.

The modern-day Brazilian Jewish community emerged in the 20th century with the arrival of Russian Jews. The Jewish Colonialization Association (JCA) established a number of Jewish agricultural colonies in southern Brazil. At the onset of World War I, there were 5,000 to 7,000 Jews in Brazil. After the war, immigration accelerated, and by 1930 there were close to 30,000 Jews. In 1930 the Brazilian government changed its immigration policy, and in 1937 secret instructions were given to Brazilian consulates throughout the world to deny visas to Jews who were desperately trying to flee the threat of Nazism. Limited Jewish immigration continued, despite the restrictions. In the postwar period, Jewish immigrants from Hungary, Syria, Lebanon, Turkey, Morocco, and Egypt bolstered the community.

Jewish architects are responsible for much of the modern architecture in Brazil. Russian-born Gregori Warchavchik built the first modern house in the country, in Sao Paulo in 1930. The most prolific Brazilian architect, working in the American skyscraper style, was Rino Levi. Henrique Mindlin's work changed the skyline of Rio de Janeiro and Elias Kaufman worked on the plans for the country's new capital city, Brasilia.

✦ C O M M U N I T Y ✦

Brazil is a federation; consequently the Jews in each state have an organization of their own. The central body representing all the federations and communities in Brazil is the Confederacao Israelita do Brasil (CONIB), founded in 1951. This umbrella organization includes 200 associations engaged in promoting Zionist activity, Jewish education, culture, and charity. Most Jewish activity takes place in the Hebraica clubs, exclusive social clubs that are privately owned and traditionally headed by leaders of the community. All major international Zionist organizations are represented in Brazil.

The large communities run welfare institutions and hospitals for the needs of their members. The Hospital Israelita Albert Einstein, supported by the Sao Paulo community, is considered the best in the country.

Brazilian Jews have in general enjoyed comfort, security, and prosperity in a country characterized by the harmonious coexistence of various ethnic groups. Nevertheless, there have been occasional manifestations of anti-Semitism. Brazil has an impressive coalition of intellectuals, clergymen, and statesmen who lead the struggle against racism and anti-Semitism. The success of the Jews, and the liberal and tolerant atmosphere in which they live, has accelerated the pace of assimilation.

✦ R E L I G I O U S   L I F E ✦

The majority of the Jewish community in Brazil identifies itself as secular Zionist. Until the 1930s, under the influence of the east European immigrants, the main religious stream was Orthodox. With the arrival of Jews from central Europe, the Reform movement was introduced as well. Today most synagogues are Conservative or Reform. In recent years, the Chabad movement has made inroads in Sao Paulo, establishing a synagogue, a *mikva*, and a kindergarten.

In both large communities, kosher food is readily available, and there are a number of kosher restaurants.

✦

◆CULTURE AND EDUCATION◆

Jewish education is organized by the National Institute for Education and Culture, and each state has its own committee. Sao Paulo has four Orthodox schools and four traditional ones. There are several Jewish schools in Rio de Janeiro, among them the 500-student Bar-Ilan School, which also has a kosher dining room and a synagogue. The University of Sao Paulo offers Judaic studies. There are several Jewish newspapers and journals published both in Yiddish and in Portuguese, including *Resenha Judaica, O Hebreu, Menorah,* and *Shalom.*

The Hashomer Hatzair, B'nai Akiva, and Habonim Dror youth movements are active in Brazil. The Syrian and Lebanese Jewish communities have their own youth groups. There are sport clubs affiliated with Hebraica in Sao Paulo and Rio de Janeiro, and these provide sporting and cultural facilities.

◆ISRAEL◆

Israel and Brazil maintain full diplomatic relations.

Aliya: Since 1948, 8,103 Brazilian Jews have emigrated to Israel.

◆SITES◆

For a glimpse of Rio's old Jewish neighborhood, visitors should stop at the area around Rua Alfandega. The Jewish museum in Rio de Janeiro chronicles the history and culture of the city's Jewish community. Visitors to Sao Paulo will want to stop at the city's Hebraica Club, a self-contained Jewish resort community with swimming pools, gym, tennis courts, theater, ballroom, library, kosher snack bar, and other attractions. Another Sao Paulo sight is the Lasar Segall Museum, which presents the work of the Lithuanian-born Jewish artist who was active in the German Expressionist movement and later made his home in Brazil.

Confederacao Israelita do Brasil (CONIB)
Avenida Nilo Pecanha, 50—Gr. 1601
20020–100 Rio de Janeiro
Tel. 55 21 240 0034, Fax 55 21 240 2717

Embassy
Avenida das Nacoes lote 38
70424–900 Brasilia
Tel. 55 61 244 7675/ 244 7875
Fax 55 61 244 6129

Guests at the Hotel Palestina in the Quatro Irmaos colony, 1920s

CHILE

GP 14,421,000 ◆ JP 21,000

◆DEMOGRAPHY◆

Most of the Jews live in Santiago, but there are also communities in Vina del Mar (Valparaiso), Concepcion, Temuco, and Valdivia. The great majority are Ashkenazim. There are also some sects of Indians in the southern region who consider themselves Jews. They observe some Jewish laws and customs and call themselves "Iglesia Israelita."

◆HISTORY◆

The first Jews who came to Chile were Conversos. One, Rodrigo de Organos, was among those who discovered the country in 1535. This community grew but eventually disintegrated with the arrival of the Inquisition in Chile and the subsequent persecution of the Converso community. Only in 1810, when Chile became independent from Spain, were Jews legally allowed to immigrate to Chile. Yet it was not until the beginning of the 20th century that a significant number of Jews actually chose to settle there. By 1914 there were about 500 Jews, but the community remained small until the immigration of Jews from Germany in the late 1930s. These refugees were able to gain entrance, despite strict immigration restrictions. With the considerable growth of the community, anti-Semitism also increased,

The ark in the Circulo Israelita Synagogue, Santiago, 1981

and the Comite Representativo, a central organization representing Chilean Jewry, was established in response.

◆COMMUNITY◆

The Comite Representativo de las Entidades Judias de Chile (formerly the Comite Representativo) is the umbrella organization of the community and represents every Jewish organization in the country.

The Federacion Sionista de Chile is the largest Zionist body. There are quite a few other Jewish and Zionist organizations including B'nai B'rith, WIZO, and *bikur cholim*.

◆RELIGIOUS LIFE◆

Most of the Jews are religiously unaffiliated. A small minority of the community keeps kosher. In Santiago there are several synagogues representing the various streams of Judaism. Synagogues exist in several other places including in Vina del Mar. Santiago has several kosher food shops.

◆CULTURE AND EDUCATION◆

There are two Jewish day schools, the Haim Weizman–ORT Hebrew Institute in Santiago and a smaller school in Vina del Mar. In addition there is a Talmud Torah and the Ben-Gurion Zionist Institute. The University of Chile has a Jewish studies department.

The Santiago community maintains a volunteer fire department called "Bomba Israel." Among the firefighters are several rabbis, and the two fire engines fly both Chilean and Israeli flags. In a number of other Latin American and Caribbean countries, the first fire departments were also established by Jews.

The community publishes three weekly newspapers: the Ashkenazi *La Palabra Israelita*, the Zionist *Mundio Judio,* and the Sephardi *El Vocero*. The community also has a Sephardi museum and a B'nai B'rith documentation center.

✦ISRAEL✦

Chile and Israel maintain full diplomatic relations.

Aliya: Since 1948, 4,723 Chilean Jews have emigrated to Israel.

✦SITES✦

The striking sanctuary of the Circulo Israelita Synagogue in Santiago is distinguished by the stained glass windows that encircle the *bimah,* casting flame-like colors under the Ten Commandments.

Comite Representativo de las Entidades
Judias de Chile
Avenida Miguel Claro, 196, Santiago
Tel. 56 2 465 927, Fax 56 2 235-2459

Embassy
San Sebastian 2812 Piso 5
Casilla 1224, Santiago
Tel. 56 2 246 1570, Fax 56 2 231 0197

✦

COLOMBIA

GP 36,500,000 ✦ JP 5,650

✦DEMOGRAPHY✦

While the Jewish population is concentrated in the capital city of Bogota, there are also small communities in Cali, Barranquilla, and Medellin. The community has an even mixture of Ashkenazi and Sephardi Jews.

✦HISTORY✦

The first Jewish presence in the country dates back to the 16th century, when Conversos came with the Spanish conquerors. With the establishment of the Inquisition in Cartagena, many of those who practiced Judaism in secret were discovered and executed. Only in the beginning of the 19th century did Jews openly enter the country. Mass immigration began after World War I, when Jews arrived from both the Middle East and eastern Europe. Large numbers of Jews from central Europe also arrived on the eve of World War II. The 1939 ban on Jewish immigration severely restricted Jewish settlement until 1950.

✦COMMUNAL AND RELIGIOUS LIFE✦

The central organization of the community is the Confederacion de Asociaciones Judias de Colombia and is located in Bogota. The east Europeans, Sephardim, and Germans of the community each have their own organizations. In addition there are community centers, youth organizations, and Zionist organizations such as WIZO and B'nai B'rith. There are nine synagogues, four of which are

Jorge Isaacs (1837–1895) was the Colombian national writer and one of the great literary figures of Latin America. The son of a converted English Jew and a Colombian mother, his novel Maria, *a story about his love for one of his Jewish cousins from Jamaica, became one of the classics of Latin American literature and was translated into many languages. The Colombian government presented a bust of Isaacs to the Hebrew University, in Jerusalem, where it stands to this day, highlighting the Jewish origins of this great writer.*

located in Bogota, with a total of 13 rabbis officiating in the community. Kosher food is readily available. Bogota, Cali, Barranquilla, and Medellin each has a Jewish school. In Bogota there is also a *kollel* and many Jewish study groups. Jews have an active cultural life, with six publications and two Jewish radio programs. The Museum of Alfredo de la Espriella has dedicated a gallery to Judaism and Jewish subjects.

◆ISRAEL◆

Israel and Colombia maintain full diplomatic relations.

Aliya: Since 1948, 1,570 Colombian Jews have emigrated to Israel.

Centro Israelita de Bogota
Apartado Aereo 12.372
Santa Fe de Bogota
Tel. 57 1 625 4377, Fax 57 1 274 9069

Embassy
Edificio Caxdac
Calle 35, No. 7-25 14 Piso, Bogota
Tel. 57 1 287 7962, Fax 57 1 287 7783

COSTA RICA

GP 3,500,000 ◆ JP 2,500

◆HISTORY◆

The first Jewish settlers were Sephardi Jews from Curacao, Jamaica, St. Thomas, and Panama who arrived in the 19th century. Most of these Jews mixed with the local population and settled in Cartago, San Jose, and Puerto Limon. After World War I, Jews arrived from Poland and, in smaller numbers, from Turkey. Costa Rica did not encourage Jewish settlement, and laws were later passed against peddlers, foreign merchants, and foreign land ownership.

◆COMMUNITY◆

The leading communal organization is the Centro Israelita Sionista, founded in 1930. The Centro includes WIZO and other Zionist groups, B'nai B'rith, and the Jewish Women's Welfare Association, affiliated with the International Council of Jewish Women. The Jewish sports center is the venue of Jewish athletics. The Centro publishes a monthly called *Hayom* and also a bulletin devoted to bettering Christian–Jewish relations.

San Jose has a synagogue, Shaarei Zion, which is served by a rabbi. There is a burial society and a Jewish cemetery. Kosher food is imported from abroad. The Haim Weizmann School, a primary and secondary institution, is attended by the majority of Jewish children.

◆ISRAEL◆

Israel and Costa Rica enjoy full diplomatic relations, and Costa Rica maintains an embassy in Jerusalem.

Centro Israelita Sionista de Costa Rica
Apartado Postal 1473–1000, San Jose
Tel. 506 233 9222, Fax 506 223 5801

Embassy
Calle 2 Avenidas 2 y 4
Apartado 5147-1000, San Jose
Tel. 506 221 0684, Fax 506 257 0867

Ecuador

GP 11,700,000 ✦ JP 1,000

✦ Demography ✦

In the last few years there has been an influx of Jews from other Latin American countries which has bolstered the community. The majority of Ecuadoran Jews are of German ancestry and most live in Quito. There are also small communities in Guayaquil, Riobaba, Ambato, and Cuenca. The Ecuadorian Jewish community is fairly homogeneous and insular. There have been relatively low levels of assimilation and intermarriage, since the Jews of Ecuador form a middle class between the largely European Catholic upper class and the native population.

✦ History ✦

The Jewish presence in Ecuador dates back to colonial times, when Conversos were among the Spanish settlers of the country. In 1904 European Jews began to arrive. Immigration accelerated with the rise of the Nazi regime in Germany. Following the establishment of a liberal constitution in 1936, Ecuador eased its restrictions on Jewish immigration and thus became a haven for many refugees. In 1939 Ecuador admitted 165 Jews who had fled Germany on the ship *Koenigstein* after several Latin American countries had refused them entrance permits. In the ten years preceding World War II, approximately 3,000 Jews came to Ecuador, and in 1950 the Jewish population reached 4,000. Since that time and until very recently, there has been a steady decline due to emigration.

✦ Communal and Religious Life ✦

The central body in the Ecuadorian Jewish community is the Asociacion Israelita de Quito. There is a parallel organization in Guayaquil, the Comunidad de Culto Israelita. Both function independently. There is a synagogue in Quito served by a rabbi. A Zionist organization, the Federacion Sionista del Ecuador, functions in Quito. WIZO, the Jewish Women's Society, and B'nai B'rith.

✦

The Jewish People's Library pavilion set up by the Latin American Jewish Congress

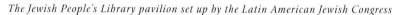

◆CULTURE AND EDUCATION◆

There is no official Jewish school in Ecuador, although teachers are hired by the community to train children in Jewish subjects. There are Jewish community centers in both Quito and Guayaquil.

◆ISRAEL◆

Ecuador and Israel maintain full diplomatic relations.

Aliya: Since 1948, 137 Ecuadorian Jews have emigrated to Israel.

Asociacion Israelita de Quito
Apartado 17–03–800
Avenida 18 de Septiembre 954, Quito
Tel. 593 2 502 734, Fax 593 2 502 733

Embassy
Av. Eloy Alfaro 969 y Amazonas
P.O. Box 2138, Quito
Tel. 593 2 565 509, Fax 593 2 504 635

Jose Abel Castillo y Albornoz (1854–1940) was the founder of El Telegrafo, one of the first newspapers in the country. He was also a pioneer in the establishment of air mail service to Ecuador. In the 1930s, Albornoz worked to help central European Jews settle in Ecuador.

EL SALVADOR

GP 5,780,000 ◆ JP 120

◆HISTORY◆

Except for the occasional transit of Portuguese Conversos, there were no Jews in the country until the first half of the 19th century when Sephardim from France settled in the town of Chaluchuapa. They were joined by Jews from Alsace who moved to San Salvador in the second half of the 19th century. At the start of the 20th century, Jews from Germany and eastern Europe arrived. In 1976 there were some 370 Jews in El Salvador, but during the civil war many left the country. With the return of peace, some families have resettled.

◆COMMUNAL AND RELIGIOUS LIFE◆

The Comunidad Israelita de El Salvador was established in 1944. A Jewish center was opened in 1945 and a synagogue in 1950. Since 1980 services have been conducted in a private house. A Zionist organization was established in 1945, and WIZO is also active.

◆ISRAEL◆

Israel has an embassy in San Salvador, and El Salvador an embassy in Jerusalem. During the civil war, the Israeli Honorary Consul was kidnapped and murdered by guerrillas.

Comunidad Israelita de El Salvador
Apartado Postal (06) 182, San Salvador
Tel. 503 814 444, Fax 503 215 264

Embassy
85, Av. Norte No. 619, Colonia Escalon
Apartado Postal 1776, San Salvador
Tel. 503 298 5331, Fax 503 279 0040

Dr. Juan Lindo, the son of a Jewish father, Don Joaquin Fernandes Lindo, has the unique distinction of having served as president of two different countries. From 1841 to 1842, he served as president of El Salvador, where he established the national university. From 1847 to 1852, Lindo was president of Honduras and founded the national educational system.

GUATEMALA

GP 10,930,000 ♦ JP 1,200

♦HISTORY♦

Although Inquisition documents indicate the presence of Conversos in Guatemala during the Spanish colonial period, the origins of the present Jewish community date back only to the middle of the 19th century. At that time, Jews from Germany settled in the country, having been attracted by the possibilities of developing the coffee trade and building cotton mills. At the beginning of the 20th century, they were joined by Jews from eastern Europe and the Middle East and, with the advent of Nazism, by German Jewish refugees. Guatemala was one of the very few countries in Latin America that had legislation aimed at excluding Jews. In 1932 an expulsion decree against "peddlers" (but aimed at Jews) was enacted. This was followed by a 1936 ban on immigration from "Asian countries," under which category Guatemalan authorities included Poland, a measure designed to block Jewish immigration. Still, by 1939 there were some 800 Jews in the country, mainly in Guatemala City and Quetzaltenango. In recent years nearly all the Jews in the provinces settled in the capital.

Guatemala can boast of two "firsts" in Israeli history. It was the first country to announce its recognition of Israel— announced by Jorge Garcia Granados in the U.N. immediately after the proclamation of the state. Guatemala was also the first country to open an embassy in Jerusalem under the same Garcia Granados. Later, under the weight of international pressure, the embassy was moved to Tel Aviv.

♦COMMUNAL AND RELIGIOUS LIFE♦

The Jewish organizations are united under the Consejo Central. The three main Jewish groups are the Sociedad Israelita de Guatemala (Beth-El), which is Reform and mainly of German origin; Magen David, which is Sephardi; and the Centro Hebreo, which is composed of people with roots in eastern Europe. Each of the organizations maintains its own synagogue. There is also a B'nai B'rith lodge, a Maccabi club, and a branch of WIZO, all of which function under the Consejo Central umbrella. The Consejo operates a Jewish kindergarten.

♦ISRAEL♦

Israel and Guatemala enjoy full diplomatic relations.

Comunidad Judia Guatemalteca
Apartado Postal 502, Guatemala, C.A.
Tel. 502 2 311 975, Fax 502 2 325 683

Embassy
13a Avenida 14-07, Zona 10,Guatemala City
Tel. 502 363 5674, Fax 502 333 6950

♦

HONDURAS

GP 5,820,000 ♦ JP 40

♦HISTORY AND COMMUNITY♦

Until the first half of the 20th century, there were only isolated Jewish families. In 1920 several families from eastern Europe arrived, and with the rise of the Nazi rule, Jews from Germany came to the country. By 1947 the Jewish population numbered 130. The Jews are divided between the capital, Tegucigalpa, and San Pedro Sula, the second largest town. With the arrival of the German Jews, the Jewish Relief Committee of Honduras was established. The only synagogue in the country is located in San Pedro Sula and there is a Jewish Sunday school. There is also a local WIZO chapter.

♦ISRAEL♦

Israel and Honduras enjoy full diplomatic relations. Israel is represented by its ambassador in Guatemala City.

Comunidad Hebrea de Tegucigalpa
Apartado Postal 5091, Tegucigalpa, D.C.
Tel. 504 32 8555/ 374968

MEXICO

GP 92,720,000 ♦ JP 40,700

♦DEMOGRAPHY♦

All but a handful of Mexican Jews live in Mexico City (37,500). Most of the rest live in Guadalajara (200 families), Monterrey (200 families), and Tijuana (60 families). Close to 300 families are scattered in other towns such as Veracruz, Puebla, and Cuernavaca. The number of people registered as "Israelites" in the official census includes Protestant sects and *mestizos* (Mexicans of mixed Indian and European ancestry) who profess to Jewish roots, such as the "Iglesia de Dios" and "Casa de Dios." None of these groups is recognized by the rabbinate in Mexico or in Israel.

Today the community is equally divided between Sephardim and Ashkenazim. The original Spanish Jews were totally integrated into the general population and lost their Jewish identity. The modern-day Jewish community has remained ethnically, culturally, and religiously distinct but has developed an identity based on the synthesis of Jewish and Mexican cultural patterns. The rate of intermarriage is estimated at between 5% and 10%.

♦HISTORY♦

The first Jews in Mexico were Conversos who arrived with the Spaniards in 1521. In the Diego Rivera Hall of the Nation in Mexico City, there is a mural portraying the arrival of Cortes at the port of Veracruz. Hernando Alonso, "the first Jewish jewelry merchant," appears at the explorer's side.

Despite various persecutions, Conversos continued to settle and prosper in Mexico, and the development of trade and commerce was largely due to their industriousness.

Some even held high positions in the service of the king of Spain and the Catholic Church. The main concentrations of Conversos were in Mexico City, Veracruz, and Guadalajara. After the abolition of the Inquisition in the 19th century, the Jews continued to be accused of deicide and the original cry of "death to Judas" and "death to the Jews" remains a custom in some small Mexican villages. After Mexico attained independence in 1821, the number of Jews diminished. From 1825 to 1867 there was some immigration from Germany. The Emperor Maximilian brought with him many Belgian, French, and Austrian Jews.

At the beginning of the 20th century, Jewish immigrants arrived from Russia, Poland, and Germany, as well as Syria, Turkey, Greece (especially Salonika), and Lebanon. Consequently, both Ashkenazi and Sephardi communities were established. The new immigrants settled in every part of the country. They prospered as peddlers

A Mexican–Indian Jew praying in the synagogue at Venta Prieta, 1986

and proprietors of small stalls in public markets and introduced the system of buying on credit. Anti-Semitic incidents eventually forced the Jews to abandon their trade in the market and to open private stores. This ultimately raised their economic status. In the 1920s and 1930s, the Ashkenazi community established a *chevra kaddisha*, the Zionist Federation, and the Socialist Bund. The two communities, Ashkenazi and Sephardi, founded separate and parallel welfare and women's bodies, as well as separate social and cultural associations. Mexican Jewry was divided by a linguistic gulf. Yiddish was prevalent in the Ashkenazi organizations and Ladino in the Sephardi.

◆ C O M M U N I T Y ◆

Mexican Jewry is highly organized. It comprises four different Jewish communities, based on place of origin: Aleppo, Damascus, eastern Europe, and the Balkans. Each of these groups is represented in the Comite Central Israelita. Each constituent community has its own synagogues. The Tribuna Israelita promotes close ties with Mexican society and monitors anti-Semitism. Women are represented by the Mexican Council of Jewish Women.

Almost all the Jews in Mexico City are members of the Comite Central de la Comunidad Judia de Mexico, which offers extensive social and cultural activities. There are other social clubs and sports centers in Monterrey, Tijuana, and Guadalajara.

The Zionist Federation, WIZO, Na'amat, and associations of friends of Israeli universities are all active. There are some 16 youth movements with approximately 2,000 members. Every year several hundred young people visit Israel. The Federation of Mexican–Jewish University Students (FEMUJ) and the Federation of Zionist Students of Latin America (FUSLA) serve the Jewish student population.

Although there have been some manifestations of anti-Semitism, there has been little violence directed at Jews.

◆

◆ RELIGIOUS LIFE ◆

Mexico City has 23 synagogues; all but two are Orthodox. The others are Conservative. Kosher food is readily available, and there are a number of kosher restaurants.

◆ CULTURE AND EDUCATION ◆

The Education Committee, *Vaad Hachinuch*, is an umbrella body that coordinates all the educational institutions and their activities. The extensive Jewish education network, composed of more than a dozen day schools in Mexico City, is run by professional Jewish educators. It is estimated that 80% of the Jewish children of school age receive their education within the Jewish educational system. All the schools offer both primary and secondary education. There are also several *yeshivot* and a number of *kollelim*. Almost every community and congregation has a Talmud Torah for bar mitzvah preparation, as well as classes and lectures on Jewish subjects. The Hebraic University provides specialized training for Jewish teachers.

The Universidad Iberoamericana offers a program of Judaic studies. There are about ten Jewish newspapers and magazines.

The Ashkenazi community maintains the Tuvia Maizel Museum, dedicated to the history of Mexican Jewry and to the Holocaust. There are also plans to build the first Institute for Holocaust Documentation in Latin America.

◆ ISRAEL ◆

Israel and Mexico enjoy full diplomatic relations.

Aliya: Since 1948, 3,200 Mexican Jews have emigrated to Israel.

◆ SITES ◆

In the capital's downtown area, where the first Jewish immigrants settled, one can find the first synagogue (founded in 1912) and the National School of Medicine, which formerly housed the Inquisition authorities. The most Jewish atmosphere is in Polanco, a middle-class neighborhood with several synagogues. In the Nidhei Israel, Mexico City's Ashkenazi Community Center, there is a small Holocaust museum. The CDI offers many cultural attractions and has an art gallery and theater. It also sponsors an annual Jewish music festival.

Comite Central Israelita de Mexico A.C.
Cofre de Perote 115
Lomas Barrilaco, 11010 Mexico DF
Tel. 52 5 540 3273, Fax 52 5 540 3050

Embassy
Sierra Madre No. 215
Mexico City 10, D.F.
Tel. 52 5 201 1500, Fax 52 5 201 1555

◆

Sidney Franklin (1903–1977), a Brooklyn-born Jew, came to Mexico in the 1920s and became one of the country's most celebrated bullfighters. He later befriended the author Ernest Hemingway, who wrote of the Jewish matador "…one of the most skillful, graceful, and slow manipulators of a cape fighting today." After his retirement, Franklin became a broadcaster of televised bullfights in Mexico City.

GP 4,238,000 ♦ JP 10

♦HISTORY AND COMMUNITY♦

It is believed that Conversos lived in Nicaragua in the 16th and 17th centuries. Modern immigration began in 1848, when Jews arrived from Germany, France, and Holland. Following World War II, there was also an influx of Jews from eastern Europe. The community reached a peak in 1972 with approximately 250 members, most living in Managua. But in the aftermath of an earthquake that destroyed much of Managua in December 1972, many Jews emigrated. The Sandinista government sequestered the synagogue and other Jewish property and also imprisoned the community leader. He managed to escape and fled the country together with most of the Jews.

The Congregacion Israelita de Nicaragua was the central Jewish organization until 1979. The community maintained a synagogue and social center, and there was a B'nai B'rith lodge and WIZO chapter. Since 1979, however, the Jewish community has been dormant.

♦ISRAEL♦

With the ouster of the Sandinista regime, Israel and Nicaragua have restored diplomatic relations. Israel is represented by its ambassador in Guatemala City.

Jewish cemetery in Managua, 1975

Kabbalat Shabbat in a Jewish school in Panama City, 1983

✦HISTORY AND DEMOGRAPHY✦

Most of the Jews live in Panama City, but there are also communities in Colon, David, and the former American Canal Zone. In the last two decades, immigration has tripled the number of Jews in the community, which includes more than 1,000 Israelis.

Although Panama was a Spanish colony, due to its geographic location it served as a transit point for many Spanish–Portuguese Jews enroute from North to Latin America or from the Atlantic to the Pacific oceans. Spanish Jews camouflaged as "New Christians" and as "Portuguese merchants" settled there. However, the Inquisitions of Lima and Cartagena sent emissaries to prevent any Jewish activity. Settlement by Jews openly practicing their Judaism started in 1836 with the arrival of Portuguese Jews from Jamaica, Guadeloupe, and Curacao. They were joined by Jews from the Virgin Islands and later from central Europe.

In 1876 the Spanish–Portuguese synagogue Kol Shearith Israel was founded in Panama City and in 1890 the Kahal Kodesh Yaacov in Colon. With the construction of the Panama Canal, and especially following World War I, Jews came from Syria, Turkey, and Eretz Israel, and these founded Shevet Ahim in Panama City, Ahvat Ahim in Colon, and a small community in David. American Jewish officials and service men stationed in Balboa in the former American Canal Zone established their own community.

✦COMMUNAL AND RELIGIOUS LIFE✦

The representative body of the Jewish community is the Consejo Central Comunitario Hebreo de Panama. Panama has active B'nai B'rith and WIZO chapters. The community has three synagogues—including a Reform congregation. The largest is the Sephardi (Orthodox) Shevet Ahim, which also has a *mikva* on the premises. Kosher food is readily available and there are five kosher restaurants.

Panama is the only country besides Israel that has had two Jewish presidents in the 20th century—Max Shalom Delvalle (1969) and Eric Delvalle Maduro (1987–1988).

✦CULTURE AND EDUCATION✦

There are two Jewish high schools with a total enrollment of 1,300 students. The Hebrew cultural center in Panama City sponsors many communal cultural and sports activities.

✦ISRAEL✦

Israel and Panama have full diplomatic relations.

Aliya: Since 1948, 180 Panamanian Jews have emigrated to Israel.

Consejo Central Comunitario Hebreo de Panama
Apartado Postal 55–0882, Paitilla
00001 Panama
Tel. 507 293 733

Embassy
Edif. Grobmaes, 5 piso
Calle Manuel Maria Icaza 12
Apartado 6357, Panama City 5
Tel. 507 264 8022, Fax 507 642 706

PARAGUAY

GP 4,960,000 ✦ JP 1,000

✦HISTORY AND DEMOGRAPHY✦

The great majority of Jews live in the capital, Asuncion. A small number of European Jews came to the country at the end of the 19th century but were soon absorbed into the native community. Sephardi Jews from Palestine began to settle in Paraguay on the eve of World War I and, together with Jews from Turkey and Greece, founded the first synagogue. In the 1920s, a second wave of Jews arrived from Poland and Russia and established an Ashkenazi community. The largest migration occurred between 1933 and 1939, when over 15,000 Jews from Germany and elsewhere in central Europe found refuge in Paraguay. The majority continued on to neighboring countries once they were able to obtain visas. Paraguay has historically served as a rest stop for Jews on their way to Argentina and other Latin American countries with more restrictive emigration policies.

✦COMMUNAL AND RELIGIOUS LIFE✦

The Paraguayan community is publicly represented by the Consejo Representativo Israelita de Paraguay. There are at least ten other Jewish organizations, including WIZO, B'nai B'rith, and several youth movements. There are three synagogues: one Ashkenazi, one Sephardi, and one affiliated with Chabad that distributes kosher food to the community. These institutions function without a rabbi. The community maintains a Jewish school, the Colegio Integral Estado de Israel, which provides both primary and secondary education for the majority of Jewish children. There is a Jewish museum with a Holocaust memorial in Asuncion.

The community is concerned about the current rate of assimilation and intermarriage. Most of the intermarried couples provide their children with a Jewish education.

✦ISRAEL✦

Israel and Paraguay maintain full diplomatic relations.

Consejo Representativo Israelita de Paraguay
Casilla de Correo 756
General Diaz 657, Asuncion
Tel. 595 21 441 744, Fax 595 21 448 289

Embassy
Calle Yegras 437 C/25 de Mayo
Edificio San Rafael, 8 piso
P.O. Box 1212, Asuncion
Tel. 595 21 495 097, Fax 595 21 496 355

PERU

GP 23,944,000 ◆ JP 3,000

◆DEMOGRAPHY◆

Almost the entire Jewish population, the vast majority of whom are Ashkenazim, is located in the capital city of Lima. The population has been shrinking since the 1940s.

◆HISTORY◆

Jews first entered the country with the leaders of the Spanish invasion in 1532. Yet, with the start of the Inquisition, these Conversos were subjected to persecution. Many were executed and even burned at

The Colegio Leon Pinelo (Hebrew day school) in Lima, founded in 1951

the stake. Modern Jewish immigration began around 1870 with the arrival of groups of central European Jews. This community largely assimilated into the general population. In 1880 a second wave of immigrants came from North Africa. Numerous refugees from Turkey settled in the country following World War I and the Jewish community reached its peak of 6,000 after World War II.

◆COMMUNAL AND RELIGIOUS LIFE◆

The central communal body is the Asociacion Judia del Peru, which both represents the Jewish community to the public and coordinates the activities of the community's three synagogues. The community also maintains a B'nai B'rith lodge, a Hebraica Club, Zionist youth movements and many social assistance institutions. A majority of the school-age children attends the Colegio Leon Pinelo. The community publishes two Jewish newspapers.

◆ISRAEL◆

Peru maintains full diplomatic relations with Israel.

Aliya: Since 1948, 1,150 Peruvian Jews have emigrated to Israel.

Asociacion Judia del Peru
Apartado 1943
Husares de Junin 163, Lima 11
Tel. 51 14 241 412/ 244 797
Fax 51 14 312 412

Embassy
Natalio Sanchez 125, 6 Piso
Santa Beatriz
Apartado 738, Lima
Tel. 51 14 334 431, Fax 51 14 338 925

◆

In 1870 Henry Meiggs arrived in Peru, a fugitive from justice in the United States. Meiggs, a native of Catskill, New York, had made a name for himself as both a builder of railways and as a financial trickster. Once in Peru, he designed and supervised construction of a railway that, at the time, was the highest in the world—a line that "broke the back of the Andes." Nothing was known of Meiggs's Jewish origins until 1875, when he donated a plot of land to the Sociedad de Beneficencia Israelita in Lima for the specific purpose of establishing a Jewish cemetery. The Jewish community was grateful for his generosity because until then they had no choice but to bury their dead in Lima's Protestant burial ground. As was later explained, Meiggs wanted to be buried as a Jew, but he understood that this would only be possible if he established a Jewish cemetery.

URUGUAY

GP 3,205,000 ♦ JP 30,000

A kosher bakery in Montevideo, 1980s

♦DEMOGRAPHY♦

Nearly all the Jews of Uruguay live in Montevideo. There are several hundred families living in Paysande and in other small towns. Some 75% of Uruguayan Jews are of eastern European origin, 14% of western European descent, and 11% are Sephardim.

♦HISTORY♦

The history of Uruguay's Jewish community parallels that of the country, which has been a geographic buffer between Argentina and Brazil. Uruguay did not have an active Inquisition, and there are some traces of Conversos who lived in the 16th century. Today's Jewish community dates back to 1880. For many Jews, Uruguay was a temporary station on their way to Argentina or Brazil. In 1909 there were 150 Jews living in Montevideo. By 1916 there were enough Ashkenazi Jews to form a *chevra kaddisha*, and in 1917, to open the first synagogue. In 1918 there were some 1,700

Jews in Uruguay, 75% of them Sephardim (from the Balkans, Syria, Cyprus, Morocco, Egypt, Greece, Turkey, and France) and the rest from eastern Europe (mostly from Russia, Poland, and Lithuania). In the years from 1925 to 1928 and in 1933, many Jews passed through on their way to Argentina. At the outset of World War II, Uruguay imposed immigration quotas. Nevertheless, in 1939 some 2,200 Jews succeeded in entering the country, mostly from Germany, as did an additional 373 Jews who arrived in 1940. After the war, Jews from Hungary and from the Middle East also sought refuge in the country.

Jews have always been well integrated in the cultural, economic, and political life of Uruguay. That integration brought with it an increase in assimilation.

♦COMMUNITY♦

The Jewish community of Uruguay is made up of some 10,000 families, organized into four separate religious communities—Polish–Russian, Sephardi, German, and Hungarian.

The 60 Jewish organizations in Uruguay are all under the auspices of the Israelite Central Committee. There are several Zionist social and cultural organizations, B'nai B'rith, eight youth movements, several women's organizations, and the Association of Friends of Israeli Universities.

There is little tradition of organized anti-Semitism in Uruguay. The attitude of the government, political parties, and the press has generally been supportive, and there is an awareness of the dangers of anti-Semitism and racism to the country.

◆RELIGIOUS LIFE◆

There are 14 Orthodox synagogues in Uruguay and a Conservative one (the German community). Two Orthodox rabbis and two Conservative rabbis cater to the needs of the religious communities. The Chabad Center, which has its own rabbi, is not affiliated with the community organization. Kosher food, both locally produced and imported, is readily available. There are several kosher restaurants, mainly in Jewish institutions.

◆CULTURE AND EDUCATION◆

Uruguayan youth have four Jewish schools with curricula both in Spanish and Hebrew. The "Integral" school is the largest and includes classes from pre-school through high school. The Chabad Center also runs an "integral" school. There are also several vocational schools offering special training. About a third of the country's Jewish children attend these schools.

There are a few Jewish weekly and monthly publications and a regular radio program.

◆ISRAEL◆

Uruguay was the first country in South America to officially recognize Israel, and the first Israeli Embassy on the continent was opened in Montevideo in November 1948.

Aliya: Since 1948, 6,850 Uruguayan Jews have emigrated to Israel.

◆SITES◆

Montevideo has a Jewish museum and documentation center, as well as a Holocaust memorial museum that has been declared a historic national landmark. A monument to Golda Meir stands in the square named for the late Israeli leader, adjacent to the opera house Teatro Solis. In Rodo Park by the seaside stands the Albert Einstein Monument. Within the Jewish cemetery there are monuments in memory of the victims of the Shoah, Israeli soldiers who fell in battle, and victims of the terrorist attack on the AMIA building in Buenos Aires. The old Jewish neighborhood of Goes contains traces of its Jewish past.

Comite Central Israelita del Uruguay
Casilla de Correo 743
Rio Negro 1308, Piso 5–Esc. 5
Montevideo
Tel. 598 2 916 057, Fax 598 2 906 562

Embassy
Bulevard Artigas 1585/89
Montevideo
Tel. 598 2 404 164, Fax 598 2 495 821

◆

During his term as president of Uruguay, Dr. Luis Alberto Lacalle participated in the "World Conference on Anti-Semitism and Prejudice in a Changing World" in Brussels in 1992 as a guest of the World Jewish Congress. On that occasion, the Uruguayan statesman declared that "Uruguay, a relatively new state in Latin America, conducts itself according to Judeo–Christian principles that are the basis of our political and cultural life... The special relationship towards the Jewish people and Israel may stem from the probable Jewish roots of many of our Spanish ancestors."

VENEZUELA

GP 22,315,000 • JP 30,000

•DEMOGRAPHY•

More than half of the Jewish population of Venezuela lives in Caracas. The other large community is in the oil center of Maracaibo. The Jews are evenly divided between Ashkenazim and Sephardim.

•HISTORY•

The first Jewish settlement in Venezuela was in the coastal town of Coro, where Jews from the nearby island of Curacao settled presumably around 1820. Jewish merchants in Curacao maintained trade ties with the Venezuelan government, which was in need of essential supplies. As trade relations between the Dutch colonies in the nearby islands increased, and following the enactment of the Venezuelan constitutions of 1819 and 1821 that granted religious freedom, Jews settled in the country.

The Jews of Curacao gained an important place in Venezuelan history as supporters of Simon Bolivar. When the Venezuelan-born liberator of Latin America fled to Curacao, he and his sister found sanctuary from the Spaniards at the home of the Jewish lawyer Mordecai Ricardo. After the Spanish defeat in 1822, Jews from Curacao began settling on the nearby mainland, first in Coro, then in Cabello, and finally in Caracas. Since Venezuela was a relatively secular country with a flexible social structure, many of the Jews attained positions of prominence. These Jews were only loosely organized, and the majority were assimilated.

Communal bat mitzvah ceremony in a Caracas synagogue, 1981

The modern community began to evolve at the beginning of the 20th century with the immigration of Jews from North Africa, Lebanon, Syria, and the Balkans. These newcomers founded the first Jewish communal organization, the Asociacion Israelita de Venezuela, in the late 1920s. In the 1930s, there was also immigration from central and eastern Europe, particularly from Romania, Poland, and Hungary, but the community still numbered fewer than 1,000. They formed their own organization, the Union Israelita de Caracas. During World War II, Jewish immigration was restricted. In 1950 an estimated 6,000 Jews lived in Venezuela. In the late 1950s, however, the community was enlarged by the arrival of Jews from Egypt, Hungary, Israel, and neighboring countries in Latin America.

General Juan (Isaac) de Sola (1795–1860), a scion of a prominent Jewish family in Curacao, was a hero of the Latin American war of liberation. He joined Simon Bolivar in Curacao and travelled with him to South America. De Sola lost a hand in the battle of Carabobo, but after the war he became one of the most outstanding citizens of newly-liberated Venezuela.

✦COMMUNITY✦

The central umbrella organization is the Confederacion de Asociaciones Israelitas de Venezuela which encompasses four organizations: Asociacion Israelita de Venezuela (Sephardi), Union Israelita de Caracas (Ashkenazi), the Zionist Organization, and B'nai B'rith. Also affiliated to the central body are the Union of Jewish Women, several youth movements, and representatives from smaller towns. Use of community educational facilities, sports and social clubs, and membership in the Zionist Organization or B'nai B'rith is reserved for registered members of one of the kehillot. All Zionist organizations are represented in the Confederacion. There are also organizations of friends of the various universities in Israel. The union in Caracas runs an old-age home. Despite the separate organizations, the Ashkenazi and Sephardi Jews are united in political, social, cultural, and educational matters. The rate of intermarriage is increasing.

There are some sporadic outbursts of anti-Semitism, but they do not represent a widespread phenomenon. Jews have not played a prominent role in political life.

✦RELIGIOUS LIFE✦

There are some 15 synagogues in Venezuela, all but one considered Orthodox. The majority of Ashkenazi and Sephardi synagogues are in Caracas. Synagogues are to be found in Maracaibo, Porlamar, Valencia, Maracay, and Puerto La Cruz. The Ashkenazi Beth Din meets in the Great Synagogue in Caracas. Both the Ashkenazi and Sephardi kehillot offer mikvaot. The Chabad House caters to the needs of the small number of ultra-Orthodox Jews. It also operates a yeshiva. In Caracas kosher food is available at several stores and at the Hebraica club.

✦CULTURE AND EDUCATION✦

Between 70% and 90% of the school-age Jewish children from the two religious communities attend the Jewish school, the Colegio Moral y Luces Herzl/Bialik, which merged with the Colegio Hebraica. The schools offer kindergarten, primary, and secondary schooling. Colegio Cristobal Colon Sinai provides an Orthodox education, as does the Kolel Nahalat Yacov. The Colegio Bilu in Maracaibo also educates children from neighboring communities. Higher education is provided by the Yeshiva Guedola de Venezuela and the Higher Institute of Jewish Studies.

The main social and cultural organization is the Hebraica Jewish Sports and Social Center, which also has a training center attached

✦

to it. It sponsors lectures, performances, and concerts. The Sephardi community holds a Sephardi Week every other year with conferences and presentations on culture. WIZO runs an annual two-week art exhibit, considered one of the most important in the country.

The main Jewish paper is the weekly *Nuevo Mundo Israelita*. There is also a weekly radio program on Jewish affairs called "Shalom." Several plays written on the Jewish experience in Venezuela have been produced, including *My Life with Mother* by Elisa Lerner and works by Johnny Gavlovsky and Isaac Chokrun, a former director of Venezuela's national theater. There is a Jewish bookstore in Caracas.

⋄ I S R A E L ⋄

There are full diplomatic relations between Israel and Venezuela.

Aliya: Since 1948, 820 Venezuelan Jews have emigrated to Israel.

⋄ S I T E S ⋄

The oldest Jewish cemetery still in use in South America is in Coro, where the oldest tombstone dates from 1832.

Confederacion de Asociaciones Israelitas de Venezuela (C.A.I.V.)
Av. Marques del Toro 9—San Bernardino
Apartado de Correos 14.452
Caracas 1011A
Tel. 58 2 510 368, Fax 58 2 515 253

Embassy
Centro Empresarial Miranda
Av. Francisco de Miranda
con Av. Principal de los Ruices
Apartado 70081, Caracas
Tel. 58 2 239 4511/921, Fax 58 2 239 4320

Ornamental rimonim originally brought from Livorno, Italy, to Aleppo, Syria, and later taken to Caracas by Syrian Jewish immigrants

WESTERN EUROPE

*Spice box,
western Europe,
ca. 18th century.
Silver filigree
with biblical scenes
on enamel*

AUSTRIA
BELGIUM
CYPRUS
DENMARK
FINLAND
FRANCE
GERMANY
GIBRALTAR
GREECE
IRELAND
ITALY
LUXEMBOURG
MALTA
MONACO
THE NETHERLANDS
NORWAY
PORTUGAL
SPAIN
SWEDEN
SWITZERLAND
UNITED KINGDOM

AUSTRIA

GP 8,106,000 ♦ JP 10,000

◆ DEMOGRAPHY ◆

Vienna is the home of the great majority of Jews in Austria. There are also several smaller communities, none with more than 100 Jews, including Baden, Bad Gastein, Graz, Innsbruck, Linz, and Salzburg. Present-day Austrian Jewry is primarily composed of Holocaust survivors (and their children), returning Austrian expatriates, and refugees from eastern Europe. In recent years, Austria has offered sanctuary to many Soviet and Iranian Jews. Among the newcomers from the former Soviet Union are a large number of Caucasian (mainly Georgian) Jews who have set up their own Caucasian Jewish Center.

◆ HISTORY ◆

The Jewish presence in Austria can be traced back more than 1,000 years. The first Jews probably arrived with the Roman colonists. Documentation from the 12th century refers to "Shlom[o]," commissioned by Duke Leopold V of Babenberg to operate the Vienna mint. But that millennial history has been filled with long periods of horrific suffering and torment, especially from the 14th century onward. In some communities Jews were often killed and their property plundered. From 1420 to 1421, they were expelled from the country and not allowed to return until 1451. After that time, the Jewish community of Vienna increased and in 1624 was granted its own quarter, later known as Leopoldstadt. In 1670, however, the Jews were again expelled from Vienna. The economic consequences of that move were so severe that the Austrians gradually encouraged the Jews to return. Conditions improved somewhat until the reign of Maria Theresa, a rabid anti-Semite who oppressed her Jewish subjects. In 1782 her son and successor, Joseph II, lifted many of the restrictions that she had imposed. The constitution of 1848 granted Jews equality of rights, but it was not until 1867 that all legal prohibitions were lifted. Over the years, Vienna also became home to a small, but vibrant, Sephardi community.

Jews made tremendous contributions to the development of the arts, the sciences, and commerce in Austria, especially in Vienna. Many of the city's outstanding writers and artists were Jews. Vienna became a dynamic city of opportunities and was a magnet for Jews living in various parts of the Austro-Hungarian Empire. A steady stream of immigrants

♦

Robert Stricker (1879–1944) was one of the most important figures in Jewish public life in the period between the wars and was an outstanding representative of Austrian Jewry. Stricker was an ardent Zionist and already in the 1930s, in unambiguous language, called for the establishment of a Jewish state—not merely a homeland. A pioneer in Jewish journalism, Stricker established the only German-language Jewish daily, the Wiener Morgenzeitung. *He was also one of the founders of the World Jewish Congress and headed its Austrian section. Afforded an opportunity to flee Austria after the Anschluss, he refused to abandon his community: "I cannot. I must stay with my constituents." He and his wife were incarcerated in Theresienstadt, where he forecast the demise of Nazi Germany and the rise of a Jewish state. Sadly he lived to see neither. Stricker was deported to Auschwitz in 1944 and was gassed upon arrival.*

Chanukah lamp, Viennese, ca. 1880

from the provinces (especially Bukovina, Galicia, the Czech lands, and Hungary) came to the imperial capital. Many of the Jews from these lands regarded themselves as Austrians, and thousands of them laid down their lives for the "Fatherland" in World War I. Yet Vienna was also a hotbed of anti-Semitic activity, and its anti-Jewish mayor from 1897 to 1910, Karl Lueger, had an influence on the young Adolf Hitler.

The situation of Jews in the Austrian Republic that emerged out of the ashes of World War I was relatively stable until the mid-1930s, by which time the Jewish population numbered some 200,000 (180,000 in Vienna). Most Austrians enthusiastically welcomed the Anschluss. Austrians joined the Nazi Party and were active in the death camp apparatus in proportionally greater numbers than the Germans. Both Hitler and Adolf Eichmann were Austrian-born. Many Austrian Jews managed to flee the country after the 1938 Anschluss, when Austria merged with Germany. Nevertheless, nearly 70,000 were killed in the Holocaust.

In 1996 a public auction of heirless art owned by Jews murdered in the Holocaust was organized by the Austrian government at the Mauerbach Monestary. The funds generated from the sale were transferred to a humanitarian fund for Holocaust survivors. There are still many outstanding claims for looted Jewish property.

✦ COMMUNITY ✦

The Bundesverband der Israelitischen Kultusgemeinden is the primary communal organization. The Sephardi Federation operates independently. There are Austrian branches of many international Jewish organizations, such as B'nai B'rith and WIZO. The Zionist Federation is the principal outlet for Zionist activity. Youth organizations include B'nai Akiva, Hashomer Hatzair, and the Austrian Jewish Students Union. The community operates a hospital and a home for the aged.

Jews in Austria have had to contend with frequent outbursts of anti-Semitism on both a grassroots and state level. These have included vandalism, swastika daubings, and attacks in the press. The election campaign of President Kurt Waldheim, former U.N. secretary general, who lied about his Nazi past, was accompanied by blatant manifestations of anti-Semitism. However, this episode forced many Austrians to confront their history. More recently the success of the extreme right in the form of Joerg Haider's Freedom Party has been cause for concern.

✦ RELIGIOUS LIFE ✦

The only synagogue in Vienna to survive the

Shoah is the Stadttempel (built in 1826), where the community offices and chief rabbinate are located. There are a number of *shtiebelach* and prayer rooms catering to various Chassidic groups and other congregations. Prayer rooms can be found in the smaller communities. Vienna has two kosher restaurants and a kosher supermarket, as well as kosher butcher shops and a kosher bakery. There is also a kosher hotel in the health resort of Bad Gastein.

⋆Culture and Education⋆

There are Jewish kindergartens and a primary school. The Zwi Perez Chajes Gymnasium was recently reopened after a hiatus of nearly 50 years. The ultra-Orthodox maintain their own separate school system. The Vienna University has an institute for Jewish studies. The Institute for the History of Jews in Austria is located in the former synagogue in St. Polten. The Jewish sports club S.C. Hakoah has long traditions in Austria and is responsible for physical training and athletics.

The Jews of Austria publish a number of journals and papers, which also have a wide readership among expatriate Austrian Jews. The two largest are the monthly *Die Gemeinde,* the official organ of the community, and *Illustrietere Neue Welt.* The Austrian Jewish Students Union has its own bulletin called *Noodnik.* The chief rabbi has a radio program. There is a Jewish bookshop in Vienna.

⋆Israel⋆

Austria and Israel enjoy full diplomatic relations, although during the Waldheim presidency, Israel was only represented by a charge d'affaires.

Aliya: Since 1948, 5,400 Austrian Jews have emigrated to Israel.

⋆Sites⋆

The Jewish Welcome Service in Vienna (Tel. 533–8891) aids Jewish visitors, including newcomers who plan to remain in the city for extended periods. Austria has numerous sites of Jewish interest, including several synagogues and cemeteries. The Jewish Museum of the City of Vienna chronicles the rich history of Viennese Jewry and the outstanding role that Jews played in the development of the city. The Jewish Museum in Eisenstadt is housed in the one-time residence of Samson Wetheimer, the Hapsburg court Jew. There is also a museum in Hohenems. The concentration camp at Mauthausen, in the Danube Valley near Linz, offers grim evidence of the Holocaust.

Federation of Austrian Jewish Communities
Seitenstettengasse 4, Postfach 145
1010 Vienna
Tel. 43 1 53 104 0, Fax 43 1 53 15 77

Embassy
20 Anton Frankgasse
1180 Vienna
Tel. 43 1 470 47 41 , Fax 43 1 470 47 46

Professor Sigmund Freud's clinic, Vienna

BELGIUM

GP 10,160,000 ♦ JP 40,000

♦DEMOGRAPHY♦

The communities of Brussels (15,000) and Antwerp (15,000) are the main centers of Belgian Jewry. Significantly smaller communities are located in Arlon, Liege, Mons, Ostende, Charleroi, and Ghent.

♦HISTORY♦

Some Jews lived in the area now known as Belgium during the 13th century. However, a combination of expulsions and allegations that they were responsible for the Black Death in the mid-14th century resulted in Jews being either killed or forced to flee. The first Jews to return to Belgium were Sephardim, including many Conversos. Their main community was in Antwerp.

The French Revolution improved the climate for Jews, and

Chassidim in the Jewish quarter of Antwerp

they gained wider acceptance in society. Consequently the late 18th century saw the immigration of more Sephardim, along with some Ashkenazim, who settled in Brussels and Antwerp. The Napoleonic pattern of communal organization was adopted and is still reflected in the communal structure of today. Immigration increased in the 19th and 20th centuries. Many Jews were eager to leave eastern Europe during this period, and a large number were attracted by the development of the diamond bourse in Antwerp.

At the outset of World War II, more than 100,000 Jews were in Belgium, many of them refugees from central and eastern Europe who were hoping to reach the New World. Some managed to escape in this direction, but considerable numbers were still in Belgium when the Germans invaded. During four years of Nazi occupation, and with the help of Belgian collaborators, 25,631 Jews were assembled in the transit camp in Mechelen (Malines) and were deported to death camps; very few of them survived.

♦COMMUNITY♦

The Comite de Coordination des Organisations Juives de Belgique (CCOJB) is the community's roof body.

The relative openness of French-influenced Wallonia, in comparison to the Flemish-dominated region of Flanders, has resulted in a strong cultural affiliation between Brussels Jewry and the dominant culture. On the other hand, the Antwerp community is traditional, tightly-knit, and features a large ultra-Orthodox element.

Belgian Jewry has played an active role in the struggle against political extremism. In the past decade, the Vlaams Blok and the Front National Belge, both nationalist anti-foreigner movements, have been successful in gaining and holding positions in town councils, in the federal parliament, and in the European Parliament. The response to the growth of these movements has been the initiative of mainstream parties to enact laws prohibiting Holocaust denial (1995) and the strengthening of laws forbidding the propagation of intolerance.

As Brussels is the capital of the European Union, the Belgian community also takes a special interest in issues on the European level. In addition, the World Jewish Congress has a Brussels office, and the European Union of Jewish Students is headquartered there.

RELIGIOUS LIFE✦

Antwerp has some 30 synagogues, all Orthodox. A number of these also serve as houses of study for the ultra-Orthodox sects, which are present in the city. Indeed, Antwerp has one of the largest communities of ultra-Orthodox Jews in the Diaspora—it includes Chassidic Jews who follow the traditions of Belz, Ger, Czortkow, Lubavitch, Satmar, and Vishnitz. There are more than 10 synagogues in Brussels, including one Reform temple and one Sephardi synagogue. The chief rabbi of Belgium is appointed by the community, and he officiates at the country's main synagogue near the heart of old Brussels. Both the chief rabbi and the main synagogue are funded by the government. Antwerp has an abundance of kosher restaurants, food stores, and Jewish bookshops. Kosher facilities are relatively sparse in Brussels.

✦CULTURE AND EDUCATION✦

The constitutional recognition of minority religions means that the various levels of government welcome independent schooling systems and provide funding for religious schools. There are seven Jewish schools in Antwerp and four in Brussels. The great majority of Jewish children in Antwerp are educated in the Jewish school system and receive an intensive religious education.

Among the main publications of the Brussels community is *Regards*. In Antwerp the leading Jewish newspaper is the *Belgisch Israelitisch Weekblad*. Individual organizations also produce magazines addressing particular agendas, such as the two Israel-focused publications, *Israel Aujourd'hui* and *La Tribune Sioniste*, and *Los Muestros* which is dedicated to Sephardi culture.

✦ISRAEL✦

Belgium and Israel enjoy full diplomatic relations. Brussels is also the seat of the Israeli ambassador to the European Union.

Aliya: Since 1948, 4,000 Belgian Jews have emigrated to Israel.

✦SITES✦

The Jewish museum in Brussels has both permanent and temporary exhibitions. The Mechelen transit camp can also be visited.

Coordinating Committee of Jewish
*   Organizations in Belgium (CCOJB)*
68 Avenue Ducpetiaux
1060 Brussels
Tel. 32 2 537 1691, Fax 32 2 539 2295

Embassy
40 Avenue de l'Observatoire
1180 Brussels
Tel. 32 2 373 5500, Fax 32 2 373 5617

✦

Antwerp, with its concentration of Chassidic Jews, is sometimes regarded as the last shtetl *in Europe. The Jewish involvement in the diamond trade there is such that the lingua franca on the Antwerp diamond exchange is Yiddish. When a deal is made, both Jews and non-Jews seal it by saying* mazel u'bracha *(luck and blessing), which has the value of a written agreement.*

CYPRUS

GP 756,000 ✦ JP 20

✦HISTORY✦

Jewish merchants arrived in Cyprus during the period of the Roman Empire. A major revolt by Jews resulted in the destruction of the city of Salamis in approximately 116 or 117 C.E. Jews were subsequently expelled from the island.

There are, nevertheless, traces of a Jewish presence throughout the centuries, and in the 12th century, Benjamin of Tudela visited communities in Nicosia, Famagusta, Paphos, and Limassol.

After 1933 several hundred German Jews found refuge in Cyprus. The British established detention camps for Holocaust survivors from many European countries who were caught attempting to enter British-ruled Palestine. From 1946 until the founding of the State of Israel, the British incarcerated over 50,000 European Jewish refugees on the island.

Since 1948 only tiny numbers of Jews have lived in Cyprus. At different times, the Israeli Embassy has served as the place for some communal activity, such as religious services.

✦ISRAEL✦

Israel had diplomatic relations with the British protectorate of Cyprus from the Jewish state's earliest days, initially at consular level.

Deportees to Cyprus, 1948
by Paul Georghiau. Oil on wood

These ties were expanded when Cyprus attained independence in 1960.

The Jewish Community of Cyprus
P.O. Box 3807, Nicosia
Tel. 357 2 441 085, Fax 357 2 445 995

Embassy
4 Gripari S.T., P.O. Box 1049, Nicosia
Tel. 357 2 445 195, Fax 357 2 453 486

✦

In the latter decades of the 19th century, as Jews in Europe became increasingly anxious to escape from European hardships, Cyprus became the focus of a number of plans for new Jewish settlements. Between the 1880s and the 1900s, various groups of Russian and Romanian Jews traveled to Cyprus and began to establish agricultural settlements. All of these ended in failure. Theodor Herzl raised the possibility of Jewish sovereignty in Cyprus with the British government in 1902. However, nothing came of these efforts.

DENMARK

GP 5,237,000 ✦ JP 8,000

✦ DEMOGRAPHY ✦

Most Jews reside in Copenhagen. There are also small communities in Odense and Aarhus.

The great majority of Danish Jews are Ashkenazim with roots in central and eastern Europe. Although intermarriage has taken its toll, Jewish life has been bolstered by the arrival of Jewish immigrants, particularly from Israel and from other European countries. Moreover, in recent years, children of some of the refugees from Poland, with tenuous Jewish links, have begun to take an active part in communal life.

✦ HISTORY ✦

Denmark was the first Scandinavian country to permit Jewish settlement. In 1622 King Christian IV invited Sephardi Jews from Amsterdam and Hamburg to settle in Gluckstadt on the Elbe estuary (then in Denmark). While these Jews were granted economic and religious freedom, Ashkenazim from Germany were subject to many restrictions. In 1684 the unified Jewish communty of Copenhagen was established by ordinance of King Christian V. Civic equality was eventually granted to Jews in 1814, and by 1849 they had attained full citizenship.

Between 1901 and 1921, the community was bolstered by the arrival of Jewish refugees from Russia. With the advent of Nazism, Jews from Germany, Austria, and former Czechoslovakia also found sanctuary in Denmark, in the period before the German occupation.

In 1943, with a German roundup of Jews imminent, about 90% of the Jewish population was spirited to safety in neutral Sweden. All in all, 5,191 Jews, 1,301 people of part Jewish parentage, and 686 Christians married to Jews were secretly transported to Sweden. Some 472 Jews were captured and deported to Theresienstadt, and 49 lost their lives there. After the war, the Jewish community was reconstituted.

In 1968, 2,500 refugees from Poland, victims of a Communist Party witch-hunt, settled in the Copenhagen area.

In Jerusalem a boatlike monument was erected on the 25th anniversary of the rescue of Danish Jewry, and a school was named in Denmark's honor. Many cities and towns in Israel have a street or square commemorating the heroism of the Danes. Moreover, one of the prominent items on display in Yad Vashem is a small boat that was used to ferry Jews to safety in Sweden. In Copenhagen's Israelplads there is a monument from Eilat stone with an inscription in both Danish and Hebrew, a gift of the people of Israel. Denmark's Queen Margrethe II was the patron of the 1993 events marking the 50th anniversary of the rescue operation of Danish Jews.

✦ COMMUNITY ✦

The central body is the Mosaiske Troessamfund i Kobenhavn (Jewish Congregation in Copenhagen). Most of the Jewish organizations and institutions have their offices in the Jewish community center. The Dansk Zionistforbund (Danish Zionist Federation) is the leading Zionist body. B'nai B'rith and WIZO have chapters in the community, as does B'nai Akiva. There are three homes for the aged, run in cooperation with the Copenhagen Municipality.

Anti-Semitism has not been a great problem, at least on the part of Danes. Denmark,

✦

Lighting the Sabbath Candles.
Stamp commemorating the 300th anniversary of the establishment of the Jewish community

however, has been the venue of a number of acts of Arab terror, including a bomb blast at the Great Synagogue in 1985 and a foiled plan to assassinate the chief rabbi and other prominent Danish Jews. Denmark's liberal laws on the freedom of expression have made it a favorite sanctuary for European hate groups.

✦ RELIGIOUS LIFE ✦

The Great Synagogue in Copenhagen was completed in 1833. It is the seat of the chief rabbinate. There is also another Orthodox synagogue which maintains a *mikva*. Kosher food is readily available, and Denmark exports kosher meat to Sweden and Norway, where *shechita* is not permitted. There is a kosher hotel in Hornbaek.

✦ CULTURE AND EDUCATION ✦

The Caroline Jewish Day School, founded in 1805, has an enrollment of some 300 pupils, about half the Jewish children in the 6- to 16-year age group. There are also two Talmud Torahs and three kindergartens. Since 1989 strong cultural ties have been established with the Jewish communities of the Baltic states.

A Jewish newspaper, *Jodisk Orientering* is published in Copenhagen and a quarterly, *Israel*, is published by the Dansk Zionistforbund. Other publications cater to the needs of youth.

The royal library in Copenhagen is an important repository of Judaica and houses the famous Biblotheca Simonseniana, as well as a Jewish department.

✦ ISRAEL ✦

Israel and Denmark maintain full diplomatic relations.

Aliya: Since 1948, 1,320 Danish Jews have emigrated to Israel.

✦ SITES ✦

Copenhagen's Great Synagogue, designed by one of Denmark's most famous architects, Gustav Friedrich Hechst, is an important site. The city has a burial ground dating back to 1693 and another, consecrated in 1886, that is the site of a monument to the 49 Danish Jews who perished in Theresienstadt. In the Liberty Museum, there is a special section devoted to the resistance movement and a section dealing with the persecution of the Jews.

Det Mosaiske Troessamfund i Kobenhavn
Ny Kongensgade 6, 1472 Copenhagen K
Tel. 45 31 128 868, Fax 45 31 141 332

Embassy
Lundevangsvej 4, 2900 Hellerup, Copenhagen
Tel. 45 3962 6288, Fax 45 3962 1938

✦

FINLAND

❖

GP 5,1263,000 ✦ JP 1,200

❖ HISTORY AND DEMOGRAPHY ❖

There are 900 Jews in Helsinki, the capital, and another 200 in Turku. Jewish settlement in Finland is of relatively recent origin, dating back to 1825. The first Jews to settle in the country were Russian Army conscripts—the so-called Cantonists who served in Russian-ruled Finland and who were permitted to remain there upon completion of their military service. These Jews were later joined by others from Russia, Poland, and Lithuania. Jews living in Finland were subject to many restrictions, including obligatory registration. These were abolished once the country became independent in 1917. In the late 1930s, admission was granted to about 250 Jewish refugees from central Europe, and in recent years, a number of Jews from the former Soviet Union, Poland, and elsewhere in eastern Europe found sanctuary in the country.

Finnish Jewry was spared the horrors of the Holocaust, in part due to the resolute stand of the Finnish authorities, who refused to surrender Finnish Jews to the Germans. When Himmler demanded that Finnish Jews be turned over to the Germans, Prime Minister Rangell is reported to have said that the Jews of Finland were decent people and loyal citizens whose sons fought in the army like other Finns. "We have no Jewish question here," Rangell declared. However, seven Jewish refugees from central Europe who had fled to Finland were deported to Germany, and only one survived.

❖ COMMUNITY ❖

The Central Council of Jewish Communities in Finland is the leading communal body. The community's outstanding priority is the preservation of the Jewish heritage, including stemming the tide of assimilation. Most Finnish–Jewish youth are sent to Israel as teenagers in order to bolster their sense of Jewish identity. The community maintains a home for the aged. Finnish Jews have been active in reaching out to their Jewish neighbors across the Baltic, particularly in Estonia.

While anti-Semitism has not been a serious problem in Finland, there have been a number of isolated incidents that have raised concern. These include the desecration of Jew-

✦

In World War II, Finland was allied with Germany, and Finnish troops fought against the Soviet Union in an effort to regain the territory it lost in the Russo-Finnish War (1939–1940). Fulfilling their obligations as loyal citizens, Finnish Jews answered the call to arms. Twenty-three of them lost their lives in the fighting, and most are buried in the Jewish cemetery in Helsinki.
In gratitude for their heroism and loyalty in Finland's darkest hour, the country's leader, Marshal Mannerheim, paid a visit to the synagogue in Helsinki and presented the Jewish community with a wreath, which is preserved to the present day as one of the most treasured heirlooms of Finnish Jewry. The community has also demonstrated fervent love for Israel, and this, together with its martial spirit, found expression during the War of Independence, when the Jews of Finland sent 29 volunteers—proportionally the largest contingent of any Diaspora community.

ish cemeteries, swastika daubings, and threatening telephone calls to members of the Jewish community.

✦COMMUNAL LIFE✦

There are synagogues in Helsinki and Turku. Services are conducted according to Orthodox practice. Most Finnish Jews, however, are less observant in their private lives. Kosher food is available and there is a kosher butcher. There is a Jewish day school in Helsinki, in which 100 students are enrolled from grades one to nine, and a Jewish kindergarten. The community also operates a Talmud Torah.

✦ISRAEL✦

Formal relations were established between Israel and Finland in 1948.

Aliya: Since 1948, 723 Finnish Jews have emigrated to Israel.

✦SITES✦

The leading sites in Helsinki are the synagogue, the adjacent community center, and the Jewish cemetery where a section is devoted to the Jews who fell in the Finnish Army in the Russo-Finnish and Continuation wars.

Central Council of Jewish Communities
*   in Finland*
Malminkatu 26, 00100 Helsinki 10
Tel. 358 0 694 1303, Fax 358 0 694 8916

Embassy
Vironkatu 5A, 00170 Helsinki 17
Tel. 358 0 1356 177, Fax 358 0 1356 959

✦

Demonstration on behalf of Soviet Jewry, Congress of
Scandinavian Jewish Youth Organization (SJUF), 1982

GP 58,333,000 ✦ JP 600,000

✦DEMOGRAPHY✦

More than half the Jews in France live in Paris and its suburbs (350,000), but there are other large communities in Marseilles (70,000), Lyons (25,000), Toulouse (23,000), Nice (20,000), Strasbourg (16,000), Grenoble (8,000), Metz, and Nancy (4,000). In addition there are a dozen communities, each with some 2,000 Jews, scattered throughout the country. Altogether there are approximately 230 Jewish communities in France.

In the 1950s and 1960s, the Ashkenazi community of veteran French Jews and immigrants from eastern Europe underwent a major demographic transformation with the arrival of 300,000 Jews from North Africa, mainly from Morocco, Tunisia, and Egypt. As a result, the Sephardi Jews now comprise 60% of the French Jewish community.

Prayer for the welfare of the French Republic

✦HISTORY✦

Archeological findings of a Jewish nature indicate a Jewish presence from the 1st, 4th, and early 5th centuries in Arles, Bordeaux, and Lyons. Written sources show that Jews were present also in Metz, Poiters, Avignon, and Arles. During the 6th century, under the Merovingian Dynasty, the Jews suffered forced conversions and other repression. Despite this their numbers increased and there were many Jews engaged in commerce and medicine.

In the 9th century, Jews enjoyed many privileges and judicial equality, and they were also intensely active in commerce, viniculture, and administration. During the Middle Ages, France was a center of Jewish learning, both in Provence and in the north, where Rashi and Rabenu Tam were among the best-known scholars. From the Crusades period and throughout the following centuries, the Jews suffered persecutions, blood libels, and expulsions.

After the French Revolution, Jews were granted equal rights as citizens. At the beginning of the 19th century, Napoleon Bonaparte convoked the Grand Sanhedrin, and in 1808, the consistorial system of religious–communal organization was established at his decree. During the 19th century, France became a center of Jewish philanthropy, and organizations such as the Alliance Israelite Universelle became active. The Damascus Affair (1840) and the Dreyfus Affair (1894) had a great impact on the community and its internal communal structure.

✦

Entrance to the Yeshiva at Aix-les-Bains

On the eve of World War II, there were 300,000 Jews living in France. In 1940 the Germans invaded the country. In Paris and elsewhere in occupied France, French policemen actively ferreted out Jews in hiding. French Jewry thus suffered at the hands of both the Germans and the French. In the unoccupied zone, the Vichy government enthusiastically cooperated with the Germans. About 70,000 French Jews perished in the Holocaust.

Between 1945 and 1948, about 80,000 Jews arrived from central and eastern Europe. In 1955, 10,000 Egyptian Jews settled in the country, and in the years from 1956 to 1963, a great wave of immigrants from the Maghreb arrived.

French Jewry has made great contributions to every facet of French life, and Jews have attained the highest positions in government—Leon Blum and Pierre Mendes-France were elected as prime ministers.

·COMMUNITY·

The political umbrella organization officially representing all the communities and organizations before the government is the Representative Council of French Jewry (CRIF), founded in 1944. The Consistoire Central is the body responsible for the religious affairs of the community. It also supervises the chief rabbinate and *bet din*, which enjoy national recognition. The United Jewish Social Foundation (FSJU) was founded in 1950 to centralize and supervise major social, cultural, and educational enterprises.

All the major Zionist organizations are active, and there are several youth movements. Despite the variety of outlets for Jewish expression, only 40% of the community are registered members of synagogues or Jewish organizations. Statistics show an increase in *aliya* and tourism to Israel in recent years. Along with assimilation, there is also a noticeable religious revival, including a growing section of ultra-Orthodox, which has created tensions within the organized community.

In recent years, and especially with the advent of the trial of the Vichy police commander of Lyons, Paul Touvier, France has been forced to confront its record of collaboration with the Germans, particularly its active assistance in rounding up the Jews of France and deporting them to the death camps. In 1995 President Jacques Chirac publicly apologized to the Jewish people on behalf of the republic.

In 1996 reports in the media on the confiscation of hundreds of apartments and works of art from French Jews during the Holocaust led to the establishment of a government commission to investigate this matter.

There have been several serious anti-Semitic incidents in France, including bombings and vandalism. Anti-Semitism is disseminated in regularly published newspapers and magazines, including those of Muslim fundamentalists. The strong electoral support for the extreme-right National Front, headed by Jean-Marie Le Pen, is a source of worry to the Jewish community.

Annual magazine for newlyweds

◆ RELIGIOUS LIFE ◆

The major religious stream in France is the moderate Orthodox, which includes most Sephardi Jews and accounts for 48% of the Jewish community. It has dozens of synagogues and rabbis. The ultra-Orthodox stream (7%) has some 10 synagogues. Five percent are Reform or Liberal and are served by a number of synagogues and rabbis. In 1992 the first Conservative community was established in Paris. About 40% of French Jewry are religiously unaffiliated.

Approximately 25% of French Jews observe *kashrut,* and the number of kosher butchers, restaurants, and shops in Paris and elsewhere is growing.

◆ CULTURE AND EDUCATION ◆

In Paris alone, there are more than 20 Jewish day schools, both elementary and high schools, as well as kindergartens and religious seminaries. Jewish schools are also to be found in Strasbourg, Nice, Toulouse, Marseilles,

◆

Around the turn of the century, there was an enormous surge of Jewish art, and there emerged a stream of Jewish artists who made their mecca the School of Paris in France. Among the outstanding names were Pissarro, Soutine, Modigliani, Pascin, Mane Katz, and especially Chagall. Pissarro, one of the greatest and most well-known of the Impressionists, was of Sephardi origin. Since many of the artists in the School of Paris were eastern European Jews, the term "Jewish School of Paris" was coined to refer more specifically to a school of painting that gravitated around the existing schools of modern art in France, but also developed certain unique features.

Bordeaux, Metz, and Aix-les-Bains. Most French universities offer courses in Judaic studies, including courses in Yiddish, Ladino, and Hebrew. The Mercaz Rashi, which contains the University Center for Jewish Studies, provides courses for academics and students. The Rabbinical Seminary ordains rabbis to serve in

theater companies are also active.

A lively Jewish press exists in France, featuring two weeklies and a number of monthly journals. Weekly Jewish programs are broadcast on both radio and television, and several local Jewish radio stations are on the air in Paris and in other major cities.

Interior of the Great Synagogue of Paris (rue de la Victoire)

French-speaking countries. About 4% of the school-age children are enrolled in Jewish day schools. The Alliance Israelite Universelle supervises an international network of French-oriented schools in other countries.

Every year there is a Jewish Book Week, a Jewish Music Week, an intellectual colloquium, and a variety of symposia and seminars on Jewish issues. Jewish dance and

✦ I S R A E L ✦

France established diplomatic relations with Israel in 1949. During the 1950s, France was Israel's major source of arms and participated in developing its nuclear program. In 1967 on the eve of the Six-Day War, France declared a total arms embargo on Israel. In addition to the embassy in Paris, there is a consulate general in Marseilles.

Decoration for the eastern wall (mizrah) of a Jewish home, Alsace, ca. 1800.
Reverse painting on glass

Aliya: Since 1948, 34,000 French Jews have emigrated to Israel.

⋆SITES⋆

Old synagogues in Carpentras and Cavaillon are considered national monuments. There are old Jewish cemeteries in Landes and in Alsace. The Provence region also contains many historic synagogues and cemeteries. Paris has several Jewish libraries, among them the Medem Library, which is the largest Yiddish library in Europe, and the Centre de Documentation Juive Contemporaine. Paris is also the site of the Museum of Jewish Art and the Cluny Museum, which houses the Strauss-Rothschild Collection. The Memorial to the Unknown Jewish Martyr and the adjacent Holocaust documentation center were among the first institutions of this type.

⋆CORSICA⋆

Jewish settlement dates back to the end of the 19th century. There are some 200 Jews in Corsica divided between Bastia and Ajaccio. The only synagogue is in Bastia.

CRIF
39 Rue de Broca
75005 Paris
Tel. 33 1 42 17 11 11, Fax 33 1 42 17 11 13

The European Jewish Congress
78 Avenue des Champs Elysees
75008 Paris
Tel. 33 1 43 59 94 63, Fax 33 1 42 25 45 28

Embassy
3 Rue Rabelais
75008 Paris
Tel. 33 1 40 76 55 00, Fax 33 1 40 76 55 55

⋆

GERMANY

GP 81,922,000 ◆ JP 60,000

◆DEMOGRAPHY◆

The largest community in Germany is Berlin (10,000), followed by Frankfurt-am-Main (6,000) and Munich (5,000). Some 80 small Jewish communities are scattered throughout Germany. There are 43,000 registered, dues-paying members of the official Jewish community. The rest are non-affiliated. Most of these Jews arrived from the former Soviet Union immediately before and after the reunification of Germany in 1990. These immigrants, mainly from the Baltic states, Russia, and Ukraine, are relatively young and well-educated but have scant knowledge of Jewish tradition. Their presence has injected new life into the aging community. In such places as Schwerin, Potsdam, Bremen, and Hamburg, about 70% of the Jews are native Russian-speakers. The majority of the veteran Jews in Germany are not descendants of the original pre-war German community, but east European Ashkenazim who came after the war. There are also several thousand Israelis. Due to the influx of Soviet Jews, today Germany has the third largest Jewish population in western Europe.

Albert Ballin (1857–1918) epitomized the patriotism of German Jewry before the rise of Nazism. One of Germany's outstanding shipping magnates, he was responsible for the phenomenal growth of the Hapag–Lloyd shipping concern and pioneered the introduction of faster and more comfortable ocean liners. Many of the Jews who emigrated from Europe to the New World arrived on Hapag–Lloyd ships. Ballin was the only unbaptized Jew in Kaiser Wilhelm II's inner circle, and the German ruler came to rely on him for advice on economic matters. During World War I, Ballin played a leading role in the distribution of food supplies. Crushed by the Kaiser's flight to Holland and the collapse of the empire, he committed suicide.

◆HISTORY◆

Jewish settlement in Germany began in the 4th century and continued throughout successive centuries, resulting in flourishing communities with an active and intellectual life. In the medieval period, the cities of the Rhineland became outstanding centers of Jewish life and learning. During the Crusades and thereafter, the Jews suffered massacres and expulsions. Many fled eastward, taking with them the Yiddish language that first developed in Germany. In the 17th century, conditions improved, and in the 19th century, Jews were granted emancipation, which found official expression in the 1871 Constitution.

It was the German Jew Moses Mendelssohn who laid the foundation for the Jewish Enlightenment, which was to have a profound impact on Jewish thought. In fact, much of modern Jewish thinking originated in Germany. The Reform movement was founded in Germany in the early 19th century and spread to other parts of the Diaspora. The roots of modern Orthodoxy can also be traced back to such German Jews as Samson Raphael Hirsch.

Prior to 1933, the Jews of Germany attained great success in all walks of life, including commerce, industry, art, and science. German Jewry included representatives of many streams of Judaism, from the devoutly Orthodox to those who desired total integra-

◆

tion with the German nation and its culture and ultimately converted to Christianity.

With the rise to power of the Nazi party in 1933, the 503,000 Jews living in Germany found themselves rapidly excluded from the German society of which they had felt so much a part. In 1935 the Nuremberg Laws were instituted, prohibiting marital or extramarital relations between Jews and German Gentiles. Beginning in 1938, their exclusion from the economy was more strongly en-

◆COMMUNITY◆

The Jewish communities have local organizations that are united under the umbrella organization, the Zentralrat der Juden in Deutschland (the Central Council of Jews in Germany). Following the reunification of Germany in 1990, the small Jewish community of East Germany was gradually integrated into the larger German Jewish community.

The council is the official representative of German Jewry and looks after Jewish po-

Megilla, Germany, ca. 18th century

forced. On the night of November 9, 1938, which became known as Kristallnacht, hundreds of Jews were killed and injured and tens of thousands were arrested. Most of the synagogues in Germany were put to the torch, and many Jewish homes and businesses were ransacked.

In 1938 demand for emigration increased, but despite the convening of the Evian Conference, immigration to most countries remained difficult and often became almost impossible. For the most part, those who remained in Germany were unable to save themselves. In October 1941, the deportations to the death camps began. It is estimated that some 180,000 German Jews were killed in the Holocaust.

After the war, the Jewish community was reconstituted, but displaced persons (DPs) from various countries in eastern Europe accounted for the majority of its members.

litical interests, matters of restitution, and other issues.

The Jewish communities are corporations under the law and are funded by a special religious tax that serves to maintain the community expenses. A wide range of Jewish institutions, such as museums, archives, and centers for learning and research, is supported by federal, state, or municipal funds.

Major Jewish organizations, such as the Zionist Organization, B'nai B'rith, WIZO, and several youth movements, are represented in Germany.

Fifty years after the defeat of Nazi Germany and the end of World War II, there is a new openness and readiness within German society to confront and deal with its Nazi past. Moreover, Holocaust denial has been declared illegal and is punishable by law.

Still, there are about 80 extreme-right splinter groups and organizations with a total of perhaps 65,000 members. More than 20 of these groups are classified officially as neo-Nazi. Anti-Semitic activities in Germany include desecration of cemeteries and attacks against synagogues, memorial sites, and Jewish property. A special office of the German Ministry of Interior Affairs keeps a watchful eye on such activities and publishes an annual report on the activities of hate groups.

School of Jewish Studies that offers academic degrees. The school curriculum in German high schools includes Holocaust studies.

The largest weekly paper is the *Allgemeine Judische Wochenzeitung*, published in Bonn. A German and a Yiddish weekly are published in Munich. The Frankfurt community publishes a monthly magazine, *Judische Gemeinde-Zeitung Frankfurt*. In Berlin the

Jewish shops in Goöppingen, the morning after Kristallnacht

✦RELIGIOUS LIFE, CULTURE AND EDUCATION✦

All major communities have their own rabbis. There are synagogues, cemeteries, community centers, and offices of Jewish organizations in numerous cities and towns. Kosher food is available in all major Jewish centers.

There are three Jewish primary schools in Germany (as compared to 23 before the war), but the enrollment is small. In 1993 a Jewish high school in Berlin was reopened for the first time since World War II. Due to an increase in interest in Judaic studies, particularly among non-Jewish students, there are more than five such programs in universities throughout Germany. In many of these programs, the majority of students and faculty are non-Jews. Such is the situation in the new Mendelssohn Center of Potsdam University. In Heidelberg there is a special, autonomous

monthly paper *Judische Korrespondenz* appears in German and in Russian.

There are some 30 museums that wholly or partially have sections dealing with Judaism. The best-known Jewish museums are in Frankfurt-am-Main, Cologne, and Berlin, where a new building is under construction.

✦ISRAEL✦

In 1951 Chancellor Konrad Adenauer declared before the Bundestag his readiness to enter negotiations with representatives of the Jewish people and Israel about reparations and in 1952, together with Nahum Goldmann, president of the World Jewish Congress, and with Moshe Sharett, foreign minister of Israel, signed the Luxembourg Indemnification Agreement. The hundreds of millions of U.S. dollars that were transferred to the State of Israel helped alleviate the economic and social burdens of the young Israeli society. West Germany expressed a special commitment to ensure the security of the new Jewish state. Throughout the years, it has concluded special military agreements with Israel and has supported it in international forums. Diplomatic relations were established in 1965.

From its establishment in 1949 until its collapse in 1990, East Germany assumed a hostile stance toward Israel and refused to acknowledge its people's moral responsibility for the Holocaust. Moreover, it furnished military aid to Arab states and terrorist organizations.

In addition to the embassy in Bonn, Israel maintains a consulate in Berlin.

Aliya: Since 1948, 18,830 Jews have emigrated to Israel from Germany. This number excludes the mass *aliya* of DPs between 1947 and 1949.

＊SITES＊

The most famous of the ancient Jewish sites in Germany are the synagogue in Worms (1034), the adjoining *mikva* (1186), and the Rashi Chapel (1624). All have been reconstructed since the war. The ancient Worms cemetery was saved from destruction. In Speyer one can see the oldest *mikva* in Germany, dating from the 11th century. Friedberg has a *mikva* from 1260, and in Andernach there is a 14th century *mikva*. There is an historic synagogue in Odenbach with baroque paintings, and there are ancient cemeteries in Wurzburg, Heidengsfeld, Hochburg, and Frankfurt-am-Main. In Berlin the impres-

The ruins of the synagogue on Oranienburgerstrasse in Berlin before its reconstruction

sive synagogue on Oranienburgerstrasse has been reconstructed as a Jewish center. During the war, the Germans constructed a concrete bunker in the main hall of the synagogue, and the building was heavily damaged by Allied air raids. Restoration, funded in part by the American philanthropist Ronald Lauder, was begun by the East German regime a short time before its collapse and was completed several years later.

Memorials can be found at the sites of the Buchenwald, Dachau, Bergen–Belsen, and Ravensbruck concentration camps. The Gestapo headquarters and the Wannsee villa, where the machinery of the Final Solution was set in motion, are also museums. In Munich there is a monument marking the destruction of one of the city's synagogues in 1938 and another commemorating the Israeli sportsmen murdered by terrorists at the 1972 Olympic Games.

Zentralrat der Juden in Deutschland
Rungsdorferstrasse 6
5300 Bonn 2
Tel. 49 228 35 70 23, Fax 49 228 35 54 69

Embassy
Simrockallee 2
53173 Bonn
Tel. 49 228 934 6500, Fax 49 228 934 6550

＊

GIBRALTAR

GP 28,000 ♦ JP 500

♦HISTORY♦

The first Gibraltan Jews arrived at the fortress from Spain as early as the 14th century. These Sephardim were joined by larger numbers in the following century, fleeing Spanish persecution.

The Treaty of Utrecht, according to which Britain officially took control of the peninsula, stated that Jews were permanently excluded from settlement. By 1729, the British agreed with the Sultan of Morocco that a number of Jews could visit Gibraltar as traders, and in 1749 Jews were permitted to settle there. With the arrival of these North African Jews, synagogues were established, and the community began to play a prominent role in the life of the territory. In the 19th century, when Gibraltar was at the height of its strategic and commercial importance to the British, the Jewish community flourished, numbering up to 2,000 people.

During the Shoah, most of the community of 2,000 was evacuated to relative safety in Britain. However, some did not return to Gibraltar. Today's community is composed of returnees and their descendants.

♦COMMUNAL LIFE♦

Four synagogues and a *kollel* are in regular use, presided over by a communal rabbi. Almost all Jewish children attend the community's primary schools, and both boys and girls can attend the Jewish secondary school. There are

Aaron Nunez Cardozo, a Jewish Gibraltan who lived in the 18th and 19th centuries, discovered and exposed a French plot to take over the territory. Cardozo later served as a prominent regional diplomat, and today his mansion is used as Gibraltar's city hall.

two kosher restaurants, a kosher bakery, and a kosher restaurant. A weekly newsletter is published by the community. A social club and a WIZO branch are active. The Jewish community enjoys good relations with the other ethnic groups in the colony—British, Arabs, Indians, and others—and for many years both the prime minister and mayor were Jews.

♦ISRAEL♦

Israel maintains a consulate in Gibraltar.

♦SITES♦

The four synagogues can be visited by arrangement with the community. The old Jewish cemetery, in the Upper Rock, also attracts the interest of Jewish tourists.

Jewish Community of Gibraltar
10 Bomb House Lane, Gibraltar
Tel. 350 726 06, Fax 350 404 87

Consulate
39 Glacis Road, Marina View
P.O.Box 141, Gibraltar
Tel. 350 777 35, Fax 350 743 01

Itzhak Mesas, a Jewish policeman, in front of Nefusot Yehuda Synagogue

GREECE

GP 10,490,000 ♦ JP 5,000

♦DEMOGRAPHY♦

Jews have left their imprint in Greece in many cities and towns over the 2,000 years of the community's history. The current centers of Greek Jewry are Athens (3,000) and Salonika (1,000), although the latter is only a remnant of the huge community that thrived in the city for some 500 years. Jews are also present in Corfu, Chalkis, Joannina, Larissa, Rhodes, Trikala, and Volos.

♦HISTORY♦

The small Jewish community of Greece is the heir to a long history shaped by the development of Hellenism, the influences of Rome and of Byzantium, the impact of the expulsions from Spain and from Portugal, and a continuous tie with the Jews of the Land of Israel.

The first record of a Jewish presence in Greece is found in a 3rd century B.C.E. inscription. It is likely that the anti-Hellenistic Maccabean uprising, in the second century B.C.E., resulted in the transfer of many Jews—as slaves—to Greece.

Refugees from the Spanish expulsion increased the Greek Jewish population in the 15th and 16th centuries. This wave of immigration helped create the great community of Salonika that, by the end of the 16th century,

had reached 30,000, half the city's population. Over the course of successive centuries, Jews from many countries moved to Salonika, introducing German, French, Flemish, Egyptian, and Italian flavors. The city became an important trading port, a center of Jewish learning, and one of the places in which the Ladino (Judeo-Spanish) language flourished.

Prior to World War II, over 70,000 Jews lived in Greece. Once the Axis powers (Germany, Italy, and Bulgaria) divided up control of the country, the fate of the Jews was sealed. Those residing in the German-controlled zone were subject to the most immediate and dire threat. The 45,000-strong community of Salonika, which fell under German administration, was almost totally destroyed in the first few months of the occupation. In Athens the community was initially protected by the Italian authorities' reluctance to enact anti-Jewish laws. After Germany took direct control of Athens, the leadership of chief rabbi Elijah Barzilai and the urging of Archbishop Damaskinos for Christians to protect Jews meant that a considerable number of Jews either escaped or were hidden. The regions of Macedonia and Thrace were placed under Bulgarian administration. However, in stark contrast to the protection that was pro-

♦

A few years before World War II, a Jewish sailor arrived in an unfamiliar Greek island port and was astounded to find that it was similar to his home port of Jaffa. When he docked and encountered some locals, he mentioned that he was from the Land of Israel. To his great surprise his hosts began to speak to him in Hebrew. They explained that they were Cretan Jews who had come across the island bay at the time of King Solomon. Because of its similarity to Jaffa, they had made their homes on the island and had even planted citrus orchards. These Jews had created rituals which sanctified their seafaring: in addition to the familiar bar mitzvah Torah reading, boys were required to sail solo beyond the confines of the harbor and back. After the war, when the sailor returned to visit the port, he found that the Germans had deported the entire Jewish community to Auschwitz and that none had survived.

vided the Jews of Bulgaria, the Bulgarian occupation authorities deported the 11,000 Jews in their zone to German death camps in Poland. In all, 65,000 Greek Jews were murdered. Most of the 10,000 Jews who were in Greece when the Axis occupation ended, including the remnants of Macedonian and Thracian Jewries, made their way to Israel and other countries in the following decades.

✦COMMUNITY✦

Most of the Jewish organizations, including women's, youth, and athletic groups, are uni-

schools operate in Athens, Salonika, and Larissa. The community publishes the monthly *Gegonota*.

✦ISRAEL✦

Diplomatic relations were upgraded to the highest level in 1990.

Aliya: Since 1948, 3,860 Greek Jews have emigrated to Israel.

✦SITES✦

Ancient synagogues can be visited in Aegina, Corfu, Delos, Joannina, Kos, and at Canea on Crete and on Rhodes. Jewish quarters can be

A Jewish family in Salonika, end of 19th century

fied by the Kentriko Israelitiko Symvoulio Ellados (Central Board of Jewish Communities in Greece).

Organized anti-Semitism is mostly generated by nationalistic movements and is propagated by a number of small-circulation magazines. In the past few years, anti-hate movements have been established, prominent among which is the Citizens' Movement Against Racism.

✦RELIGIOUS LIFE✦

There are eight synagogues throughout the country, all of them Sephardi. These are served by rabbis permanently based in Athens, Salonika, and Larissa.

✦CULTURE AND EDUCATION✦

The Athens community center contains meeting rooms and a communal library. Small

found in Arta, Chalkis, Chios, Corfu, Crete, Drama, Ioannina, Ipati, Kyparissa, Naxos, Patras, and Veria. The Jewish Museum in Athens presents the story of Greek Jewry.

Central Board of Jewish Communities in Greece
2, Sourmeli Street
10439 Athens
Tel. 30 1 883 9953
Fax 30 1 823 4488

Embassy
Marathonodromou 1
Paleo Psychio
154 52 Athens
Tel. 30 1 671 9530
Fax 30 1 674 9510

♦DEMOGRAPHY♦

The Jewish community of Ireland is almost exclusively concentrated in the capital city of Dublin. Irish Jewry has been experiencing a great decline over the past 30 years, in part due to economic stagnation and a lack of opportunities. During this period, the emigration of young Jews to the United Kingdom, Israel, and the United States has halved the community's population and diminished its activism.

♦HISTORY♦

A few Jews lived in Ireland in the Middle Ages but none were there after the English expulsion of 1290. After Jews returned to England in 1656, some ex-Conversos moved on to Dublin and founded a community. Later, Ashkenazim arrived, but the community passed out of existence at about the end of the 18th century. It was revived in 1822 and was strengthened by immigrants from England, and from central and eastern Europe. About 400 were living there in 1881 when Jews, especially from Lithuania, began arriving in large numbers and—apart from Dublin—communities flourished elsewhere, including Belfast, Cork, and Limerick. At its peak, the community numbered 7,000 to 8,000.

Jews played a role in the struggle for Irish independence, and the constitution of the Irish Republic, adopted in 1937, recognizes Jews as a minority and accords special status to the Irish chief rabbi.

The Proverbs of Solomon in Hebrew, Gaelic, and English, Dublin, 1819

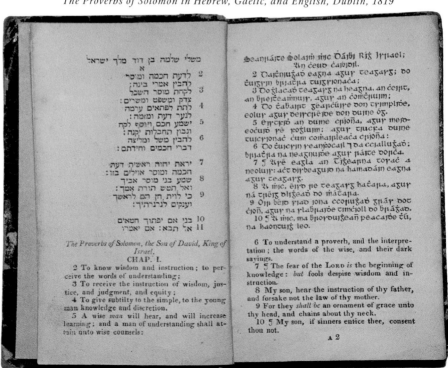

·COMMUNAL LIFE·

The Jewish Representative Council of Ireland brings together various Zionist, youth, and women's organizations.

Ireland's chief rabbi supervises the republic's synagogues (all in Dublin except for one in Cork). Past chief rabbis of Ireland have included Rabbi Isaac Herzog and Rabbi Immanuel Jakobovits (who became, respectively, the chief rabbis of Israel and of the British Commonwealth). The chief rabbi also supervises the *kashrut* of Dublin's two kosher butchers.

Apart from the Orthodox religious establishment, a Progressive congregation is also active in Dublin. There is a Jewish school, including a high school called Stratford that also has many non-Jews among its student body and faculty.

The Dublin Jewish News is published four times each year.

·ISRAEL·

Israel's first ambassador to Ireland arrived in 1994.

Aliya: Since 1948, 673 Irish Jews have emigrated to Israel.

·SITES·

The Jewish Museum in Dublin presents the history of Irish Jewry.

Jewish Representative Council of Ireland
Herzog House
Zion Road
Rathgar—Dublin 6
Tel. 44 353 1 9492 2599
Fax 44 353 1 9492 4680

Embassy
Carrisbrook House
122 Pembroke Road
Ballsbridge—Dublin 4
Tel. 44 353 1 668 0303
Fax 44 353 1 668 0418

Robert Briscoe (1894–1969) was a great Irish and Jewish patriot. He supported Eamon de Valera and from 1917 to 1924 played a leading role in the Irish struggle against the British. Briscoe was an admirer and friend of Vladimir Jabotinsky and greatly aided the Zionist Revisionist Movement in its struggle for a Jewish state. His experience in clandestine military activity inspired the Jewish underground, called the Irgun Zvei Leumi. Briscoe was later elected lord mayor of Dublin—the first Jew to attain that honor. Upon being told of the election of a Jew as mayor of Dublin, Yogi Berra, the American baseball player, allegedly remarked, "Only in America!"

ITALY

GP 57,226,000 ✦ JP 30,000

Italian map of holy places in the Land of Israel, ca. 1800

✦DEMOGRAPHY✦

Italy's widely dispersed Jewish community has, at different periods of its long history, been present in scores of cities and towns across the country. Italian Jewry is today concentrated in Rome (15,000) and Milan (10,000). Smaller communities are situated in Turin (1,600), Florence (1,400), and Leghorn (Livorno) (1,000). A few hundred Jews are also organized in Bologna, Genoa, Trieste, and Venice, and smaller numbers of Jews are found in Alessandria, Ancona, Asti, Ferrara, Gorizia, Mantua, Merano, Modena, Naples, Padua, Parma, Perugia, Pisa, Siena, Spezia, Vercelli, Verona, Viareggio, and Casale Monferrato.

A number of eastern European Ashkenazim, mainly Holocaust survivors, found sanctuary in the country after World War II. In more recent years, Italian Jewry has been bolstered by some 3,000 Libyan Jews who moved to Italy in the late 1960s and early 1970s.

✦HISTORY✦

The experiences of Jews who have lived in the lands known today as Italy have been precursors of the experiences of Diaspora Jewry throughout the world.

After the Maccabean uprising against Greek dominance in the Land of Israel, it is recorded that Judah Maccabee sent a diplomatic representative to Rome, marking the first Jewish presence in Rome (2nd century B.C.E.). These political ties were soon to result in the Roman suzerainty over Palestine. During the pagan period, Roman attitudes towards Jews wavered between hostility and acceptance, setting a pattern for the subsequent 21 centuries. Jewish traders gravitated towards the center of the empire, and Jewish slaves and prisoners wound up there as well. These Jews, numbering up to 50,000, formed the first community of Rome.

The Jewish community of Turin benefited from the enlightened attitude of the House of Savoy some years before Jews were emancipated in united Italy. In 1862 it decided to construct a sky-scraping synagogue as a monument to Jewish emancipation. Construction was commenced on a grandiose scale, but due to the magnitude of the project and its proportionate expense, the community quickly ran out of funds. Consequently it presented the project to the city. Despite decades of alternative finance and usage proposals, today the building—the Mole Antonelliana — stands at its full height but without a permanent use. Serving as a lookout point and a venue for temporary exhibitions, the incomplete Mole remains the tallest building in Turin.

The Roman conversion to Christianity signaled a distinctive change of perception of Jews. Unpredictable ambivalence gave way to a tendency towards restrictions on, and isolation of, the Jewish population. Changes in regional restrictions kept Jews moving from one town or area to another, having to change professions, dress, and living arrangements as laws changed. In 1492 the Italian lands under the Spanish throne enacted an expulsion that sent 40,000 Jews away from Sicily and Sardinia, and, 50 years later, also from Naples.

The 16th century Counter-Reformation was intensely experienced by Italian Jews; Catholic officialdom chose to place some blame on the Jews for this severe threat to Papal control over Christianity. The first ghetto, created by the Venician senate in 1516, became the model for anti-Jewish laws as the Counter-Reformation developed. In 1555, the Pope sanctioned and encouraged the establishment of ghettos. Attacks on Jews and the destruction of manuscripts and holy books characterized this period and the successive pre-emancipation centuries.

The emancipation of Italian Jewry was prefaced by Napoleonic control over Italy. The French armies granted equal rights to all, but after the defeat of France the Jews found themselves stripped of their equality by reactionary regimes. Yet, in the decades to come, freedoms were slowly granted on a region-by-region basis, starting in Tuscany in 1815. The Papal state was perhaps the most resistant, requiring Jews to attend proselytizing sermons until well into the middle of the century. Between the years 1848 and 1860, as the Italian unification movement embraced more and

Pope John Paul II, accompanied by Italian Chief Rabbi Toaff, during his visit to the Great Synagogue of Rome, April, 1986

more of the country, Jewish emancipation spread. When Rome was liberated from papal control in 1871, Roman Jews were finally emancipated. In subsequent decades, Italian Jews contributed to many fields of public life, and an Italian Jew, Luigi Luzzatti, became premier (head of the Council of Ministers) in 1910.

In its early years, Benito Mussolini's Fascist movement was not characterized by anti-Semitism. Indeed, some Italian Jews were enthusiastic Fascists until the alliance of Italy with Germany, and even after it. Nazi pressure to implement discrimination against Jews was for the most part ignored or enacted half-heartedly. The appearance of anti-Semitism in Mussolini's speeches, however, was a hint of the tragedy that was to come. In 1931 there were 48,000 Jews in Italy. By 1939 up to 4,000 had been baptized, and some thousands more chose to emigrate, leaving 35,000 Jews in the country. During the war, Jews were interned in labor camps in Italy, but when the north of the country was effectively occupied by the Germans in 1943, the threat to Jews became critical. In spite of German efforts to deport Italian Jewry to death camps, the willingness of much of the Italian popula-

tion to shelter Jews meant that many Nazi efforts were stymied. By the end of the war, the Nazis and some Italian Fascists had murdered 7,750 Jews.

✦COMMUNITY✦

The community's organization, the Unione delle Comunita Ebraiche Italiane, is directly involved in providing religious, cultural, and educational services, and, significantly, represents the community politically. Individual communities and associations are independent but maintain firm cooperative links with the Rome-based union. Until Israel and the Vatican secured a diplomatic accord in 1993, the union was a critical link between the Catholic Church, Israel, and world Jewry.

International organizations such as B'nai B'rith and WIZO are active in the main cities in Italy, and a number of them also provide for youth (B'nai Akiva and Hashomer Hatzair), welfare, and cultural concerns.

Anti-Semitism is propagated by people often linked to the extreme, right-wing political movements and skinhead groups. The community, with the support of many politicians and intellectuals of various political persuasions, has been vocal in its concern about the intolerant elements of the Lega Nord

(Northern League) and the reformed Allianza Nazionale, which is tied to Mussolini's legacy. The latter parties' participation in the governing coalition of Silvio Berlusconi in 1994 caused alarm about the apparent re-legitimization of fascism. Italian Jewry is the source of a number of the country's liberal voices, stressing the need for tolerance and respect for democratic processes.

Prior to the collapse of the Soviet Union, the town of Ladispoli, near Rome, was used by the JDC as a transit station for Soviet Jewish emigrants. During the 1970s and 1980s, Italy also became a focus of pro-Palestinian activity, and a number of huge rallies took place during the Intifada to protest Israeli policies. Pope John Paul II's visit to the Great Synagogue of Rome in 1986 marked the rapprochement between Jews and the Vatican.

✦ RELIGIOUS LIFE ✦
The continual presence of a Jewish community in Rome for more than two millennia has produced a distinctive tradition of prayer—comparable to the Sephardi or Ashkenazi traditions—called the Nusach Italki (Italian rite). A number of synagogues in Rome, including the Great Synagogue, follow this tradition. The *nusach* has its own order of prayer and tunes. Most synagogues in Italy are Sephardi.

The Italian chief rabbi officiates at the Great Synagogue of Rome and heads the country's rabbinical council. Kosher food is available, and there are kosher restaurants in Bologna, Florence, Milan, and Rome.

✦ CULTURE AND EDUCATION ✦
Jewish schools are established in Rome, Milan, Florence, Genoa, Livorno, and Trieste. The community tends to use the primary-level schools at a high rate (more than 60% of the Jewish children in Rome attend) and sends its children to regular schools for secondary education. Advanced studies—including those for rabbinical students—are available in institutes in Rome, Turin and Milan.

The monthly *Shalom* is the Roman community's key publication, while its counterpart, the *Bollettino delle Comunita*, is published in Milan. Numerous organizations have their own publications. *La Rassegna di Israel* is an academic quarterly. Milan and Rome have Jewish cultural clubs for the community-at-large and for youth.

✦ ISRAEL ✦
Israel and Italy enjoy full diplomatic relations. In addition to its embassy in Rome, Israel maintains a consulate general in Milan. Since 1994 Israel has also had an ambassador to the Holy See.

Aliya: Since 1948, 4,170 Italian Jews have emigrated to Israel.

✦ SITES ✦
The Venician ghetto, with its remaining synagogue and museum, is a prime Jewish tourist attraction. The catacombs in Rome include a number of Jewish tombs, and the Arch of Titus (opposite the Roman Forum) depicts the destruction of Jerusalem. The remains of a 4th-century synagogue can be seen in Ostia Antica, near Rome, constructed on the site of a synagogue from the 1st century B.C.E. Jewish history museums are found in Rome (where the city's ghetto can be visited in the San Angelo district), as well as in Venice, Casale Menferrato, and Asti.

Unione delle Comunita Ebraiche Italiane
Lungotevere Sanzio 9
00153 Rome
Tel. 39 6 580 3667/580 3670
Fax 39 6 589 9569

Embassy
Via Michele Mercati 14
00197 Rome
Tel. 39 6 3619 8500
Fax 39 6 3619 8555

GP 412,000 ◆ JP 600

◆HISTORY AND DEMOGRAPHY◆

From the 1300s until the era of Napoleonic dominance over Europe, very small numbers of Jews settled in Luxembourg and Arlon (today Belgium). However, frequent persecution, such as massacres at the time of the Black Death (1349) and expulsions (1391 and 1530) prevented communities from developing deep roots in the grand duchy.

Napoleon's influence laid the foundation for a religious framework established along the French model in 1838, and this remains as the Consistoire Israelite. A synagogue was built for the first time in 1823, and by 1880, there were 369 Jews in the capital city and some 60 families elsewhere in the duchy. A second synagogue was dedicated in 1899, as was one in Esch-sur-Alzette in 1899.

In the 1930s, the Jewish population swelled from 1,500 to 4,000, thanks to immigration from Germany. Evacuations to France and efforts by Christian rescuers enabled the majority of these Jews to survive. Some 720 Jews were eventually deported, of whom 690 were murdered.

The post–World War II population is dominated by returning Luxembourgers and their descendants, but recent Jewish immigrants have also made their home in the country.

◆COMMUNITY◆

The Consistoire Israelite is constitutionally recognized as the community's representative to the government and is the organ through which the chief rabbi and one communal functionary are appointed. Both are financed by the government.

The community's main synagogue is situated close to the town center. Orthodox traditions are followed. Kosher food is not locally produced, but families who observe *kashrut* obtain meat and other foodstuffs from Brussels and Strasbourg.

◆ISRAEL◆

Full diplomatic ties were established between Israel and Luxembourg in 1949. Israel's ambassador to the grand duchy resides in Brussels.

Aliya: Since 1948, 84 Luxembourg Jews have emigrated to Israel.

Consistoire Israelite de Luxembourg
45 Avenue Monterey
2018 Luxembourg
Tel. 352 452 914, Fax 352 473 772

◆

Postage stamp commemorating the Great Synagogue of Luxembourg

MALTA

GP 369,000 ♦ JP 60

♦ HISTORY AND COMMUNITY ♦

Almost all the Jews of Malta live in Valletta. Traces of evidence show that Jews were on Malta during Roman rule some 2,000 years ago. From the 8th to the 11th centuries, the Arab rulers allowed the presence of perhaps a few dozen families. In the following centuries, when the island was under Sicilian rule, Jews lived on Malta until their expulsion in 1492.

During the rule of the Knights of St. John (16th to 18th centuries), Jewish prisoners captured in raids on Turkey were held on Malta until ransomed. Due to the island's proximity to North Africa, it is from this area that most of today's Jewish community is descended. A synagogue was opened in Valletta in 1984.

♦ ISRAEL ♦

Israel has full relations with Malta and is represented by its ambassador in Rome.

Jewish Community of Malta
P.O. Box 4, Birkirkara, Malta
Tel. 356 44 59 24

Interior of the new synagogue in Valetta,
consecrated on Rosh Hashanah, 1984

MONACO

GP 32,000 ♦ JP 1,000

♦ HISTORY ♦

Prior to World War II, a small number of Jews, mostly originating from France, lived in Monaco. During the Holocaust, the government protected its Jewish citizens by falsifying records which would have revealed their Jewish identity. In the post-war period, Jewish families have come to settle in Monte Carlo primarily as retirees from France and the United Kingdom. In addition, North African and Turkish Jews have joined the community.

♦ COMMUNAL LIFE ♦

The Association Culturelle Israelite de Monaco, established in 1948, is recognized as the official Jewish representative body. The community maintains a synagogue in a house con-

verted for that purpose. A community rabbi is employed who also oversees Monte Carlo's kosher food store, and teaches at the community's Hebrew school. B'nai B'rith, WIZO, and several other organizations are active.

♦ ISRAEL ♦

Israel and Monaco have diplomatic relations and Israel is represented by its consul in Marseilles.

Association Culturelle Israelite de Monaco
15 Avenue de la Costa
98000 Monte Carlo
Tel. 33 93 30 16 46

THE NETHERLANDS

GP 15,575,000   JP 30,000

✦DEMOGRAPHY✦

Amsterdam (15,000) is the focus of the Netherlands' Jewish community. There are medium-size communities in Rotterdam and The Hague, and small ones in Amersfoort, Arnhem, Bussum, Eindhoven, Enschede, Groningen, Haarlem, Hilversum, Leeuwarden, Leiden, Utrecht, and Zwolle. Contemporary Dutch Jewry is overwhelmingly Ashkenazi.

✦HISTORY✦

It is possible that Jews lived in the present-day Netherlands during the Roman period, but the first documented communities date from the late Middle Ages. As in neighboring regions, the Black Death in the 14th century wiped out these communities, either by disease or in massacres following allegations that Jews had brought on the plague.

The history of contemporary Dutch Jewry begins at the end of the 16th century, when Conversos fleeing the Inquisition in Portugal found refuge and security in Protestant Holland. They were welcomed because their international connections were invaluable in developing Amsterdam-based commerce. They received freedom of worship early in the 17th century and were able to practice Judaism openly. These Sephardim were to evolve into a prominent commercial and cultural group during the Netherlands' Golden Age.

Ashkenazi Jews from Germany, Lithuania, and Poland also made their way to the Netherlands in the 16th century, and their skills allowed them to work as tradespeople and small merchants. However, broad religious liberties were not allowed until the 18th century, when freedom gradually spread across the land. At that time, the 10,000 Jews of Amsterdam constituted the largest community in western Europe. The Napoleonic armies were the catalyst for the Dutch emancipation of the Jews in 1796, one year after the creation of the Batavian Republic. By this time, the number of Jews had increased to some 55,000 (50,000 Ashkenazim and 5,000 Sephardim). Efforts were made to assimilate the Jewish community into Dutch society by emphasizing a difference only of religion. At

✦

Copper plate engraving of Jewish women preparing for Pesach
by Bernard Picart, early 18th century

one stage during the 19th century, the government campaigned for the replacement of Yiddish with Dutch as the language of the Ashkenazi Jews.

Prior to the Holocaust, 140,000 Jews were living in the Netherlands. During the 1930s, the community was active in helping Jews leave Germany, so that by the outbreak of the war, some 30,000 had found sanctuary in the Netherlands. The tragedy of Dutch Jewry during the Shoah was marked by a paradoxical response by the Dutch people. Many of the Dutch collaborated with the Germans, while many others strove to rescue their Jewish neighbors. By the war's end, over 100,000 Dutch Jews had been murdered. Some 10,000, including 3,500 children, had been hidden until the danger passed.

A number of Hebrew words have entered the Dutch language. In the Netherlands, as in Israel, it is not unusual for one friend to describe another friend as a chabber. *Similarly if one needs to pay a price of 100 guilders, it is common to be asked for a* meier.

◆COMMUNITY◆

Dutch Jewry is organized into three councils based on affiliation: Ashkenazi Orthodox, Reform, and Sephardi Orthodox. These councils are, respectively, the Nederlands–Israelitisch Kerkgenootschap, the Verbond van Liberaal Religieuze Joden, and the Portugees–Israelitisch Kergenootschap.

The Netherlands is the venue of much Zionist activity. WIZO and B'nai B'rith are present, as well as five youth movements, a student union, and Maccabi.

A comprehensive welfare structure has been created in the post-war period. There is a Jewish hospital in Amstelveen and retirement homes in Amsterdam and Scheveningen.

Political extremism, particularly the activities of a number of right-wing movements, are deeply troubling to Jews and other minority groups. The Netherlands' 900,000 resident foreigners—mostly from North Africa and Turkey—are the prime targets of extremism, but anti-Semitism and Holocaust denial are also elements of these movements' ideologies. Extremists have managed to gain minimal representation in the national parliament.

◆RELIGIOUS LIFE◆

Amsterdam has ten Ashkenazi and two Sephardi synagogues. The communities of The Hague and Rotterdam have Ashkenazi Orthodox synagogues, as do the cities of Amersfoort, Arnhem, Bussum, Eindhoven, Groningen, Haarlem, Hilversum, Leiden, Leeuwarden, Utrecht, and Zwolle. The Netherlands' Liberal congregation has synagogues in Amsterdam, Arnhem, Enschede, The Hague, Rotterdam, Tilburg, and some other towns. Kosher food is readily available.

◆CULTURE AND EDUCATION◆

Two Jewish day schools operate in Amsterdam, one each for the traditional communities (primary and secondary school) and the ultra-Orthodox community (primary and secondary school). Furthermore, there are three institutes of higher learning—a kollel, a seminary, and the Institute of Jewish Studies in Leiden.

The weekly *Nieuw Israelitisch Weekblad* is widely read by the community. The journal *Studia Rosenthaliana* is published twice a year by the Bibliotheca Rosenthaliana (the Judaica library of Amsterdam University).

◆ISRAEL◆

The Netherlands since 1948 has had diplomatic links with the State of Israel.

Aliya: Since 1948, 6,120 Dutch Jews have emigrated to Israel.

◆SITES◆

Amsterdam features a number of sites of great Jewish interest, starting with the famous Por-

Interior view of the Portuguese Synagogue in Amsterdam, dedicated in 1675.
The sanctuary is lit by candlelight.

tuguese Synagogue, directly opposite the Jewish Historical Museum, which is housed in four old Ashkenazi synagogues. The Anne Frank House draws an enormous number of visitors from all over the world. It also houses an exhibition exposing contemporary European intolerance. The Resistance Museum has many sections of particular Jewish interest. In recent years, synagogues have been restored in Amsterdam, Middelburg, Rotterdam, and Breda. The detention camp at Westerbork has also been preserved and a commemoration center established there. At the Hollandsche Schouwburg, where Amsterdam Jews were assembled prior to deportation, there is a small museum. The Spinoza House and the Portuguese Synagogue in The Hague (which has served as the synagogue of the Liberal congregation for 20 years) and the old Jewish cemetery at Ouderkerk-on-the-Amstel are other recommended sites of interest.

Federation of Dutch Jewish Communities
Van der Boechorststraat 26
1081 BT Amsterdam
Tel. 31 20 644 9968, Fax 31 20 644 2606

Embassy
Buitenhof 47
2513 AH, The Hague
Tel. 31 70 376 0500, Fax 31 70 376 0555

✦

♦ DEMOGRAPHY ♦

Norwegian Jewry is centered in Oslo, but there is also a small community in Trondheim (120, mostly elderly). Some 500 Jews, about half of them Israelis, are not affiliated with the community.

♦ HISTORY ♦

Norway, for centuries part of the Danish kingdom, shared the same Lutheran-inspired laws which effectively restricted Jews from settling in the western regions of Scandinavia. Some flexibility was allowed for Portuguese Jews to have links with Norway, but this practice was essentially in order to make use of these Jews' trading connections.

> *Norwegian Jews can boast of having the northernmost synagogue in the world, located in Trondheim, which is at the same time the only synagogue known to have at one time served as a railway station.*

In the 1840s, the liberal literary figure Henrik Wergeland initiated a campaign to lift restrictions on Jewish immigration. After 10 years of public debate and lobbying, Wergeland's initiative succeeded in having the Storting (parliament) accept a resolution allowing Jewish migration to Norway. Only a small number of Jews took the opportunity to immediately make Norway their home, but by the end of the 19th century, some 650 Jews had arrived, mostly from central and eastern Europe. The two focuses of settlement were Oslo and Trondheim.

When Norway was invaded by Germany in 1940, 1,800 Jews were living in Norway; all but 200 were Norwegian citizens. When the army surrendered and the state was taken over by the collaborationist government led by Quisling, Nazi demands for anti-Jewish legislation were accepted and implemented quickly. In 1942 when the Germans requested that Norwegian Jews be sent to Nazi concentration camps, the government complied by sending 770 Jews; 760 were killed in death camps. The Norwegian underground succeeded in smuggling 900 Jews across the Swedish border to safety. In 1996 after revelations in the media and public pressure the Ministry of Justice appointed a commission to examine the issue of restitution of Jewish property confiscated by the Quisling regime.

♦ COMMUNAL LIFE ♦

The Mosaiske Trossamfund (Mosaic Community) represents the Jews of Norway.

There is one rabbi in Norway, who officiates at the synagogue in Oslo and who also supervises the kosher food shop in the capital (*shechita* is prohibited). Some 150 to 200 people attend *shabbat* services. There is a second synagogue in Trondheim. The Oslo community runs a kindergarten and an after-hours Hebrew school for primary and secondary school students. There are local chapters of B'nai B'rith, WIZO, and the Union of Jewish Women. B'nai Akiva organizes seminars and camps for all ages. Maccabi is also active. The community owns a country estate that is used for summer camps and *shabbat* seminars. In 1988 a Jewish old-age home was opened. The Oslo community produces a magazine called *Hatikwa*.

✦ISRAEL✦

Israel and Norway have full diplomatic relations. Norway played an essential role in bringing together Israeli and Palestinian leaders and precipitated the Oslo agreement. For their efforts, Nobel Peace prizes were awarded to Yitzhak Rabin, Shimon Peres, and Yasser Arafat. Nearly two decades earlier, Menachem Begin and Anwar Sadat had been similarly honored.

Aliya: Since 1948, 320 Norwegian Jews have emigrated to Israel.

✦SITES✦

At the Ostre Gravlund cemetery, there is a monument to the victims of the Shoah.

Det Mosaiske Trossamfund
Bergstien 13
0172 Oslo
Tel. 47 2 2606 826, Fax 47 2 2416 573

Embassy
Drammensveien 82C,
0244 Oslo 2
Tel. 47 2 2244 7924, Fax 47 2 2256 2183

✦

A postcard of the northernmost synagogue in the world, Trondheim

Trondheim – Norway

Foto: B. Johansen

Greetings from the most northern situated Jewish Community in the World

PORTUGAL

GP 9,808,000 ♦ JP 900

♦DEMOGRAPHY♦

Lisbon is the main center of Jewish life, but there are some 200 Conversos in Belmonte who are in the process of returning to Judaism. A still smaller Converso community is found in Oporto.

♦HISTORY♦

Until the 12th century, when Portugal began to emerge as an entity separate from Spain, Portuguese Jewry's historical experiences were essentially the same as those of Spanish Jewry, dating back to Roman times.

The kings who most contributed to the formation of Portugal employed prominent Jewish courtiers. This relationship contributed to the considerable autonomy granted to the Jewish community during the early years of independence. In exchange for significant tax payments and confinement to Jewish quarters, *juderias*, Jews were allowed to administer their own laws and practice their religion. The monarch appointed a Jewish leader, the *arraby mor*, to represent Jewish needs to the government, but Jews were themselves permitted to choose local leaders and rabbis. This security and tight-knit framework allowed Jews to prosper commercially and culturally.

Yet the Church developed a deep hostility to Judaism. The Black Death in 1350 presented the Church with an opportunity to vent its anti-Semitic anger. By blaming Jews for the creation and spread of the malady, anti-Jewish riots were sparked in many cities

A Belmonte Converso kindling the Sabbath lights, 1970s

Isaac ben Yehuda Abrabanel was a 15th-century, Lisbon-born Jew who, as well as being a student of Jewish and Renaissance philosophy and a successful merchant, served as treasurer to King Alfonso V of Portugal and later as financial advisor to the Spanish royal couple, Ferdinand and Isabella. His closeness to the Spanish dynasty gave him the opportunity to appeal against the 1492 expulsion of the Jews, albeit without success. Making his new home in Italy, Abrabanel was a scholar and a statesman, alternating between authoring works of Jewish philosophy and serving as an advisor in Italian courts.

and towns. From this point onwards, Portuguese Jews suffered from diminishing protection and tolerance.

Although Jews exiled from Spain were allowed to enter Portugal in 1492, the spreading influence of the Spanish monarchy resulted in Portugal issuing an expulsion edict of its own four years later. The Portuguese dynasty's fear that the Jews' departure would economically cripple the kingdom resulted in the forced conversion of tens of thousands of Jews to Christianity. The status of these Conversos—whether or not they welcomed their new faith—was never fully accepted by the "Old Christians." In the 16th century, an Inquisition was introduced that remained in force until 1821. The number of Conversos declined throughout these centuries of limbo, and many escaped to western Europe and the Americas. By the time the Inquisition ended, the number of Conversos was unknown.

Jews have begun to trickle back into Portugal during the past 150 years. Communities were permitted to settle there in 1892, a development that was reconfirmed at the time of the Portuguese Revolution in 1910. Prior to World War II, 380 Portugese Jews were in the country, together with some 700 Jewish refugees from other parts of Europe. During the war, neutral Portugal served as an escape corridor for thousands of refugees.

◆COMMUNAL LIFE◆

Today's community has a Sephardi majority, but there is also a sizeable Ashkenazi group made up of post-war migrants from Germany and Poland. The Comunidade Israelita de Lisboa is the organization which unites local communal groups and links communities throughout the country. In Lisbon there are both a Sephardi and an Ashkenazi synagogue, but only the former is active. There are also synagogues in both Belmonte and Oporto. Kosher food can be obtained in Lisbon and Belmonte.

In recent years, a number of Portuguese have traced their roots back to Conversos. Some of these individuals, primarily in Belmonte, but also in Oporto, Macao, and Ortiga, have decided to return to Judaism.

◆ISRAEL◆

In 1977 Portugal and Israel established diplomatic ties, and the consulate general in Lisbon was raised to the rank of an embassy. Portugal opened an embassy in Israel in 1991.
Aliya: Since 1948, 248 Portuguese Jews have emigrated to Israel.

◆SITES◆

An ancient synagogue can be found in Tomar and remnants of a Jewish quarter in Castelo de Vida. The old Jewish cemetery in Faro is often visited.

Comunidade Israelita de Lisboa
Rua Alexandre Herculano, 59
1250 Lisbon
Tel. 351 1 385 8604, Fax 351 1 388 4304

Embassy
Rua Antonio Enes, 16
1000 Lisbon
Tel. 351 1 570 251, Fax 351 1 352 8545

◆

SPAIN

GP 39,647,000 ♦ JP 14,000

♦DEMOGRAPHY♦

The two major centers of Jewish life in Spain are Madrid (3,500) and Barcelona (3,500), followed by Malaga, where a smaller number of Jews live. Other communities are found in Alicante, Benidorm, Cadiz, Granada, Marbella, Majorca, Torremolinos, and Valencia. In Spanish North Africa, Jews reside in Ceuta and Melilla. The Jewish community of modern Spain is primarily based on waves of post-war migration from Morocco, from the Balkans, from other European countries, and, most recently (in the 1970s and 1980s), from Latin America. The majority are Sephardi.

♦HISTORY♦

Spanish Jewry first appeared in the Roman period, but not until the Visigoth invasion of the Iberian peninsula did Jewish communities develop in a number of centers. At the beginning of the 4th century, the newly dominant Christian Church enacted detailed restrictions on interaction with Jews in the Council of Elvira. In the following four centuries, the Visigoths ruled the peninsula. At times they were well disposed toward the Jews, but after they adopted Christianity in 589, their attitude changed. In 613, Jews were given the option of conversion or emigration, and in 694, the remaining Jews were enslaved.

The Muslim invaders of 711 were welcomed by the Jews of Spain as liberators.

Lighting shabbat and festival candles in buckets was one technique used by Conversos to hide their Jewish identity, but other practices were used to convince neighbors that the "New Christians" were genuine: playing cards on the night of Yom Kippur and disguising mezuzot as crucifixes are two examples. Even less known were the tricks of deception used in the kitchen. Jews would refrain from cooking stews in case it was suspected that they were cooking for shabbat, and pork sausages were hung in kitchen windows as if to wave the culinary flag of Christianity.

Spain's Muslim rulers released Jews from slavery and gave them the freedom to organize communities. The Moors came to rely on Jews to add stability to economic development, to settle sites abandoned by Christians, and to serve as diplomats and court advisors. The opportunity created by a societal role allowed Jews to contribute in medicine, philology, literature, and other pursuits, as well as to cultivate great centers for traditional Jewish learning. The Muslim influence on Jewish art and expression, in architecture, and in literature was significant.

For the next eight centuries, Spanish Jewry played a vital role in the peninsula's history. Both the Muslims and the reconquering Christians relied on Jewish courtiers and communities to spread and secure dominance over particular regions and towns. While Christians and Muslims wrestled for control over Spain, there was always a role for Jews. However, as soon as the Christians had repossessed Spain in its entirety, any Church tolerance of Jews ended.

The Church's hostility toward Judaism was somewhat diluted during the earlier centuries of Christian rule, although a considerable number of restrictions were implemented at different times, requiring Jews to dress according to a specific code and prohibiting Jews from independently holding positions of

119

authority. Jewish communities were, for the most part, allowed internal autonomy, and for many years, communities' *betei din* were respected as being the general law-interpreting bodies for Jews.

By the 13th century, Christian dynasties had reconquered most of Spain, and the need for Jews as intermediaries had diminished. The Church was granted increasing power to separate Jews from Christians and to pressure the Jews to renounce their religion. In 1250 the first Spanish blood libel case was recorded. These pressures caused tensions within the Jewish communities. Some turned to mysticism and produced the Zohar. In 1391 persecution of Jews became violent and intolerably oppressive. Thousands of Jews were killed in riots, synagogues were seized and turned into churches, and holy books were stolen or censored. A public disputation—a debate between Christian and Jewish theologians— at Tortosa in 1413 and 1414 led Jews to convert by the thousands.

The statue of Maimonides at his birthplace in the former Jewish quarter of Cordoba.

The union of the two Spanish dynasties by the marriage of Isabella de Castilla to Fernando de Aragon started the process by which Catholic Spain was unified. To purify Christian Spain, the Inquisition was introduced in 1481. When in 1492, Muslims were driven out of Granada—their stronghold on the peninsula—the monarchs were moved to complete Spanish unity by expelling Spanish Jewry. By the end of July 1492, more than 100,000 Jews had fled Spain.

Years of persecution had taught Jews that they could be baptized and still practice Judaism in secret. These Conversos or New Christians were called *marranos* (swine) by the non-Jewish population. Tens of thousands were discovered and burned at the stake. After the Expulsion, some of these Conversos escaped to western Europe and Latin America, where they could revert to open practice of Judaism. A considerable number of Conversos married into the Spanish aristocracy.

Small numbers of Jews came to Spain in the 19th century, perhaps responding to the Spanish republic's 1868 pledge to religious tolerance. The reconstituted community opened synagogues in Barcelona and Madrid in the first decades of the 20th century. Spanish neutrality in World War II allowed 25,600 Jews to use Spain as an escape route from the European theater of war. Furthermore, Spanish diplomats protected some 4,000 Jews in France and the Balkans. In 1944 Spain took part in the effort to rescue Hungarian Jewry by accepting 2,750 refugees. However, the vast majority of the Jews who took refuge in Spain later left for other countries.

Under the Franco regime, Jewish communities in Madrid and Barcelona kept a low profile. In 1968, however, a new synagogue was opened in Madrid. To mark the event, the government officially repealed the 1492 expulsion edict. In 1992 King Juan Carlos also repealed—in a symbolic gesture—the expulsion order. In recent years, new synagogues have been constructed in other Spanish cities.

◆COMMUNITY◆

The Federacion de Comunidades Israelitas de Espana, which unites the Spanish communities from different parts of the country, represents Jewish interests to the government. A sizable proportion of the community is affiliated to the synagogue-focused communal centers in Barcelona and Madrid, which, in turn, are linked to the Federacion.

In the absence of laws restricting hate propagation or Holocaust denial, Spain serves as a publishing and distribution center for neo-Nazis and other extreme rightists. Indeed, Spain serves as a refuge for a number of Nazi war criminals and neo-Nazis convicted elsewhere of promoting racial hatred or historical revisionism.

◆CULTURAL AND RELIGIOUS LIFE◆

The Latin American immigrants, who come from communities with a strong secular tradition, have formed organizations that bring Jews together for cultural and intellectual events. The Circulo de Reflexion group, the Baruch Spinoza Center, and the magazine *Raices* (Roots) are initiatives of these secular-oriented Jews.

In Barcelona the Sephardi and Ashkenazi communities pray in separate synagogues in the same building. Apart from the two major centers, synagogues operate in Alicante, Benidorm, Malaga, Marbella, Melilla (North Africa), Seville, Torremolinos, and Valencia. Kosher food is provided at the Madrid communal center.

Jewish day schools exist in Barcelona, Madrid, and Malaga. Groups such as WIZO and B'nai B'rith are active in Spain.

◆ISRAEL◆

Israel and Spain did not establish diplomatic ties until 1986, when Spain recognized the State of Israel. Prior to recognition, the Span-ish Jewish community, through cultural friendship associations, provided an unofficial linkage between the two countries.

Aliya: Since 1948, 1,412 Spanish Jews have emigrated to Israel.

◆SITES◆

Toledo features the Museo Sephardi (situated in the El Transito synagogue), the nearby Church of Santa Maria La Blanca (an ancient synagogue), and the former Jewish quarter. The synagogue of Maimonides can be visited in Cordoba, and ancient synagogues can be seen in Avila, Bembibre, Caceres, Estella, Montblanc, and Seville. Most of these have long since been used as churches. Former Jewish areas, the *juderias*, can be seen in Barcelona, Besalu, Burgos, Caceres, Gerona, Granada, Hervas, Madrid, Montblanc, Segovia, Seville, Tarazona, Tarragona, and Tudela.

◆CANARY ISLANDS◆

The first Jews in the Canary Islands were Conversos. However, the foundation of the modern community was laid by immigrants from North Africa in the 1950s. There are several Jewish families in Tenerife and a synagogue in Gran Palma.

◆MAJORCA◆

The Jewish community was reconstituted in 1971 after a hiatus of 536 years. Today there are about 300 Jews in Majorca, and the community maintains a synagogue.

Federacion de Comunidades Israelitas de Espana
Balmes 3
28010 Madrid
Tel. 34 1 445 9843, Fax 34 1 445 9835

Embassy
Velasquez 150-7
28002 Madrid
Tel. 34 1 411 1357, Fax 34 1 564 5974

SWEDEN

GP 9,000,000 ♦ JP 18,000

♦DEMOGRAPHY♦

Sweden's main Jewish communities are situated in Stockholm, Malmo, and Gothenburg. Small communities are found in Boras and Uppsala, and a number of Jews live in Helsingborg, Lund, Norrkoping, and Vaxjo.

The contemporary Swedish community is primarily composed of descendants of prewar refugees and of Shoah survivors who arrived after the war. It also includes refugees who fled Hungary in 1956 and others who left Poland in 1968. In recent years, Sweden has become home to migrants from the former Soviet Union.

The Great Synagogue of Stockholm, completed in 1870

♦HISTORY♦

The dominance of anti-Jewish hostility propagated by the Lutheran Church prevented Jews from settling in Sweden until the late 18th century.

King Gustav III, motivated by the need to add momentum to Sweden's economic development, lifted the ban on Jewish immigration and granted Jews the right to settle in Stockholm, Gothenburg, and Norrkoping. The economic freedoms allowed to Jews were encouraging, but religious liberties were not generous. Nearly complete emancipation was granted in 1838. However, a negative reaction from certain sectors of the population forced the monarch to maintain limitations on cities of residence and on the holding of political office. The final restriction on Swedish Jewry, the right to hold ministerial office, was removed in 1951.

From the moment of emancipation, when Swedish Jewry numbered perhaps 1,000 people, the community's size grew steadily to 3,000 in 1880 and to 7,000 in 1933. The community tended to favor the liberal model of religious practice influenced by the German Reform movement.

In the years preceding World War II, Swedish Jews were alert to the dangers facing their co-religionists to the south, but Sweden's hostility towards the acceptance of refugees prevented many Jews from finding safety there. From 1933 to 1939, 3,000 Jews were accepted into Sweden, and another 1,000 were allowed to use Sweden as a point of transit. By 1942, when the intensity of Nazi brutality began to reveal itself, and Germany's military fortunes deteriorated, the Swedish government had a dramatic change of heart and welcomed refugees.

Sweden's doors were opened to 900 Norwegian Jews in 1942, setting a precedent for the rescue of Danish Jewry in October 1943. At that time, some 8,000 Danish Jews and partly Jewish relatives or spouses escaped to Sweden on scores of fishing boats and other small seacraft. The remarkable efforts of the Budapest-based Swedish diplomat, Raoul Wallenberg, have been given considerable attention in Sweden, and are a source of national pride. In 1997 the Swedish government established a committee to investigate the issue of Nazi gold transferred to Sweden during the war.

♦COMMUNITY♦

The communities are linked by the Official Council of Jewish Communities in Sweden.

The first Jew to try to make his home in Sweden was Aron Isak, a seal engraver, who came from Germany in 1774. He was officially informed that "a Jew has not lived in our kingdom since the beginning of time. But as it is the King's wish, we have decided to allow you to remain here. You cannot do this as a Jew, because that would be against our laws; but if you accept Christianity, you will have immediate citizenship."
"I wouldn't change my religion for all the gold in the world," Isak replied. "I can tell you that the fundamental doctrine of Judaism is to fear God and to love one's neighbors...and this I will do as long as I live."
The Lord Mayor of Stockholm was so impressed by Isak's dignity and determination that he advised Isak as to how to make a legal protest to the King. Isak became Sweden's first Jew.

The absorption of thousands of wartime refugees greatly influenced the Swedish community. As a result, Swedish Jewry is particularly active in international Jewish welfare activities and in supporting development projects in Israel. The community includes organizations such as WIZO, the General Organization of Jewish Women, Emunah, B'nai B'rith, and B'nai Akiva.

1959 meeting of the World Jewish Congress in the hall of the Swedish Parliament

The legal system in Sweden generally allows the free expression of anti-Semitic, racist, and xenophobic ideas, including Holocaust denial. Right-wing extremist groups, often with neo-Nazi sympathies, have perhaps a few thousand members. Some of these groups have links to Europe-wide extremist networks.

◆ RELIGIOUS LIFE ◆
Stockholm has three synagogues (two Orthodox, one Conservative) and two rabbis. Synagogues are also operating in Gothenburg (one Orthodox, one Conservative) and Malmo (Orthodox). Because of the law prohibiting *shechita*, kosher meat is imported and readily available in Stockholm and Malmo. Stockholm boasts several kosher shops and a bakery.

◆ CULTURE AND EDUCATION ◆
A Jewish primary school and a separate kindergarten operate in Stockholm. The Judaica House maintains a communal library and hosts activities such as Hebrew-speaking and Yiddish-speaking groups, Israeli dancing, and sporting events. The bimonthly *Judisk Kronika* is published by the community, and each week a Jewish radio program is broadcast.

◆ ISRAEL ◆
Israel and Sweden have full diplomatic relations.
Aliya: Since 1948, 1,465 Swedish Jews have moved to Israel.

◆ SITES ◆
The Great Synagogue of Stockholm dates from 1876. There is a small Jewish museum in Stockholm.

Official Council of Jewish Communities in Sweden
Wahrendorffsgatan 3 B, 10391 Stockholm
Tel. 46 8 679 2900, Fax 46 8 611 2413

Embassy
Torstenssonsgatan 4
P.O.Box 14006, 10440 Stockholm
Tel. 46 8 663 0435, Fax 46 8 662 5301

SWITZERLAND

GP 7,224,000 ✦ JP 18,000

✦DEMOGRAPHY✦

The largest communities are Zurich (6,800), Geneva (4,400), and Basel (2,600). Jews are also to be found in other cities and towns throughout the Swiss Federation. Some 61% of the Jews live in the German-speaking part of the country and 36% in the French-speaking part.

✦HISTORY✦

Jews first appeared in the area today known as Switzerland in the 13th century and were mostly permitted to fulfill classical medieval functions associated with Jews—moneylending and peddling. Many came from the German lands to the

The synagogue in Geneva, built in 1859

north and spread throughout the German-speaking part of Switzerland to form 30 small communities by the end of the 14th century. From the beginning of the 14th century, responding to the expulsion from France in 1306, the French-speaking Swiss lands also accepted Jews, who soon founded 14 communities. In 1348 many Jews were accused of responsibility for the Black Death and were murdered as a result.

Immediately prior to the French Revolution, only three communities were in existence: Aargau, Lengau, and Oberendingen (today Endingen).

The French Revolution influenced the 1798 formation of the Helvetic Confederation, which, in the following decades, wrestled with the status of Jews within a state that initially defined Jews as "resident aliens." Only in 1866 were Jews granted citizenship, and the condition of participation in a Christian group was dropped.

Since 1893, following a referendum on animal protection, *shechita* has been prohibited in Switzerland.

During the Shoah, Swiss Jews were protected by the state's neutrality. However, a number of Swiss initiatives prevented the entry of Jewish refugees. These included inducing the Germans to mark the passports of Jews with the letter "J." By the war's end, 25,000 Jews had benefited from Swiss protection, but many thousands of others had been delivered back into the hands of the Nazis and their collaborators and lost their lives as a result. In recent years, under pressure from the international community and the World Jewish Congress, Switzerland was forced to confront its behavior during the Holocaust. Several committees were formed to investigate the issue of Jewish assets deposited in Switzerland and the history of Swiss banks' collaboration with Nazi Germany in laundering confiscated and looted gold and other valuables. In the beginning of 1997 the Swiss established a humanitarian fund dedicated to needy Holocaust survivors.

✦COMMUNITY✦

The Swiss community is presided over mostly by the Schweizerischer Israelitischer

Gemeindebund (SIG), founded in 1904 to oppose the restriction on *shechita*.

Ultra-Orthodox and Reform communities operate independently—i.e., without affiliation to the SIG. There are more than 20 cities and towns where Jewish populations have organized communities.

A number of international Jewish organizations have representative offices in Geneva. These include the World Jewish Congress.

✦RELIGIOUS LIFE✦

Synagogues of a variety of denominations operate in Switzerland: traditional, ultra-Orthodox, Reform, Conservative, and Sephardi. Zurich has four synagogues, Geneva three, Basel two, and Lugano two. Synagogues are also to be found in Baden, Berne, Fribourg, La Chaux-de-Fonds, Lausanne, Lucerne, Vevey-Montreux, St. Gallen, and Winterthur. Rabbis are employed in Zurich, Geneva, and Basel, where an Orthodox seminary is active. The SIG plays a role in the distribution of kosher food, which, due to the *shechita* prohibition, is mostly imported.

✦CULTURE AND EDUCATION✦

Due to the dispersed nature of the Jewish population, nine schools are operating in five cities. These are Zurich, Lausanne, Lucerne, Basel, and Kriens-Obernau.

There are three Jewish newspapers for the German-speaking Jewish community and one publication for the French-speakers, who are mostly concentrated in Geneva.

✦ISRAEL✦

Israel and Switzerland enjoy full diplomatic relations. In addition to its embassy in Berne, Israel also maintains a consulate general in Zurich and a representative mission to international organizations in Geneva.

Aliya: Since 1948, 3,220 Swiss Jews have emigrated to Israel.

✦SITES✦

The site of the first Zionist Congress in 1897, is the Musiksaal of the Stadt–Casino in Basel. The Jewish museum in Basel chronicles the history of Swiss Jewry, and in its courtyard are tombstones from the 13th century. Among the cemeteries of particular historical interest are those in Endingen and Lengnau.

Large numbers of Jewish tourists visit Switzerland at all times of the year. Consequently, in certain resort towns, there are hotels that provide kosher facilities.

Federation of Swiss Jewish Communities (SIG)
Gotthardstrasse 65
8002 Zurich
Tel. 41 1 201 5583, Fax 41 1 202 1672

Embassy
Alpenstrasse 32
3006 Berne
Tel. 41 31 351 1042, Fax 41 31 352 7916

✦

Paul Grueninger was a Swiss police chief in the St. Gallen Canton on the Swiss–Austrian border. Moved by the plight of Austrian Jewish refugees attempting to gain entry into Switzerland, Grueninger backdated the entry dates on their documents to mislead authorities into thinking that the refugees had arrived before the border between the countries was closed on August 19, 1938. In so doing, Grueninger saved up to 3,000 Jews from certain death. However, when his ruse was discovered by his superiors, Grueninger was dismissed from his job and in 1940 was convicted of fraud. He never found regular work again and died a broken man in 1972. In 1995, 55 years after his conviction, and in the very same courtroom, Grueninger was posthumously acquitted of any wrongdoing. After the trial, his lawyer, Swiss parliamentarian Paul Reichsteiner, stated, "The acquittal of Paul Grueninger means more than just an acquittal. It's a symbol for taking responsibility for your actions and against conformity and obsequiousness."

✦Demography✦

British Jewry has always been concentrated in Greater London, where two-thirds of the community now reside. Major regional centers include Manchester (30,000), Leeds (10,000), and Glasgow (6,500). In Birmingham, Brighton, Bournemouth, Gateshead, Hull, Leicester, Liverpool, Newcastle upon Tyne, Southend, and Westcliff, there are also sizeable communities, and there are dozens of smaller communities across the British Isles.

The Jewish population has experienced a marked decline in recent decades. While 410,000 Jews were thought to be in Britain in 1967, the community has declined by some 25% since then, despite the arrival of an estimated 30,000 Israelis. The community is shrinking due to a low birthrate, intermarriage, and emigration.

✦History✦

Britain's first Jews came from northern France, in the wake of William the Conqueror's successes in 1066, to help develop commercial contacts between England and France. The early Norman monarchs encouraged Jewish settlement in towns outside of London.

Acceptance of Jews did not become firmly rooted, and in the 12th and 13th centuries, blood libels, heightened tax demands, and Crusading fervor hurt the community. Some Jews were murdered, and the rights of others were denied. In 1290 Edward I decided to expel the entire community of 4,000.

A Jewish wedding in Derby, 1904

Except for a small number of Conversos who were briefly present during the Tudor reign, Jews only began to return to Britain during the 17th century. The ascension to power of the Puritans led to a more favorable perception of Jews because of their connection with the Bible. In 1656 Oliver Cromwell agreed to their readmittance, and this marked the beginning of the official Resettlement.

The first settlers were Sephardim from Holland. Ashkenazi Jews also went to England from the Netherlands and Germany, often working as small-scale merchants and artisans. The 18th century saw continuing Ashkenazi immigration. The numerical dominance of the Ashkenazim eventually brought them together with the Sephardi elite to form a common representative organization— the Board of Deputies of British Jews.

The societal reforms of the 19th century signaled progress for Jews, even though the Jewish Emancipation Bill of the 1830s was rejected by the House of Lords. The final barrier to legal acceptance fell when, in 1858, Lionel de Rothschild was allowed to take a seat in the House of Commons. By participating in the industrial development, Jews were able to establish themselves as a comfortable and confident community.

From 1881 onwards, tens of thousands of eastern European Jews flowed into Britain, seeking to exchange persecution for social and economic opportunity. Between 1881 and 1914, this wave of immigration increased the size of the Jewish community from 65,000 to 300,000. These immigrants found homes in the inner city areas of Glasgow, Leeds, Liverpool, London (predominantly in the East End), and Manchester, often working as artisans and small merchants.

Already in the mid-19th century, Sir Moses Montefiore, perhaps the most important Jewish political leader of his generation, took initiatives to support settlement in Palestine. His role set a precedent for British Jewry's involvement in the eventual creation of a Jewish state, although the community was not unified in its support for Zionism. Chaim Weizmann became a British citizen while playing a leading political role in lobbying for the acceptance of a Jewish home in Palestine. British Jewry experienced years of confusion while Jews in British-controlled Palestine fought a war of liberation against their overlords.

Prior to World War II, some tens of thousands of central and eastern European Jewish refugees arrived in the United Kingdom. The tragedy inflicted upon continental European Jewry widened support for Zionism, which became a focus of identity.

English Sephardim can claim credit for introducing high-class fare into the English fish diet—and beyond. Smoked salmon was a local Sephardi delicacy in the mid-19th century, and the oldest established purveyor of lox was a firm of Sephardi Jews called Costa. For their part, the Ashkenazim can lay claim to the more lowly fish and chips, the dish that came to characterize the English working class. This was the invention of an East London Jewish fish store proprietor who began to sell the tasty duo in 1865. In 1968 the National Federation of Fish Friers awarded a plaque to the still-extant store for the gastronomic innovation.

◆ C O M M U N I T Y ◆

The Board of Deputies links many synagogues and, together with a large number of special interest groups, brings British Jewry into a common framework. The board is the community's political representative and endeavors to encourage organizational cooperation and planning.

At the same time, this communal structure does not attract the interest of a significant number of Jews. Several initiatives have been dedicated to involving unaffiliated Jews in some form of Jewish activity.

Support for Israel is fostered by a number of pro-Israel or purely philanthropic organizations. Zionist youth movements of a variety of religious and political persuasions are active and successful in promoting *aliya* and attachment to Israel.

Welfare structures are given high communal priority, and organizations such as Jewish Care and World Jewish Relief have prominent positions. Jewish Care plays a critical role in supporting dozens of retirement homes.

Today's community is, for the most part, solidly middle class. Increasing numbers have turned to the professions, while many are involved in commerce. Relative to the population in general, British Jews have a strong tendency to attend institutes of tertiary education. Jews are active and prominent in political life, and a number have served as cabinet ministers and senior members of the judiciary.

✦ R E L I G I O U S   L I F E ✦
Organized Jewish life in the United Kingdom is largely centered around synagogue affiliation. Britain's 360 houses of worship reflect 6 forms of religious affiliation: traditional Orthodox, ultra-Orthodox, Reform, Liberal, Sephardi, and Masorati. Approximately 70% of the community is affiliated with these denominations.

A recent study suggests that these Jews are divided thusly: 47% are members of traditional Orthodox communities, 12% of Reform communities, 4% of Liberal, 4% of ultra-Orthodox, 2% of Sephardi, and 1% of Masorati. Rabbinical training centers are operated by the Orthodox, Reform, ultra-Orthodox, and Sephardi communities. Each of the denominations is serviced by an independent umbrella organization, the most prominent of which is the Orthodox United Synagogue, which is headed by the chief rabbi.

Kashrut observance is served in London by a number of kosher stores, butcheries, restaurants, and caterers. Smaller communities have more limited facilities, but kosher food can be found in most parts of the country.

✦ CULTURE AND EDUCATION ✦
A network of Jewish day schools operates in London and in other major cities. The educational institutions in Gateshead offer boarding facilities for Jews who wish to study in an ultra-Orthodox framework.

Jews College is the traditional Orthodox community's rabbinical studies center. Leo Baeck College trains Reform rabbis, and a number of *yeshivot* are operated by the ultra-Orthodox communities. One of Britain's leading centers of tertiary Jewish studies is the Oxford Centre for Hebrew Studies at Yarnton.

The *Jewish Chronicle* is the focus of communication for the community across the country. It is read by an estimated 75% of the community. The *Jewish Quarterly* is a magazine that offers commentary and articles of a

High Tea in the Sukka
by Solomon Joseph Solomon, 1906.
Ink, graphite, and gouache on paper

cultural focus. *New Moon* is a magazine targeting a young adult audience.

✦ I S R A E L ✦

Britain and Israel maintain full diplomatic relations.

Aliya: Since 1948, 26,500 British Jews have emigrated to Israel.

✦ S I T E S ✦

The Jewish Museum, the London Museum of Jewish Life, and the Bevis Marks Synagogue are all of interest. Former Jewish quarters from the early period of Jewish life in the United Kingdom can be visited in London and in a number of cities and towns. The British Library and the British Museum contain major collections of Jewish artifacts and manuscripts.

Manchester has a Jewish Museum, and the medieval home of Aaron the Jew is located in Lincoln. In 1996 a Holocaust education center—the first of its kind in the United Kingdom—was opened near Nottingham.

✦ S C O T L A N D ✦

The first Scottish Jewish community is thought to have been formed in Edinburgh in the late 18th century, but today's community is descended from a congregation founded in 1816 in the same city. Waves of immigrants from Russia and eastern Europe, who came to settle across the United Kingdom during the 19th century, brought thousands of Jews to Scotland, most of whom chose to make their homes in industrial Glasgow.

Glasgow's contemporary community has moved from the industrial parts of the city into the suburbs, where many of the city's seven synagogues are located. Edinburgh, which has a smaller community of just over one thousand Jews, has one synagogue and a number of small, but active, Jewish societies. There are also small numbers of Jews in Aberdeen and Dundee.

✦ W A L E S ✦

The Welsh Jewish community took form when Jews immigrated from Russia and eastern Europe to escape persecution and stifled opportunity. Today Cardiff has both an Orthodox and a Liberal synagogue. There is a Jewish kindergarten. Kosher food is sold in several shops. Jews also live in Llandudno, Newport, and Swansea.

✦ N O R T H E R N   I R E L A N D ✦

The current community of Belfast was founded in 1869, although historical sources record the presence of individual Jews in earlier centuries. As with the Jews of the Republic of Ireland, immigrants in the previous century boosted the community's numbers significantly. In recent decades, the civil unrest between Catholics and Protestants has seen most of Belfast Jewry migrate to England, Israel, and the United States. A modern synagogue was built in 1967, but today the community numbers only a few hundred.

✦ C H A N N E L   I S L A N D S ✦

Jews first appeared in the Channel Islands in the middle of the 18th century, and the first synagogue was built in the middle of the 19th century. Most Jews managed to flee the island in advance of the German occupation, but those that remained were handed over to the Germans by the local authorities and deported to their deaths in Auschwitz. After the war, Jews returned to the islands, where they reside mainly in Jersey. There is a synagogue in Jersey that is served by a rabbi who visits from England.

Board of Deputies of British Jews
Commonwealth House, 1–19 New Oxford St.
GB London, WC1A 1NF
Tel. 44 171 543 5400
Fax 44 171 543 0010

Embassy
2 Palace Green
London, W8 4QB
Tel. 44 171 957 9500
Fax 44 171 957 9555

✦

EASTERN EUROPE

"May this hour bring success to your house."
Prague, ca. late 19th century.
Copper clock with Hebrew letters as numerals

ALBANIA
BOSNIA AND HERZEGOVINA
BULGARIA
CROATIA
CZECH REPUBLIC
ESTONIA
HUNGARY
LATVIA
LITHUANIA
MACEDONIA
POLAND
ROMANIA
SLOVAKIA
SLOVENIA
YUGOSLAVIA

ALBANIA

GP 3,401,000 ♦ JP 10

♦HISTORY AND COMMUNITY♦

Jewish communities were established by refugees from Spain, Portugal, and Sicily at the end of the 15th century and the beginning of the 16th. Some settled along the coast, especially in the port of Durres (Durazzo), but most Jews made their homes in Berat, in central Albania. A 1930 census recorded 204 Jews in the country, mainly in Tirana and Vlore (Valora). In 1939 a small number of Jewish refugees from Germany and Austria found sanctuary in the country, and they were later joined by Jews fleeing Croatia and Serbia. The Albanian population, and even the Italian forces occupying the country from 1939, were sympathetic to the Jews. Until the collapse of Communism in 1990, the community was completely cut off from the Jewish world. All religion was strictly outlawed, and consequently there was no Jewish communal life. In 1991 nearly the entire Jewish community, numbering some 300 people, was airlifted to Israel.

In 1673 Shabbtai Tzvi, the famous false messiah, was exiled to Albania and spent the last years of his life there.

With the departure of almost the entire Jewish community, there is virtually no organized Jewish life. Most of the remaining Jews live in the capital, Tirana. There is, however, an Albania–Israel Friendship Society. A synagogue still exists in Vlore, but is no longer in use.

♦ISRAEL♦

Israel and Albania have maintained diplomatic relations since 1991. Israel is represented by its ambassador in Rome.

Aliya: Since 1948, 356 Albanian Jews have emigrated to Israel.

Albania–Israel Friendship Society
Rruga Barriskatave, 226 Tirana
Tel. 355 42 22611

The late Joseph Jakoel, author of a history of Albanian Jewry, holding an ancient ketuba, Tirana, 1991

GP 3,628,000 ✦ JP 500

✦DEMOGRAPHY✦

About half of the Jews live in Sarajevo and the balance in Mostar, Zenica, Tuzla, Doboj, and Banja Luka. Two-thirds of the community have left since the outbreak of conflict in the former Yugoslavia, but recently the tendency toward emigration has slackened. Some 90% of the community is Sephardi. However, only older people still speak Ladino.

✦HISTORY✦

Sephardi Jews established a community in Sarajevo during the second half of the 16th century. They were later joined by Ashkenazi Jews from central Europe. A special Jewish quarter was established in the second half of the 16th century, and the poorer Jews resided there until the Austrian conquest in 1878. A succession of Ottoman laws in the 19th century emancipated the Jews of Turkey and the various territories under its rule, including Bosnia and Herzegovina.

After World War I, when Bosnia and Herzegovina became a constituent part of

The Sarajevo Haggada is a 14th-century Spanish manuscript bought by the Sarajevo Museum in 1894

Yugoslavia, the Jewish community joined the all-Yugoslav Federation of Jewish Religious Communities. For the most part, Bosnian Jewry retained its unique Sephardi customs along with the the Ladino language.

On the eve of the Shoah, the Jewish population numbered some 14,000. In 1941 Bosnia was incorporated into the Croat state. When the Germans entered Sarajevo, together with a local Bosnian Muslim mob, they destroyed the Sephardi synagogue. Bosnian Jewry was decimated by a combination of German, Ustashe (Croat Fascist), and Bosnian Muslim forces. The Mufti of Jerusalem (Haj Amin-al Husseini) was active in enlisting recruits to a Bosnian Muslim S.S. unit and in encouraging local authorities to organize the deportation and extermination of Bosnian Jewry.

After the war, the Jewish community was reconstituted, and many of the survivors returned. As was the case elsewhere in

✦

In February 1994, Israel, with the aid of the World Jewish Congress and the JDC, provided sanctuary to some 90 Muslim refugees fleeing the civil war in Bosnia. Among them was the family of Mrs. Zejneba Hardaga-Susic, a Muslim woman who rescued a Jewish family in Bosnia during the Shoah. Several months after her arrival in Israel, Mrs. Hardaga-Susic passed away and was laid to rest in the cemetery at the Moshav Beit Zayit. Her daughter, son-in-law, and grandchild have converted to Judaism and are presently living in Mevasseret Zion (near Jerusalem).

Sarajevo's monument to 900 Jews whose remains were exhumed
and reburied in a common grave in the Sephardi cemetery

Yugoslavia, the rate of intermarriage was high, but most Jews retained a sense of Jewish identity. After the collapse of Yugoslavia in 1990, Jews in Bosnia shared the fate of their non-Jewish neighbors, and many elected to flee the country.

⋆COMMUNITY⋆

Since 1945 there has been a united Jewish community (Sephardi and Ashkenazi). The Federation of Jewish Communities of Bosnia and Herzegovina is responsible for both religious and secular life. There are no branches of international Jewish organizations. La Benevolencija, a Jewish humanitarian association formed 100 years ago, is active in promoting the general welfare of the population, irrespective of religion or nationality. The JDC has provided critical aid to this beleaguered community.

⋆RELIGIOUS AND CULTURAL LIFE⋆

There is only one functioning synagogue, which was rebuilt after World War II, and it is the center of Bosnian Jewish communal life. Four other synagogue buildings exist, one of which serves as the Jewish Museum. Cultural programs are held, including co-sponsored exhibitions, concerts, and lectures. There is also a Sunday school. A bimonthly paper called *Bulletin* is published, as well as occasional journals on Jewish culture.

⋆ISRAEL⋆

There are no diplomatic relations between Bosnia and Herzegovina and Israel, but Jerusalem has sent humanitarian aid to the fledgling republic.

Aliya: Until 1994 Bosnian Jews were counted together with immigrants from other parts of Yugoslavia.

⋆SITES⋆

The Sephardi Jewish cemetery in Sarajevo is one of the most important Jewish burial grounds in Europe because of the shape of the tombstones and the ancient Ladino inscriptions on them. The famous 14th century "Sarajevo Haggada" was hidden for safekeeping by the government during the conflict. The Jewish Museum chronicles the history of Sarajevan Jewry. In the Sarajevo synagogue, there is a valuable collection of Ladino and other Jewish books, some printed 200 to 300 years ago. The tomb of the *Tzaddik* Rabbi Moshe Danon in Stolac is venerated by Jews and non-Jews. On the anniversary of his death (the first Sunday in July), pilgrimages are made there.

Sarajevo Jewish Community, "La Benevolencija"
Hamdije Kresevljakovica 83, 71000 Sarajevo
Tel. 387 71 663 472, Fax 387 71 663 473

BULGARIA

GP 8,468,000 ◆ JP 3,000

◆DEMOGRAPHY◆

Nearly all the Jews are Sephardim and live in Sofia. As a result of emigration and assimilation, the elderly account for a disproportionately large share of the population.

◆HISTORY◆

Archeological findings indicate the presence of Jews as far back as the Roman period. Until the arrival of Jewish refugees from Spain at the end of the 15th century, the majority of Jews living in Bulgaria followed the Romaniot (Byzantine) prayer rite. Later Jews from Hungary, Bavaria, and elsewhere also found sanctuary in Bulgaria. By the end of the 17th century, these disparate groups had coalesced to form a unified Sephardi community.

On the eve of the Shoah, some 50,000 Jews lived in the country. They were saved from deportation largely due to energetic intervention on the part of various elements in Bulgarian society, including the clergy, the liberal intelligentsia, and the king. The Jews of Bulgarian-occupied Thrace and Macedonia, however, were deported by the Bulgarians to German death camps. In the years immediately following the war, about 90% of Bulgarian Jewry emigrated to Israel. During the course of the next 40 years, the Jewish community and its institutions were brought under the control of the Communist Party and the state. Until the fall of Communism, Jews in Bulgaria maintained only very sporadic contact with world Jewry. After the fall of the regime in 1989, the Jewish community was reconstituted.

◆COMMUNITY◆

Bulgarian Jews are represented by the Shalom Organization, which is the successor to the Social and Cultural Organization of Jews in Bulgaria. Efforts are under way to complete the renovation of the community's monumental synagogue in Sofia and to preserve other houses of worship in cities in which there are no longer active Jewish communities. Some of the Jewish community's properties have been restored, and Bulgaria is one of the few countries that has enacted thorough legislation on this issue. Although anti-Semitism has generally not been a problem in Bulgaria, in recent years, newly organized nationalist groups have attempted to rouse anti-Jewish sentiments.

Bulgaria is one of the few countries in which a Jewish monarch reigned. Czar Ivan Alexander (1331–1371) met a Jewish woman named Sarah and became so infatuated that he repudiated his Christian wife. He married Sarah, who adopted the name Theodora upon her baptism. Theodora was a great aid to her husband and was his principal advisor. Their son, Ivan Shishman III, assumed the throne in 1371, while still a teenager. He ruled until 1393, only losing his throne when his capital, Veliko Turnovo, was lost to the Turks. His sister Tamara was married off to the Turkish Sultan in order to ensure the safety of Bulgaria. A series of legends has arisen around the figure of Theodora, who is venerated in Bulgaria as a saint-like personage. Czar Ivan Shishman is also regarded as a great national hero.

◆RELIGIOUS LIFE◆

There are synagogues in Sofia and Plovdiv, but no resident rabbi. Services are conducted by lay people. No specifically kosher food is available, but wine and matzot are imported. The level of religious observance is low, and most Bulgarian Jews identify themselves in a national-ethnic, rather than religious, context.

✦CULTURE AND EDUCATION✦

Under the Communist regime, Bulgarian Jewish youth received no formal Jewish education of any kind. Today there are greater opportunities for those who wish to increase their knowledge. At the request of the Shalom Organization, all Jewish children now attend the same public school, and Hebrew has been instituted as a part of the curriculum. There is also a Sunday school attended by 100 children. The community publishes a bulletin called *Evreiski Vesti* and an annual yearbook.

✦ISRAEL✦

Relations between Israel and Bulgaria were initiated in 1948 but were severed in 1967. In 1990 diplomatic relations were resumed.

Aliya: Since 1948, 42,716 Bulgarian Jews have emigrated to Israel, 38,000 of them in the period between July 1948 and May 1949.

✦SITES✦

The neo-Byzantine synagogue in Sofia, completed in 1878, is one of the largest Sephardi houses of worship in the world and one of the largest synagogues in Europe. Adjacent to the synagogue is a small museum dedicated to the history of the rescue of Bulgarian Jews during World War II.

Shalom Organization of Jews in Bulgaria
Al. Stamboliisky 50
Sofia
Tel. 359 2 88 46 93, Fax 359 2 87 01 63

Embassy
1 Bulgaria Square
NDK Administration Building
Sofia
Tel. 359 2 543 201/2, Fax 359 2 521 101

✦

Sofia's Great Synagogue, consecrated in 1909, is one of the largest Sephardi synagogues in the world.

CROATIA

GP 4,504,000 ♦ JP 2,000

♦DEMOGRAPHY♦

More than half of Croatia's Jews live in Zagreb, the capital. There are small communities in Osijek, Rijeka, Split, and Dubrovnik. The average age is well over 60, and there are only about 250 young people.

♦HISTORY♦

Jews arrived in Croatia with the Roman armies, and there are remains of a Jewish cemetery in Solin (near Split) dating back to the 3rd century. That community ceased to exist in 641, when Solin was destroyed.

The Croats, who entered the region in the 7th century and established a kingdom in the 10th century, found established Jewish communities. Jews lived in Zagreb in the 13th and 14th centuries, and Jews were also settled in other parts of the country. Jewish communities in Split and Dubrovnik prospered, particularly during the Middle Ages, when they played an important role in commerce with Italy and the countries of the Danube basin.

However, Jews were expelled from Croatia proper and from Slavonia in 1456 and did not return until the end of the 18th century, by which time the territory was ruled by the Hapsburgs. At that time, during the reign of Emperor Joseph II, Jewish settlement was permitted, and Jews arrived from Burgenland, Austria, and from Bohemia, Moravia, and Hungary. Jews still had to contend with a number of restrictions until their full emancipation in 1870. The community was strongly influenced by Austro-German and Hungarian culture, and in many respects communal and religious life followed the pattern established in those countries.

After World War I, upon the establishment of an independent Yugoslavia incorporating Croatia, the Jewish community was integrated into the new state's Federation of Jewish Communities. In the interwar period, some 20,000 Jews lived in Croatia.

After the German invasion of Yugoslavia in April 1941, Croatia was reorganized as a semi-independent state allied with Germany. During the course of the next four years, the Croats stripped the Jews of all their property and eventually killed most of them in local concentration camps. The most notorious of these was the Jasenovac camp, in which thousands of Jews perished at the hands of the Ustashe (Croat Fascists). After the war, some of the survivors returned, and Jewish life resumed.

♦COMMUNITY♦

The Federation of Jewish Communities is responsible for Jewish religious and cultural life, and it maintains a Jewish old-age home in Zagreb. Active organizations include the Croatian Union of Jewish Youth, the Union of Jewish Women, and Maccabi.

Vid (Haj) Morpurgo (1838–1911), the scion of an eminent family, played a leading role in the struggle for national renaissance in Dalmatia, as well as in the cultural life and industrial development of the region. The esteem in which he was held is reflected by the inscription on his tombstone in the Jewish cemetery in Split: "Mighty in mind, noble in spirit, he devoted all his intellectual life to the liberation of the people from spiritual and material slavery. In the awakening of the people, he stood in the vanguard, the founder of the first bookshop, the first bank, the first industries. His passing has left us with a vacuum never to be filled."

Jews' Street in Dubrovnik

Anti-Semitism remains a problem in Croatia. There is a strong tendency toward Holocaust denial, particularly where the role of Croats is concerned, and this has at times been spearheaded by the country's head of state, Franjo Tudjman.

✦RELIGIOUS AND CULTURAL LIFE✦

There are synagogues and prayer rooms in Zagreb, Dubrovnik, Split, and Rijeka. There is no resident rabbi, and services are conducted by lay people. No specifically kosher food is available, but matzot and kosher wine are imported from Israel. The community operates a Sunday school for children aged 7 to 14. There are Hebrew classes and courses in Jewish history and tradition which cater to both youth and adults. A newsletter called *Bilten* is published, along with *Motek*, a youth review, and *Omanut*, a journal devoted to cultural issues.

✦ISRAEL✦

Israel and Croatia only established diplomatic ties in 1997 because international Jewish organizations and the state of Israel had expressed reservations about the publication of President Tudjman's book, which denies the Holocaust. President Tudjman has since apologized to the Jewish people.

Until recently, Croatian *aliya* statistics have been subsumed under those of Yugoslavia.

✦SITES✦

Dubrovnik is the site of the second oldest functioning synagogue in Europe (Prague has the oldest), established in 1352. It is located in a house on Jews' Street in what was the city's ancient Jewish quarter and has Torah scrolls that were brought from Spain by Jews fleeing the Inquisition. In the recent shelling of the city, the roof of the synagogue was damaged, but not the interior. The Jewish cemetery in Split, on the slope of Mt. Marjan, contains about 700 tombstones, some dating back to the 18th century. The site of the Jasenovac camp is mute testimony to the sufferings of Yugoslav Jewry at the hands of the Ustashe.

Jewish Community of Zagreb
Palmoticeva 16, 41000 Zagreb
Tel. 385 142 5517, Fax 385 143 4638

CZECH REPUBLIC

GP 10,251,000 ♦ JP 5,000

♦ DEMOGRAPHY ♦

Apart from Prague, in which the great majority of Jews live, there are several other communities, notably in Brno, Plzen, Olomouc, and Karlovy Vary. None of these smaller communities has more than 350 persons. Most Czech Jews are elderly. In recent years, however, the community has been bolstered by the presence of a large number of foreign Jews, primarily Americans, presently working in Prague.

♦ HISTORY ♦

The presence of many medieval Jewish sites (including Prague's Altneuschul, the oldest functioning synagogue in Europe) testifies to the deep roots of the Jewish communities in Bohemia and Moravia. Jewish settlement was initiated in the 10th century with the arrival

Kiddush cup, Bohemia, ca. late 19th century. Rubin glass

of Jews from Germany, Hungary, and the Byzantine Empire. The first reference to a Jewish community in Prague appeared in 1090. In 1096 the Jews suffered severe persecution and forced baptism at the hands of the Crusaders. Over the course of the following centuries, the situation of the Jewish community was tenuous, alternating between periods of persecution, degradation, and expulsion and periods of tolerance. Jews experienced a golden age under the reign of Rudolf II (1576–1611) and Mathias (1611–1619), during which Jewish life flourished. The expulsion of Jews from Vienna (1670) and the flight of Jews from Poland at the time of the Chmielnicki massacres (1648–1649) led to an increase in the Jewish

population. Nevertheless, subsequent rulers oppressed their Jewish subjects. When Bohemia and Moravia came under Austrian control, the situation of the Jews remained difficult. Maria Theresa ordered the expulsion of Jews, and between 1745 and 1748, they were banished from Prague. However, at the end of the 18th century, during the reign of Joseph II, conditions improved, and by 1867 the process of emancipation was complete.

Much of the Jewish population identified with the dominant German culture, and many of the great Jewish writers from Prague, notably Franz Kafka and Max Brod, wrote in German. Toward the end of the 19th century, however, and later with the independence of the country, a greater number of Jews adopted the Czech language. In the 19th century, the size of the Jewish community remained constant but actually shrank as a proportion of the general population.

The killing of a Christian girl near Polna in 1899 led to the infamous Hilsner ritual murder trial, which produced a wave of anti-Jewish sentiment (including riots) in Bohemia and Moravia. This in turn accelerated the exodus of Jews from many of the smaller Jewish communities to the large cities.

Czech Jewry failed to keep pace with the dynamic growth of other communities in the region. Assimilation, emigration, and a low birthrate took a heavy toll. Already in the 1920s, the rate of intermarriage in Prague had reached some 30%. The political status of Jews in independent inter-war Czechoslovakia was favorable, and Jewish nationality for those who identified themselves as such was recognized by the authorities. Jews played a prominent role in the arts, sciences, commerce, and industry.

About 80,000 Czech Jews (85% of the community) were killed in the Shoah. Many of the survivors attempted to rebuild Jewish life, but with the imposition of Communist rule, the atmosphere became increasingly inhospitable. The Slansky trial of 1952, in which a number of Communists of Jewish origin were charged with Zionism and other "crimes," was accompanied by a general deterioration in conditions for the Czech Jewish community. The JDC and other foreign Jewish organizations were expelled, and many Jews were arrested and imprisoned. Emigration was tightly restricted.

With de-Stalinization, the situation for Jews improved somewhat, but communal life was subject to stringent control. In 1968 there were high hopes that the liberalization would ease the plight of Jews, but these were dashed by the Soviet invasion. The 1989 Velvet Revolution, however, has led to a reawakening of Jewish consciousness and has opened up many new avenues of Jewish expression.

·COMMUNITY·

The Federation of Jewish Communities in the Czech Republic, housed in the celebrated 400-year-old Jewish Town Hall, is the leading communal organization. Among the local Jewish organizations are the Society for Jewish Culture and the Union of Jewish Youth. The Franz Kafka Society promotes Jewish culture, and the Czech–Israel Friendship Society acts to improve relations between the two countries. There are branches of B'nai B'rith and Maccabi.

The question of restitution of Jewish property is still unsettled. Anti-Semitism has been a minor problem, but from time to time, vandals have defaced Jewish sites, and in the media there have been several isolated attacks on Jews.

Statue of the Maharal
by Vladislav Saloun, Prague, 1917

The legend of the golem of Rabbi Judah Loew ben Bezalel of Prague (the Maharal) is an established part of the folklore of the city and has been the subject of stories, music, and films. Rabbi Loew is said to have created a golem as a servant and to have kept him in the Altneuschul. But the creature later went out of control, threatening the townspeople. In order to avert disaster, Rabbi Loew was forced to destroy the homunculus, reducing him to dust. Legends of this type evidently flourished throughout the Jewish world, and it is believed that the story of the golem was attributed to Rabbi Loew only in the 18th century. German writer Gustav Meyrnik's 1915 novel, Der Golem, *H. Leivick's 1928 Yiddish play, and three film versions (1920, 1936, and after World War II) brought the legend to a wide public. Today the golem is a favorite theme for souvenir vendors in Prague.*

✦Religious Life✦

Attendance at synagogues in Prague and other cities is sparse, and some of them function only on major holidays. A Reform community called "Beit Praha" was recently established in Prague and conducts High Holy Day services in the "Spanish" synagogue. For all intents and purposes Jewish life is focused on the capital—which is also the seat of the only rabbi. The community sponsors a kosher restaurant that is especially popular with foreign tourists.

✦Culture and Education✦

A Jewish kindergarten sponsored by the Lauder Foundation, has been opened in Prague. Older children attend a, once-a-week, afternoon Talmud Torah. A Jewish journal called *Rosh Chodesh* appears monthly, and there is also a radio program called "Shalom Aleichem." Books on Jewish themes are popular, and there is a steady stream of such titles available in Czech.

✦Israel✦

Israel and the Czech Republic enjoy full diplomatic relations. Czechoslovakia recognized Israel in 1948 and supplied the fledgling Jewish state with much of its modern weaponry—including airplanes. In 1967 Prague severed relations. After the collapse of Communism, Prague renewed ties with Jerusalem.

Aliya: Since 1948, 23,943 Jews have emigrated to Israel from the former Czechoslovakia, 18,788 of them between 1948 and 1951.

✦Sites✦

The Jewish quarter of Prague is a treasury of Jewish art and architecture and is one of the most outstanding Jewish sites in Europe. Its synagogues (including the 14th century Altneushul), ancient cemetery, and museum are visited by both Jews and non-Jews alike. The names of 77,291 Czech Jews killed in the Shoah were painted on the walls of the sanctuary of the 500-year-old Pinkas synagogue. During Communist rule, whole sections were erased, but the names have since been restored. Many cities and towns have Jewish relics in various states of repair. The grounds of the former concentration camp at Terezin (Theresienstadt) present the tragic history of those deported to the "model ghetto."

Federation of Jewish Communities
in the Czech Republic
Maislova 18, 11001 Prague 1
Tel. 42 02 481 0130
Fax 42 02 481 0912

Embassy
Badeniho 2, 17000 Prague 7
Tel. 42 02 322 481
Fax 42 02 322 732

The Prague Jewish cemetery, the oldest in Europe, contains the graves of famous rabbis and scholars such as Judah Loew ben Bezalel (the Maharal).

ESTONIA

GP 1,471,000 JP 2,500

◆DEMOGRAPHY◆

Most of the Jews live in Tallinn. Outside of the capital, small communities exist in Tartu and Narva.

◆HISTORY◆

Although there is evidence to indicate the presence of Jews in Estonia as far back as the 14th century, permanent settlement only dates back to the 19th century. At that time a statute of Czar Alexander II permitted Jewish veterans of the Russian army and certain categories of artisans, merchants, and those with higher education to settle there. By the beginning of the 20th century, there were two communities, Tallinn and Tartu.

In independent Estonia (1917–1940), Jews enjoyed cultural autonomy that was guaranteed by law. On the eve of the Shoah, nearly 4,500 Jews lived in the country, 2,500 of them in the capital. During the first Soviet occupation (1940–1941), all Jewish institutions were liquidated, and about 10% of the Jewish population was deported to detention centers in Siberia and elsewhere in the Soviet Union. Immediately following the German invasion, about 1,000 members of the community perished at the hands of the Nazis and their local henchmen. Others, fleeing before the German advance, escaped into the Soviet interior. After the war, some of the survivors returned, and their numbers were bolstered by Russian-speaking Jews from other parts of the Soviet Union. Consequently, the majority of Jews today are native Russian-speakers. With the end of Soviet rule, all restrictions on Jews were cancelled and communal life was reactivated.

When Nazi officials met in the Wannsee suburb of Berlin in January 1942 to discuss the "Final Solution of the Jewish Problem in Europe," they prepared a list in which the Jewish population of all the countries of Europe was enumerated. A map with the chilling drawing of a casket next to the number of Jews killed was also passed out. The German Einsatzgruppen *killing squads that followed the Nazi advance into the Soviet Union, aided by Estonian collaborators, had been so murderously efficient that on both documents, Estonia (alone among the countries of Europe) was already declared* Judenfrei *(free of Jews).*

◆COMMUNITY◆

The Jewish Community is an umbrella organization that includes all Jewish societies and groups, both religious and secular. There is a Jewish veterans group, a WIZO branch, a Union of Jewish Students, and a Maccabi Sports Club. The Jewish community of neighboring Helsinki, Finland, maintains a close relationship with Estonian Jewry.

There have been several manifestations of anti-Semitism, including Holocaust denial, that have generated concern.

◆RELIGIOUS AND CULTURAL LIFE◆

The Tallinn synagogue is housed in a small building specially adapted for this purpose (the original synagogue was razed during the Shoah). The majority of those who attend are elderly. There is no rabbi and there are very few observant Jews. Specifically kosher food is not available, but matzot, kosher wine, and other items are imported for the holidays. In 1989 a Sunday school was established in

◆

Tallinn, and in 1990, a Jewish school with 350 students from grades 1 to 12 was opened. Both institutions are housed in the building of the former Jewish Gymnasium, which was restored to the community. Tartu University offers courses on Jewish subjects. *Hashahar*, a monthly newspaper, appears in Russian, and once a month a 45-minute Jewish radio program called "Shalom Aleichem" is broadcast on Estonian State Radio.

◆ISRAEL◆

Israel is represented by its ambassador in neighboring Latvia.

Aliya: Since 1989, 1,027 Estonian Jews have emigrated to Israel.

◆SITES◆

At Klooga, a German killing field 56 miles from Tallinn, there is a memorial to those who perished in the Shoah.

The Jewish Community of Estonia
P.O. Box 3576, EE 0090 Tallinn
Tel. 372 2 43 76 93, Fax 372 2 43 85 66

Festival cup, Narva, ca.17th–18th century.
The Hebrew inscription in ornate Ashkenazi letters reads,
"So Moses declared to the Israelites the set times of the Lord."
Silver, engraved, partly gilt

HUNGARY

GP 10,050,000 ✦ JP 70,000

The synagogue of Szeged

✦DEMOGRAPHY✦

Some 80% of Hungarian Jews live in the capital, Budapest. There are also small communities in Debrecen, Miklosc, Szeged, and elsewhere. The Hungarian Jewish community is the largest in eastern Europe and has been greatly affected by assimilation. The rate of intermarriage is high, and only a minority is involved in communal life. The community has a high proportion of Holocaust survivors. By most estimates, about half the Jewish population is over the age of 65.

✦HISTORY✦

Jews have lived in what is today Hungary since Roman times. However, archeological evidence of the community's origins dates back to the 11th century, the time of the Arpads who laid the foundations of the Hungarian nation. For several centuries, the Jews played an important role in the commerce of the country and rose to high positions. But in the middle of the 14th century, this position deteriorated. Charges of ritual murder resulted in attacks that claimed the lives of many Jews. Only the Turkish occupation in the 16th century brought relief. However, once the Turks were driven out in 1696, persecution of the Jews was resumed. The situation gradually

improved, and in the 18th century, Jews from Moravia and Poland came to the country.

Under the rule of Emperor Joseph II in the late 18th century, conditions for Hungarian Jewry improved still further, and by 1840 there were some 200,000 Jews in the country (as compared to only 11,621 a century earlier). In 1867 legislation was introduced that completely emancipated the Jews, and in 1896 a law was passed recognizing the Jewish faith as the legal equal of various Christian denominations. Hungarian Jewry quickly integrated into the life of the country and made enormous contributions to the development of Hungarian commerce, industry, arts, and sciences. At the same time, as the community was strongly affected by assimilation, many Jews abandoned their faith. In the 1860s, Neology, a distinct brand of Liberal Judaism, also arose in Hungary, initially from disputes over the nature of Jewish education. Closer to Conservative/Masorati Judaism than to Reform, Neology remains the dominant outlet for Jewish religious life in Hungary.

After the defeat and dissolution of the Austro-Hungarian Empire in World War I, Hungarian Jewry, including many of the Orthodox and Chassidic communities, found

✦

themselves within the borders of Czechoslovakia, Romania, and Yugoslavia. In 1919 when the short-lived Hungarian Soviet Republic collapsed, a period of "White Terror" ensued, during which some 3,000 Jews were murdered. In the 1920s, the situation stabilized, but by the late 1930s, the first of a series of anti-Semitic laws was enacted, restricting the socioeconomic activity of the Jewish population.

Tzedaka box, 1822

Following negotiations on Jewish property, in early 1997 the Hungarians ratified a law on the establishment of a restitution fund, representing a small fraction of the value of assets seized from Hungarian Jews during the Holocaust.

◆COMMUNITY◆

The Alliance of the Hungarian Jewish Communities is the leading communal organization. This framework embraces two communities: the Neolog community

The wartime fate of the Jews of the territories detached from Hungary after World War I, but later returned, was linked to those of Hungary proper. Over 600,000 Hungarian Jews perished in the Shoah, in many instances at the hands of Hungarian Fascists or with their cooperation.

After the war, some 200 Jewish communities were reconstituted, but most dwindled through natural attrition, emigration, and migration to the capital. In 1946 anti-Jewish sentiment led to pogroms in Kunmadaras, Miskolc, and elsewhere. The imposition of Communist rule resulted in the closure of many Jewish institutions and the arrest of Jewish activists. Many Jews were expelled from Budapest but were later allowed to return. During the Hungarian Revolution in 1956, 20,000 Jews opted to leave the country. The situation of Hungarian Jewry began to improve in the late 1950s. The community was allowed to reestablish links with the Jewish world, and with the collapse of Communism, all restrictions on ties with Israel were lifted.

and the Orthodox one. Many leading international Jewish organizations are active in Hungary, including B'nai B'rith and WIZO. Moreover, the JDC and the Lauder Foundation sponsor Jewish activity. Since the fall of Communism, Zionist organizations have been revived, including most of the major youth groups, united under the umbrella of the Association of Zionist Organizations. The Maccabi Sports Club has also resumed activity. The Jewish Forced Labor Veterans Association addresses the needs of those once enslaved by the Germans and by Hungarian Fascists. The community also operates the Charity Jewish Hospital and Nursing Facility, and there are two homes for the aged, one of which is Orthodox.

The Hungarian media often deals with Jewish topics, and its coverage is sometimes tinged with anti-Semitism. During electoral campaigns in particular, there have been manifestations of anti-Semitism. A common charge is that Jews were responsible for imposing Communism on Hungary. A number

◆

of anti-Semitic publications and political parties are active.

⋆RELIGIOUS LIFE⋆
About 20 synagogues and prayer houses function in Budapest, and there are others in the principal provincial towns in which Jews live. The bulk of those Hungarian Jews who are religiously active (a small minority) attend the Neolog synagogues, but there are also four Orthodox synagogues, one of them Sephardi. Eastern Europe's only rabbinical seminary, Neolog in its practice, is in Budapest, and students from some of the neighboring countries study and receive their ordination there. The Pedagogium (teachers training college) is affiliated with the seminary. Some 20 rabbis serve the Jewish population. Chabad is also active in Hungary, and has attracted youth from assimilated homes. In Budapest there are more than 10 kosher butchers and a kosher bakery and restaurant. Hungary exports matzot, kosher wine, spirits, and meat.

⋆CULTURE AND EDUCATION⋆
In Budapest there are three Jewish day schools and a high school. One of the schools is Orthodox, another Neolog, and the third is sponsored by the Lauder Foundation. A Jewish youth camp held on the shores of Lake Balaton, attracts more than 1,500 children and teenagers each summer. In 1994 the Balint Jewish Community Center was opened. It is the venue of many Jewish cultural and educational activities, including lectures, Hebrew classes, and musical and artistic gatherings. A Center for Jewish Studies is attached to Eotvos Lorand University, and students can also pursue higher Jewish studies at the Hungarian Academy of Sciences. The number of books of Jewish interest issued by Hungarian publishers is rising, and there is a Jewish bookstore. A community newspaper called *Uj Elet* appears biweekly, and there are also several other Jewish periodicals.

⋆ISRAEL⋆
In 1989 Israel and Hungary resumed diplomatic relations severed in 1967.

Aliya: Since 1948, 30,029 Hungarian Jews have emigrated to Israel, 14,324 of them between 1948 and 1951. This figure does not include Hungarian-speaking Jews from Romania.

⋆SITES⋆
The 19th-century Dohany Synagogue in Budapest is the largest in Europe and is presently undergoing extensive repairs. The Budapest Jewish Museum has an impressive collection of Judaica. The Emanuel Holocaust Memorial is called the Tree of Life. On this modern sculpture, each leaf symbolizes a victim of the Shoah. There is also a statue honoring Raoul Wallenberg, the Swedish diplomat who rescued several thousand Jews in Budapest. Hungary has a large number of monumental synagogues. That of Szeged, constructed in a late eclectic style, was designed by Lipot Baumhorn, who was responsible for many of the most beautiful such buildings in central Europe. Today, after painstaking restoration, the Szeged synagogue is a public museum.

Central Board of Hungarian
*   Jewish Communities*
Sip utca 12, 1075 Budapest VII
Tel. 36 1 322 6475, Fax 36 1 342 1790

Embassy
Fullank Utca 8, 1026 Budapest II
Tel. 36 1 2000 781, Fax 36 1 2000 783

Hungarian Jews have proven to be outstanding athletes—statistically the best in the Jewish world. They have taken Olympic medals in canoeing, gymnastics, football, kayaking, water polo, track and field, and wrestling. They have especially excelled in fencing, winning no fewer than 34 Olympic medals in the sport between 1896 and 1968. Hungary's Jewish athletes have earned more Olympic medals than those of any other country but the United States and the former Soviet Union. One Hungarian Jew even won an Olympic medal for his literary skill. In 1928 Dr. Ferenc Mezo received a special medal for his many works chronicling the history of the Olympics.

LATVIA

GP 2,504,000 ♦ JP 15,000

♦DEMOGRAPHY♦

Riga (11,000) is the most important center of Jewish life in the Baltic States. There are several smaller communities, notably in Daugavpils (Dvinsk).

♦HISTORY♦

Jews in present-day Latvia trace their presence back many centuries to the Jewish communities in the principalities of Courland and Livonia, a history confirmed by Jewish tombstones dating back to the 14th century. These territories changed hands many times over the course of history, and the situation of the Jews there was always dependent upon the ruler in power. Latvia's geography also meant that its Jews were exposed to German, Russian, and eastern European influences while developing their own distinct characteristics.

Courland was beyond the pale of Jewish settlement, and consequently only Jews who could prove that they had lived there before the advent of Russian rule were allowed to remain. Over time, however, other Jews who were considered useful were granted the privilege of settling there.

Jews played an important role in the commercial and industrial development of independent Latvia, but the government pursued a policy aimed at squeezing them out of the economy, which brought ruin to much of the community. Latvia was an important center of Jewish life and learning. Zionism was especially strong among the Jews of Latvia, and Latvia was the birthplace of the Betar youth movement.

On the eve of the Shoah, there were about 85,000 Jews in the country—40,000 in Riga, 10,000 in Liepaja (Libau), and the rest in other communities. Immediately following the German invasion, the local population began to

The Betar maritime academy training ship Theodor Herzl, *Riga, 1938*

torment the Jews. By the end of the war, more than 90% of Latvian Jewry had perished.

Some 3,000 of the survivors returned, but today the majority of Jews in the country are descendants of those who came to Latvia from other parts of the Soviet Union after the war. As a result, the community is largely dominated by Russian-speakers. In the 1970s, Riga was a major center of Jewish dissident activity. After the collapse of Communism and the resurrection of independent Latvia, restrictions on Jewish life were removed.

✦COMMUNITY✦

The Latvian Society for Jewish Culture is the leading communal organization. There are synagogues in Riga, Daugavpils, Liepaja, and Rezhitsa. Most members of the community are non-observant. The Chabad movement, however, is active in promoting Jewish observance. There is a Jewish school attended by about 500 children who learn both Hebrew and Yiddish. The community also operates a children's theater and choir. A Jewish hospital, Bikur Cholim, is housed in the restituted pre-war Jewish hospital building in Riga.

Because the majority of present-day Latvian Jews are not descended from pre-war residents, they are unable to enjoy full civil rights. Rectifying this situation is high on the list of the community's priorities. There have been a number of disturbing manifestations of anti-Semitism on the part of both the ethnic Latvians and the sizeable Russian minority, including violent incidents. A major source of conflict between the community and the authorities has been the exoneration of Latvians who collaborated with the Germans.

✦ISRAEL✦

Israel and Latvia have full diplomatic relations.

Aliya: Since 1989, 10,831 Latvian Jews have emigrated to Israel.

✦SITES✦

The restored Peitavas Street synagogue in Riga, which dates back to 1905, was used by the Germans as a warehouse and thus spared destruction. There is also a monument on the site of the Choral Synagogue, in which hundreds of Jews were killed when the building was torched in July 1941. There is a monument to the memory of some 46,000 Jews slaughtered at Bierkernieki Forest (one of the worst massacres of the Shoah). The Jewish Center in Riga is a beehive of activity and a good place for travelers to meet local Jews.

Latvian Society for Jewish Culture
Skolas 6, LV 1322 Riga
Tel. 3712 289 580, Fax 3712 821 494

Embassy
Elizabetes 2, LV 1340 Riga
Tel. 3717 320 739 980, Fax 3717 830 170

✦

Taking advantage of their country's location on the Baltic Sea, Latvian Jews were keen mariners. In the period between the wars, the Courland Yacht Club, with its predominantly Jewish membership, repeatedly triumphed over the old, established Latvian–German club. In 1938 the Betar youth movement established a school for seafaring in Riga and purchased a sailing-training ship, which they named Theodor Herzl.
The school operated only until the Soviet invasion, but some of the Israeli navy's first officers were graduates of Betar's maritime academy.

LITHUANIA

GP 3,728,000 ♦ JP 6,000

♦DEMOGRAPHY♦

Most Jews live in Vilnius (Vilna), the capital, but there are also several smaller communities, notably in Kaunas (Kovno), Klajpeda (Memel), and Siauliai.

♦HISTORY♦

Jews trace their origins in Lithuania back to the days of Grand Duke Gedeyminus, who founded the first Lithuanian state in the 14th century. By the late 15th century, there were already thriving communities. In time, Vilnius became known as the "Jerusalem of Lithuania," a great center of Jewish religious learning. Jews from other parts of Europe flocked to the great Lithuanian *yeshivot* (including those of Slobodka, Volozhyn, Mir, and Telshe), and those who learned according to the guidelines laid down in the Lithuanian *yeshivot* were called "Litvaks." The Vilna Gaon, Elijah ben Solomon Zalman, who lived in the 18th century, epitomized the supremacy of Torah studies, and his influence on traditional Jewish scholarship remains strong. The Gaon was a determined opponent of Chassidism, and as a result, the Chassidic penetration of Lithuania was negligible. Lithuania was also home to a large Karaite community centered in Trokai.

The Jews of Lithuania lived an intense Jewish life, and their role and influence in the major Jewish political and cultural movements were far greater than their numbers would have suggested. Lithuania was also an outstanding center of Yiddish culture, and

Lithuanian Jews laid the foundations for one of the major English-speaking Jewish communities. Between 1880 and 1930, tens of thousands of Lithuanian Jews landed in South Africa, and today 85% of South African Jews trace their ancestors back to those "Litvak" immigrants. Jews sometimes called South Africa "a Lithuanian colony."

Vilnius (then under Polish rule) was the site of the YIVO Institute for Jewish Research.

On the eve of the Shoah, there were about 160,000 Jews in independent Lithuania and another 60,000 in Vilnius and the surrounding area, which were transferred to Lithuania after the Soviet conquest of eastern Poland. That population was bolstered by Jewish refugees from German-occupied Poland. During the German occupation, about 95% of Lithuanian Jewry was killed (a greater percentage than in any other community in Europe), in large measure due to the enthusiastic participation of ethnic Lithuanians.

After the war, some of the survivors remained in Lithuania, and some who had been deported or fled also returned. These were joined by non-Lithuanian Jews (primarily Russian-speakers) from other parts of the Soviet Union. Jews in Soviet Lithuania benefited from a slightly more relaxed atmosphere than in Soviet Russia or Ukraine, and in Vilnius certain limited expressions of Jewish culture were tolerated. Upon regaining its independence, Lithuania dropped all restrictions on Jewish religious and cultural life.

♦COMMUNITY♦

The Lithuanian Jewish Community is the roof organization of Lithuanian Jewry. In Vilnius there are affiliates of some of the leading international Jewish organizations. B'nai B'rith, Betar, Maccabi, WIZO, and various professional, veteran, and survivor groups are active. The rehabilitation of numerous

♦

Painting of a street in the Jewish quarter of Vilnius
by L. Werner, 1930

Lithuanian collaborators has been cause of concern not only for Jews living in Lithuania, but for Jews throughout the world. The Israeli government and Jewish bodies, especially Jews of Lithuanian origin, have been especially active in demanding the prosecution of Lithuanian Nazis. Negotiations for the restitution of Jewish property are under way.

✦ RELIGIOUS LIFE ✦

There are synagogues in Vilnius and Kaunas, but attendance is low. Matzot and other supplies, such as kosher meat and wine, are imported. The Chabad House, with its own rabbi, has been especially active in organizing classes for young people and promoting knowledge of Judaism.

✦ CULTURE AND EDUCATION ✦

There is a Jewish secondary school and kindergarten in Vilnius, and Sunday schools are maintained in other towns. The community publishes *Jerusalem of Lithuania*, a monthly newspaper in Lithuanian, Russian, Yiddish, and English. There is also a monthly 20- to 25-minute Jewish television program and a bimonthly radio presentation. The Jewish Community Building houses the State Jewish Museum, the Israel Center of Culture and Arts, the Center of Yiddish Culture and Music, and the Zalman Rejzen Foundation Supporting Jewish Culture, Education, and Science.

✦ ISRAEL ✦

Israel and Lithuania enjoy full diplomatic relations. Israel is represented by its ambassador in Riga, Latvia.

Aliya: Since 1989, 5,591 Lithuanian Jews have emigrated to Israel.

✦ SITES ✦

Important sites include the medieval Jewish quarter of Vilnius and the grave of the Vilna Gaon. The Romanesque–Moorish Choral Synagogue is the only Jewish house of worship to survive the Shoah. Among the objects in the State Jewish Museum in Vilnius are ritual items salvaged from the Great Synagogue that was destroyed by the Soviets. These include parts of the original ark and reader's desk. The museum also includes a section devoted to the destruction of

Lithuanian Jewry. In Trokai there is a museum adjacent to the Karaite Synagogue that tells the story of this community. The Nazi killing grounds such as Paneriai (Ponary), where 70,000 Jews were massacred, and the infamous Ninth Fort of Kaunas also attract visitors.

Lithuanian Jewish Community
Pylimo Street 4, 2600 Vilnius
Tel. 370 2 613 003, Fax 370 2 227 915

Poster for pre-war Hebrew production of
Jacques HaLevy's opera La Juive *in Vilnius*

MACEDONIA

GP 2,000,000 ✦ JP 100

✦HISTORY AND COMMUNITY✦

The Jewish presence in Macedonia dates back to the end of the Second Temple period. In the list of Jewish communities quoted from the correspondence of Agrippa I to Caligula, Philo refers to the Jews of Macedonia. Ruins of a 3rd-century synagogue in Stobei are evidence of a once-sizeable community situated on an important commercial crossroads between Turkey and western Europe. Until the arrival of Spanish and Portuguese Jews in the 16th century, the community followed the Romaniot (Byzantine) customs. Later the Sephardi *nusach* prevailed, and the Jews adopted Ladino.

On the eve of the Shoah, there were nearly 8,000 Jews and five synagogues in Bitola (Monastir), and some 3,000 Jews in Skopje. In 1943 the Bulgarian occupation authorities stripped the Jews of their property and deported them to Treblinka and Auschwitz.

Only 10% of the community survived, most in hiding or with the partisans. After the war, more than half of the survivors left for Israel. Since the succession of Macedonia, the Jewish community has operated independently. Most Jews live in Skopje, the capital, but there are also a handful of Jews in Stip. There are no functioning synagogues in Macedonia and little religious life. Jews maintain close contacts with the Jewish communities of Belgrade and Salonika, and there are occasional cultural and religious events.

✦ISRAEL✦

Israel and Macedonia enjoy full diplomatic relations. The Israeli ambassador in Athens represents Israeli interests.

Jewish Community
Borka Taleski 24, 91000 Skopje
Tel. 389 91 237 534

POLAND

GP 39,000,000 • JP 8,000

◆DEMOGRAPHY◆

Most of the country's Jews live in Warsaw, the capital, but there are also communities in Krakow, Lodz, Szczecin, Gdansk, and in several cities in Upper and Lower Silesia, notably in Katowice and Wroclaw. The eastern part of the country, including cities and towns that were once great centers of Jewish life, such as Lublin and Bialystok, probably has no more than 50 Jews. Yiddish is only spoken by the elderly. In the last few years, there has been a reawakening of Jewish consciousness. Young people of Jewish origin who had no Jewish knowledge are joining the community.

◆HISTORY◆

Jewish settlements in Poland can be traced back more than 1,000 years. Fleeing persecution in western and central Europe, Jews found sanctuary in Poland. In 1264 Prince Boleslaw the Pious issued the Statute of Kalisz, the first writ of privileges for Jews in Poland and the basis for subsequent protective charters. Successive Polish kings, notably Kazimierz the Great in the 14th century, encouraged Jews to settle in Poland and protected them. Jews were outstanding mint masters, and the first coins minted in Poland bore Hebrew, not Polish, inscriptions. By the middle of the 16th century, about 80%

Painting of a yeshiva bocher by Bernard (Benjamin) Rolnicki, ca. 1930s. Oil on canvas. The artist perished in the Holocaust.

of world Jewry lived on Polish lands. From the 16th to the 18th centuries, Jews enjoyed a unique form of self-government called the Council of Four Lands (*Va'ad Arba Aratsot*), which functioned as a Jewish parliament. However, from 1648 to 1649, Cossack hordes led by Bogdan Chmielnicki massacred the Jews of eastern Poland (present-day Ukraine). It is estimated that between 100,000 and 200,000 Jews perished. Much of Polish Jewry was impoverished, and Poland became fertile ground for messianic leaders such as Shabbtai Tzvi and Jacob Frank. Later it gave birth to the Chassidic movement.

The partition of Poland at the end of the 18th century meant that the Jews of the three constituent zones developed along very different lines. The bulk of Polish Jewry was concentrated in Russian and Austrian-ruled parts of the country, but there were also small communities in the territories annexed to Prussia. Russian-ruled Poland was a part of the so-called pale of settlement.

Toward the end of the 19th century, when much of Poland was a part of anti-Semitic Czarist Russia, a great wave of emigration began, and Polish Jews went to the United States, Canada, Argentina, Germany, France, and the Land of Israel. At the same time, Jews

◆

Dov Berush Meisels (1798–1870) was a pillar of both Jewish Orthodoxy and Polish patriotism and one of the most outstanding Jewish leaders of his day. In 1832 Meisels was elected chief rabbi of Krakow (in Austrian-ruled Poland). An exceedingly generous man, he distributed his rabbinical salary to various charitable institutions and to the needy. Meisels was also a fervent Polish patriot, and personally financed the purchase of weapons for Polish insurgents battling against Russian rule in the Congress Kingdom. In that spirit, he convened prayer services in the main synagogue of Krakow and called upon his congregants to aid the Polish cause. In 1848 Meisels was elected to the Austrian parliament in Vienna and to the Krakow city council. In 1856 he was appointed as chief rabbi of Warsaw and in that capacity actively aided the Polish Uprising in 1863. This resulted in his expulsion from the city. When Meisels was finally allowed to return, he devoted himself to the study of Jewish texts. His funeral in Warsaw in 1870 was attended by thousands of Polish Jews and Gentiles and was a great demonstration against the yoke of Russian rule.

from Lithuania and other parts of the Russian Empire moved to Poland. Jews played a significant role in the economic development of the country, particularly in commerce and industry. They also made many outstanding contributions to Polish arts and sciences.

In the inter-war period, despite the government's often hostile policies, Polish Jewry represented one of the most creative communities in the Diaspora. Poland was the heartland of many of the great movements that shaped Jewish life. These include Chassidism, Zionism, and Jewish socialism— and all of these currents found expression in numerous schools, organizations, political parties, and publications. Inter-war Poland was the leading center of Yiddish creativity, including the Yiddish film industry. Polish Jewry also played an especially important part in the development of Hebrew culture and maintained an impressive network of schools in which Hebrew was the language of instruction.

On the eve of the Shoah, 20 years after Poland regained independence, some 3,300,000 Jews lived in the country, constituting the second-largest Jewish community in the world. Warsaw alone had over 300,000 Jews. About 85% of Polish Jewry was wiped out in the Holocaust, and many Jews from other countries were deported to Poland and killed in the German extermination centers situated there.

After the war, most of the survivors refused to return to (or remain in) Poland, which was rocked by civil war and anti-Semitic outrages. Emigration accelerated after the pogrom in Kielce in July 1946, which claimed the lives of over 40 Jews. Although the situation eventually stabilized, the Jewish population continued to shrink through successive waves of emigration. The most recent exodus took place in 1968, in the wake of a Communist party witch-hunt directed against persons of Jewish origin. At that time, most of the remaining Jewish communal infrastructure, including the Jewish school system, was closed down. However, in the years leading up to the collapse of Communism, Poland's small Jewish community, including many "closet Jews," was gradually able to reassert its identity.

◆ C O M M U N I T Y ◆

The Coordinating Committee of Jewish Organizations in the Polish Republic (KKOZRP) coordinates the activities of the various Jewish organizations. The two major communal organizations are the Religious Union of Jewish Communities and the Social and Cultural

Organization of Polish Jews—a secular organization. Under the auspices of the Lauder Foundation, clubs have been established that organize a wide range of activities for young people, including Jewish summer camps and athletics. One Jewish group is composed of persons orphaned in the Holocaust and raised by non-Jews.

High on the community's agenda is the preservation of the large number of Jewish historical sites (including cemeteries and synagogues) that cover the length and breadth of the country. This is also tied to the issue of the restoration of property to the Jewish community, which has been the subject of negotiations with the Polish government. Catering to the needs of Jews, young and old, who are rediscovering their Jewish identity, is also a top priority.

Anti-Semitism remains a problem, but none of the political parties that ran on an openly anti-Jewish platform passed the electoral threshold for either Sejm or Senate representation. Still there are occasional manifestations of anti-Semitism in the form of vandalism of Jewish sites, graffiti, the publication and distribution of anti-Semitic tracts, and anti-Jewish utterances by public figures, including members of the clergy.

✦ RELIGIOUS LIFE ✦

There are synagogues in most of the towns mentioned above. Some of these are historic edifices, such as the Remu Synagogue and the Templum in Krakow, and the Nozyk Synagogue in Warsaw. Poland has a chief rabbi whose seat is in Warsaw and a second rabbi who caters to the needs of the youth. The JDC maintains kosher cafeterias in the largest Jewish centers. Private kosher restaurants can be found in Warsaw and Krakow. Kosher meat and other foodstuffs are available, and in recent years, Poland has become an important center for the production of kosher spirits.

✦ CULTURE AND EDUCATION ✦

A Jewish primary school and kindergarten have been opened in Warsaw. Various Jewish courses (including Hebrew) are offered at Warsaw University and the Jagiellonian University in Krakow. The Jewish Historical Institute (ZIH) is an important repository of documentation on the history of Polish Jewry, and especially on the Shoah. It also maintains a permanent exhibition of Jewish art and artifacts from the Holocaust. In Krakow the

✦

The site of the Auschwitz death camp

Center for Jewish Culture in Kazimierz is the venue of much of the city's Jewish activity, including exhibitions, lectures, films, meetings, and various courses.

The E.R. Kaminska Jewish Theater in Warsaw is the only regularly functioning Yiddish theater in the world. Audiences can listen to its productions in Polish (and occasionally in other languages) with the use of headphones. Today most of its actors are non-Jews. There are several Jewish publications including *Jidele* for young people, *Dos Yiddishe Wort* (in Polish and Yiddish), a literary journal *Midrasz*, and the *ZIH Bulletin*. There is also a journal devoted to Israel called *Polska–Izrael*. In recent years, there has been an impressive number of books, and publications on Jewish themes have appeared.

Poland is also the scene of many international Jewish youth pilgrimages that are directed toward the sites of death camps and pre-war relics of Polish Jewry. The largest of these is the "March of the Living," which brings thousands of Jewish youth to Poland from communities all over the world.

Torah mantle,
Galicia, ca. 1870.
Velvet embroidered with
beads and metallic threads

✦ISRAEL✦

Israel and Poland resumed full diplomatic relations in 1990 after a hiatus of 23 years.
Aliya: Since 1948, 171,471 Polish Jews have emigrated to Israel, 106,414 of them between 1948 and 1951.

✦SITES✦

Poland, particularly in its central and eastern parts, contains numerous places of interest for the Jewish visitor. In Warsaw there are a number of sites connected with the ghetto uprising and the life of the city's once vibrant community. These include the central ghetto

monument, designed by Natan Rapoport and the exhibition at the Jewish Historical Institute, which also houses a collection of paintings by Polish–Jewish artists. In Krakow, which was spared the destruction to which the capital was subjected, there are a number of old synagogues which can still be visited, among them the Remu and the 14th-century Stara Synagoga (the oldest in Poland), which today houses a Jewish museum. Lodz is the site of one of the largest Jewish burial grounds in Europe. Of particular interest are the mausoleums of the city's great textile magnates. Many of the smaller towns contain remnants of the Jewish presence. Among the most noteworthy is the town of Tykocin (near Bialystok), which has a magnificent 17th-century synagogue recently restored to its former grandeur. Another such synagogue can be found in Lancut. There are also many historic cemeteries, some containing the graves of famous Chassidic rabbis, such as those in Gora Kalwaria (Ger) and Lezajsk (Lezensk). The sites of former death and concentration camps are a magnet for Jewish visitors. These include Auschwitz–Birkenau, Majdanek, and Treblinka. Of the last, no trace remains, and the grounds are the site of a powerful monument consisting of thousands of shards of broken stone.

Coordinating Committee of Jewish
*   Organizations in Poland (KKOZRP)*
Pl. Grzybowski 12/16 , 00-104 Warszawa
Tel. 48 22 620 0554, Fax 48 22 620 0559

Embassy
ul. Krzywickiego 24, 02-278 Warszawa
Tel. 48 22 250 923/251 134, Fax 48 22 251 607

ROMANIA

GP 22,650,000 ✦ JP 14,000

Purim celebration at the Choral Synagogue of Bucharest, 1980

✦ DEMOGRAPHY ✦

The great majority of Romanian Jews are over the age of 70. Fewer than 1,000 are under the age of 25. Six thousand Jews live in Bucharest, and small Jewish communities exist in the principal towns of Moldavia—Iasi (Jassy), Dorahoi, Succeava, Radauti—and in Transylvania (Cluj, Arad, Timisoara, Satu Mare, Tigu Mures, Oradea), as well as in Constanta on the Black Sea coast. Only 5 of these number more than 500 people, and that number is dwindling fast. Nearly all the Jews are Ashkenazi, and the small Sephardi community has lost its distinct identity. Yiddish is only spoken by the elderly. Many of the Jews in Transylvania, which was a part of Hungary until the end of World War I, still speak Hungarian.

✦ HISTORY ✦

Jews have lived in Romania since Roman times when the country was called Dacia. Organized communal life, however, dates back to the 15th century, by which time there were communities in Iasi and several other towns in Moldavia. Although the Orthodox Church bitterly opposed contacts with Jews, various local rulers encouraged Jewish settlement from Poland and elsewhere. Jews suffered horribly in the Russo-Turkish War (1769–1774) and in later fighting on Romanian soil. In the 19th century, Jews were subjected to many restrictions and much violence. Moreover, the Romanian authorities failed to comply with the terms of the Treaty of Berlin of 1878, which required them to grant Jews equal rights. Between 1898 and 1904 some 70,000 Jews left Romania for the United States.

Only after World War I was legislation enacted to emancipate Romanian Jewry. Jews served as traditional scapegoats in the struggle between the ruling classes and the peasantry. Despite their unfavorable situation, Jews played an important role in the transformation of Romania from a feudal system into a modern economy and were also active in the country's cultural life. Romania was the birthplace of the Yiddish theater. It also produced

✦

many of the first chalutzim (pioneers) who settled in the Land of Israel. Rosh Pina and Zikhron Ya'akov, two of the oldest villages, were established by Romanian Jews. The Jews in the greater Romania that emerged from World War I (the community's population tripled) continued to be influenced by the culture prevailing in the particular part of the country in which they resided. Distinct communities lived in the Regat and in Moldavia (pre–World War I Romania), Transylvania, Bessarabia, and Bukovina.

In the second half of the 1930s, and with the rise of fascism, the situation of the Jews became increasingly desperate. In 1938 there were about 800,000 Jews in the country. On the eve of the Shoah, Romania was deprived of northern Transylvania, northern Bukovina, Bessarabia, and southern Dobruja. Of the Jews who remained under Romanian jurisdiction, about 265,000 (43%) were murdered, many by the Romanian army and the Fascist Iron Guard. The Jews in northern Transylvania, which was under Hungarian rule, fared even worse. Some 150,000 of them were, with Hungarian collusion, deported to Auschwitz or killed by local Fascists. About 400,000 Romanian Jews survived the war.

Between 1948 and 1988 about 300,000 Jews left the country. The majority moved to Israel, where they today comprise one of the largest ethnic communities. With the advent of Communist rule, all Zionist activity was prohibited, and the sole representative Jewish

Among the most popular Yiddish songs in America was one that reminisced about life in the old country: Romania, Romania, Romania! Written by Aaron Lebedeff, a star of the Yiddish stage, and arranged by the well-known cantor Sholom Secunda, Romania remains a beloved hit. Throughout the Diaspora, despite the bitter hardships to which Jews were subject, they could still be sentimental about their old homes.
"Once there was a beautiful land— Romania!
Life was so good!
No cares,
just wine,
mamaligeh
(Romanian porridge),
beautiful girls,
and merriment!"

organization was the Federation of Jewish Communities under the direction of the late Chief Rabbi Dr. Moses Rosen. Under Rabbi Rosen's leadership, Romania was an anomaly in eastern Europe. Religious and cultural life was active, and the great majority of Jewish youth received a Jewish education. Moreover, the community was able to provide kosher food for its members. Although Zionist activity was officially prohibited, Rabbi Rosen nurtured ties between Israel and Romanian Jewry, and as a result of agreements reached with the Ceausescu regime (agreements that benefited Romania economically and diplomatically), Jews were able to emigrate to Israel.

⋆ C O M M U N I T Y ⋆

The Federation of Jewish Communities represents Romanian Jewry. The communal framework which existed under Communist rule has been preserved, but the office of the president of the community and of the chief rabbi have been separated. Increasingly the community is geared toward meeting the needs of its aging population—most of whom have children or grandchildren living abroad. The JDC is especially active in Romania and ensures that all Jews receive at least basic foodstuffs and heat in the winter. There are a number of Jewish old-age homes, and it can be expected that in a few years these will be the dominant venue of Jewish life as Romanian Jewry withers away.

There has been a disturbing rise in anti-Semitic activity in Romania. A number of newspapers and political parties, including some leaders of the mainstream parties, have an active anti-Semitic agenda, and the community has been forced to contend with historical revisionism that aims at the rehabilitation of wartime Romanian leaders. Following negotiations with the WJRO, in 1997 the Romanian government agreed to begin its process of restitution of confiscated Jewish communal property.

✦ RELIGIOUS AND CULTURAL LIFE ✦

Despite the dwindling number of Jews, synagogues and a religious infrastructure are maintained in many localities. The number of operating synagogues in the provinces is in constant decline. There are kosher cafeterias in some 10 cities. Virtually all Jewish children receive at least the rudiments of a Jewish education in the community's Talmud Torah schools. There are three rabbis in Romania.

Bucharest maintains a Jewish youth choir. There is a small Yiddish theater that receives government funding and a monthly newspaper, *Revista cultului mozaic* (published in Yiddish, Romanian, Hebrew, and English). The Babes–Bolyai University in Cluj–Napoca is the seat of the Dr. Moses Carmilly Institute

for Hebrew and Jewish History, which was established in 1990. The institute, the only one of its type in Romania, offers a range of courses and encourages research on Jewish topics, particularly those related to Transylvanian Jewry.

✦ ISRAEL ✦

Romania and Israel have had uninterrupted diplomatic relations since 1948.

Aliya: Since 1948, 273,825 Romanian Jews have emigrated to Israel, 117,950 of them between 1948 and 1951.

✦ SITES ✦

Romania is one of the few countries in eastern Europe in which remnants of *shtetl* life can still be observed (primarily in towns, such as Radauti and Dorohoi in Moldavia). In Iasi there is an imposing monument in the Jewish cemetery to the 10,000 Jews massacred there in 1941. Some of the cities have impressive synagogues, notably the Choral Temple in Bucharest.

Federation of Jewish Communities of Romania
Vineri 9-11, Sector 3, 70478 Bucharest
Tel. 40 1 613 2538, Fax 40 1 312 0869

Embassy
Dr. Burghelea 5, 73102 Bucharest
Tel. 40 1 311 2299, Fax 40 1 312 0431

✦

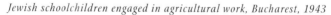

Jewish schoolchildren engaged in agricultural work, Bucharest, 1943

◆DEMOGRAPHY◆

The majority of Slovak Jews live in Bratislava, the capital, but there are also Jewish communities in Kosice, Presov, Piestany, Nowy Zamky, and other towns. Most Jews are more than 70 years old, as intermarriage has taken a heavy toll. Yet in recent years, many younger people have rediscovered their Jewish origins, injecting new life into the remnant of Slovak Jewry.

◆HISTORY◆

For close to a millennium, Slovakia was an integral part of Hungary, and the history of its Jewish community is tied to that of Hungarian Jewry. Before World War II, Bratislava was a great center of Jewish learning, and its *yeshiva* was among the most celebrated in all of Europe. Slovak Jewry included Chassidim, proponents of religious Orthodoxy, and Neolog reformers. Slovak Jews have been strongly influenced by Hungarian (and, to a lesser extent, German) culture, and many, particularly in southern Slovakia, are native Hungarian speakers.

On the eve of the dissolution of independent Czechoslovakia in 1939, there were some 150,000 Jews in Slovakia (nearly twice the number of those in the neighboring Czech lands). The government of independent Slovakia orchestrated the deportation of Slovak Jews to German death camps in Poland (paying the Germans 500 marks per head for the privilege), and in Hungarian-occupied south Slovakia, the Hungarian authorities played a

Chatam Sofer as depicted on a Slovak postage stamp, 1995

similar role. Only 25,000 Jews survived the Holocaust, and many of these elected to emigrate immediately after the war. The Jewish community was reestablished, but it gradually shrank due to aging, emigration, and assimilation. The latter two were accelerated by the hostile attitude of the authorities. The freedom that followed the collapse of Communism opened new, hitherto unimagined avenues of expression for Slovak Jews.

◆COMMUNITY◆

The Federation of Jewish Communities in Slovakia is the major communal organization. Branches of a number of international Jewish organizations have recently been established, and Slovak Jewish youth are especially active in these. Among these groups are B'nai B'rith and Maccabi.

Anti-Semitism, long concealed beneath the surface, has re-emerged as a serious problem. Certain newspapers have engaged in anti-Semitic polemics, and certain elements within the Slovak Roman Catholic Church, as well as within nationalist political parties, have engaged in the defamation of Jews. Several Jewish cemeteries have been desecrated, and the rabbi of Bratislava was beaten up by hooligans. There has been a tendency to rehabilitate Father Josef Tiso, the country's murderous wartime leader, with a number of monuments erected in his memory. Moreover, several persons with a Fascist past occupy government positions. The government is negotiating with the community and the WJRO for the restitution of properties and has initiated legislation to this effect.

✦ RELIGIOUS LIFE ✦

There are synagogues in a number of Slovak towns and rabbis in Bratislava and Kosice. Kosher meat is produced locally, and there are kosher restaurants in Bratislava and Kosice. Religious observance is increasing, and even some children of mixed marriages are returning to the community and studying Judaism.

✦ CULTURE AND EDUCATION ✦

Under Communist rule, Jewish life was suppressed, and there is still widespread ignorance of Jewish tradition. However, this is rapidly changing. There are Talmud Torahs in Bratislava and in Kosice—the home of most Slovak Jewish youth. The JDC and the Lauder Foundation are active in sponsoring cultural activities geared toward young people.

✦ ISRAEL ✦

Israel has full relations with Slovakia and is represented by its ambassador in Vienna.

Gisi Fleischmann (1897–1944) was one of the outstanding heroines of the Holocaust. Ignoring the danger to her own life, she refused to leave her community. Fleischmann was the indefatigable spirit of an underground rescue movement that sought to inform the world about German attempts to wipe out European Jewry. Through coded messages sent to Jewish leaders in neutral Switzerland and Turkey, she conveyed the first eyewitness accounts of the death camps and actively sought to aid Polish Jews who had escaped to Slovakia. In 1944 Fleischmann was arrested by the Germans and sent to Auschwitz with the instructions "return undesirable." She was gassed upon arrival.

Until 1991 *aliya* from Slovakia was subsumed under Czechoslovakia.

✦ SITES ✦

Slovakia has many interesting sites of Jewish interest, including numerous synagogues and burial grounds in various states of disrepair. Outstanding among them is the underground mausoleum in Bratislava, which contains the resting places of 18 renowned rabbis. These include Moshe Sofer Schreiber, known as the Chatam Sofer. Sofer, who lived in the 19th century, was a radical opponent of the Enlightenment. In part, thanks to his efforts, Bratislava (then known by its German name, Pressburg) became the intellectual heart of Austro-Hungarian Orthodox Jewry, and children from throughout the Empire were sent to its great *yeshiva*. A Jewish museum has been opened in Bratislava.

Federation of Jewish Communities in Slovakia
Kozia ul, 21, 814 47 Bratislava
Tel. 42 17 531 2167, Fax 42 17 531 1106

A Brooklyn rabbi and his wife on a visit to the grave of his uncle in the village of Pecovsk Nova Ves

Torah binder.
Linen emboidered with silk thread

SLOVENIA

GP 1,942,000   JP 75

◆HISTORY AND COMMUNITY◆

Jews have lived in what is today Slovenia since at least the end of the 12th century. They were active as merchants, bankers, and artisans and carried out extensive trade between central and southern Europe. Their main center was the city of Maribor. However, when this territory became part of Austria in the 15th century, the Jews were expelled. After the emancipation of Jews in Austria in 1867, a small number settled in Slovenia. During World War II, Slovenia was directly annexed to the German Reich. Some Jews escaped to Italy and others joined partisans. Those less fortunate were deported to their deaths.

The only communal organization is the Jewish Community of Slovenia, which is affiliated with the community in Croatia. There is no organized religious life.

◆ISRAEL◆

Israel and Slovenia have full diplomatic relations. Israel is represented by its ambassador in Vienna.

◆SITES◆

The old synagogue in Maribor dates back to 1429. When Jews were expelled from the city in 1496, the synagogue was converted into a church. The building is presently under restoration. There are historic cemeteries in a number of cities and towns, including Ljubljana, Lendava, and Murska Sobota. The burial ground at Rozna Dolina (Nova Gorica) is preserved as a historic monument.

Jewish Community of Slovenia
Trzaska 2 PP 4387
1101 Ljubljana
Tel./Fax 386 61 221 836

YUGOSLAVIA
(SERBIA AND MONTENEGRO)

GP 10,295,000 ✦ JP 2,500

✦DEMOGRAPHY✦

Nearly all the Jews live in Serbia. Of these some 2,000 reside in Belgrade. Most of the others live in Nis, Novi Sad, Sombor, and Subotica. The community includes both Sephardi and Ashkenazi Jews, but these differences have become less distinct with time. The level of intermarriage is high, but many of the children of such marriages have retained their Jewish identity. More than half the Jews exceed 50 years of age.

✦HISTORY✦

The Jewish presence in Serbia can be traced back to Roman times. In the 12th century, Benjamin of Tudela reported that Jews were influential in the region. During the period of Turkish rule, which commenced in 1389, Jewish merchants prospered. Refugees from Spain arrived in the 16th century. Austria ruled over part of the country for two decades in the first half of the 18th century, and for the most part, conditions were favorable. During that time, Jews arrived from Austria, Hungary, and elsewhere. In 1829, after a number of rebellions, the Turks granted Serbia autonomy, but the Jews suffered from a number of economic restrictions. The Treaty of Berlin in 1878 provided for civil rights for Jews, but it was only in 1889 that the Serbian parliament proclaimed complete equality for all Serbs, irrespective of their religion or ethnicity. Many Jews were decorated for bravery in the Serbian army during the Balkan War (1912–1913), the Serbian–Bulgarian War, and World War I.

After World War I, upon the creation of Yugoslavia, the Jews of Serbia were linked to Jews in other parts of the Kingdom. The

---

David Albala (1886–1942) was an outstanding Serbian patriot and Zionist activist. During World War I, he served on the Serbian delegation to the United States that attempted to secure support for Belgrade. At the same time, he also worked to secure recognition for Zionism and to attract recruits to the Jewish Legion. On December 27, 1917, Albala received an official letter of support for Zionist aspirations from the Serbian military representative in Washington. "There is no other nation in the world sympathizing with this plan more than Serbia. Do we not shed bitter tears on the rivers of Babylon in sight of our beloved land, lost only a short time ago? How should we not participate in your clamors and sorrows, lasting ages and generations, especially when our countrymen of your origin and religion have fought for their Serbian fatherland as well as the best of our soldiers? It will be a sad thing for us, to see any of our fellow Jewish citizens leaving us to return to their promised land, but we shall console ourselves in the hopes that they will stand as brethren and will leave with us a good part of their hearts, and that they will be the strongest tie between free Israel and Serbia." Albala continued his career of public service in Yugoslavia, and when the Germans invaded the country, he was sent to Washington as the ambassador of the Yugoslav government-in-exile.

destruction of Serbian Jewry commenced with the German invasion and occupation of the country. Already in August 1942, a German report stated that "the problem of Jews and Gypsies has been solved; Serbia is the only country where this problem no longer exists." Belgrade was the first city in Europe officially declared *Judenrein*. A number of Jews distinguished themselves in the partisan struggle against the German invasion.

After the war, the Jewish community was reconstituted. Unlike most of their brethren in eastern Europe, the Jews of Yugoslavia maintained lively contact with Jews in Israel and Western countries. In 1991 after the outbreak of the Yugoslav civil war, Serbian Jews were cut off from the communities in other parts of the country, which established their own independent communal organizations.

✦ RELIGIOUS AND CULTURAL LIFE ✦

Yugoslav Jewry is represented by the Federation of Jewish Communities in Yugoslavia, and the community center in Belgrade is the focus of communal life. There is an Ashkenazi synagogue in Belgrade, but it follows the Sephardi *nusach* according to the custom of its rabbi. Specifically kosher food is not available. Jewish children are educated in a Talmud Torah. The JDC has been especially active in providing material aid to the community.

✦ ISRAEL ✦

Israel and Yugoslavia maintain diplomatic relations.

Aliya: Since 1948, 10,016 Yugoslav Jews have emigrated to Israel. Within this number are Jews from all the various constituent parts of the former republic.

✦ SITES ✦

Turn-of-the-century synagogues in Subotica and Novi Sad, among the most impressive buildings in these cities, have been transformed into concert halls. The Jewish Museum in Belgrade records the history of Jews in the capital. In the town of Zemun the grave of Theodor Herzl's grandparents can be visited. In the Jewish cemetery in Belgrade, a monument resembling two outstretched wings symbolizes the tragedy that befell the Jews of Yugoslavia.

Jewish Community of Belgrade
Ulica Kralja Petra 71a/III
P.O. Box 841, 11001 Belgrade
Tel. 381 11 624 289, Fax 381 11 626 674

Embassy
c/o Intercontinental Hotel
Ulica V. Popovica 10, 11001 Belgrade
Tel. 381 11 132 931

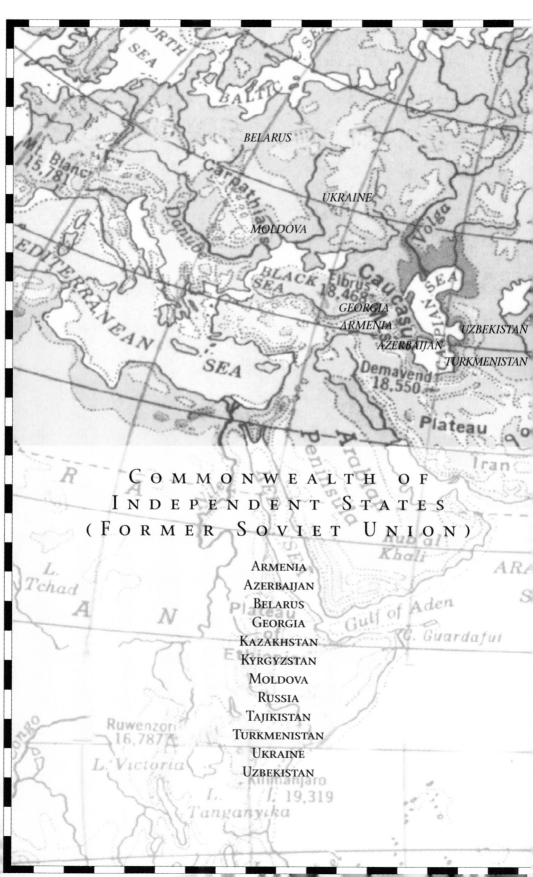

COMMONWEALTH OF
INDEPENDENT STATES
(FORMER SOVIET UNION)

ARMENIA
AZERBAIJAN
BELARUS
GEORGIA
KAZAKHSTAN
KYRGYZSTAN
MOLDOVA
RUSSIA
TAJIKISTAN
TURKMENISTAN
UKRAINE
UZBEKISTAN

RUSSIA

KAZAKHSTAN

L. Balkhash

Tien Shan

KYRGYZSTAN

TAJIKISTAN

Altai Mts.

Gobi

Kunlun Mts.

Plateau of

Himalaya Tibet

Mt. Everest Mts.
29,002

Ganges

Yangtze

Hwong

YELLOW SEA

SOUTH CHINA SEA

Comorin

Mald
Mts.
M

Equator

Borneo

Sumatra

INDONESIA

Java

Girls from Samarkand, Uzbekistan, on their way to Israel, 1990

ARMENIA

GP 3,638,000 ✦ JP 110

✦HISTORY AND DEMOGRAPHY✦

Historians claim that Jews arrived in Armenia after the destruction of the First Temple. There was certainly a community in the late Second Temple times, when there were ties between Jews in Armenia and in the Land of Israel. One of Herod's grandsons was crowned king of Lesser Armenia. However, from the 4th century, the Jewish population dwindled.

The modern-day Jews are almost all Ashkenazim who came there during the Soviet period. There are also several Georgian Jewish families. In the last five to ten years, most of the Jews of Armenia have emigrated to Israel and elsewhere. Nearly all the remaining Jews live in Yerevan, the capital.

✦COMMUNAL AND RELIGIOUS LIFE✦

In Yerevan there is a prayer house served by an Orthodox rabbi. Matzot are baked locally. The community is active in providing for the welfare of Jews. This is especially important, as living conditions are rough, and electricity and water are in short supply. An Armenian–Jewish Friendship Society is active in Yerevan.

✦ISRAEL✦

Israel is represented by its ambassador in Tbilisi, Georgia.

Aliya: Since 1989, 1,246 Armenian Jews have emigrated to Israel.

✦

Jews of the Caucasus

AZERBAIJAN

❖

GP 7,595,000 ❖ JP 20,000

GP 7,595,000 ❖ JP 20,000

❖ DEMOGRAPHY ❖

The main centers are Baku (15,000) and Quba (3,000). There are communities in several other smaller towns, but none of these numbers more than 500 people.

❖ HISTORY ❖

Azeri Jews are divided into two distinct groups: the Ashkenazim who arrived in the country during the last century and the autochthonous Caucasian Mountain Jews, or Tats, who trace their roots back many centuries and who speak a distinct Jewish dialect called Judeo-Tat (a north Iranian language that uses some Hebrew words and is sometimes referred to as Tat). The Tats claim that they arrived in the country at the time of Nebuchadnezzar. This warlike tribe inhabited a whole series of mountain villages. In dress

and in lifestyle they followed the example of their Caucasian neighbors, and in their homes (low mud huts), polished weapons were always displayed on the walls.

However, the imposition of Soviet authority gradually changed the Tat way of life. In 1928 they were forced to adapt the Tat language to the Latin alphabet, in place of the Hebrew letters that they had normally used. In 1938 the Tats were forced to adopt the Cyrillic alphabet in place of the Latin. Attempts were made to expunge the language of its Hebrew elements. Tat cultural institutions were closed down, as were some of their synagogues. Yet the Tats displayed resilience and clung to their traditions. Intermarriage was and remains minimal, and nearly all weddings were and continue to be celebrated with

The unveiling of a gravestone at the cemetery in Quba, 1990

religious ceremonies. There are also some Georgian and Bukharan Jews.

✦COMMUNITY✦

Azerbaijan Jewry has no umbrella organization. There are 10 to 15 Jewish bodies in Baku, including Zionist groups, youth associations, and an Azerbaijan–Israel Friendship Organization. In Quba and the smaller communities, the religious community is the focus of Jewish communal life, but there are also some other organizations such as Maccabi. The JDC is active in welfare work.

✦RELIGIOUS LIFE✦

Baku has three synagogues: a Mountain Jewish congregation, which is the oldest and largest of the Jewish houses of worship; an Ashkenazi synagogue; and a Georgian one. There are synagogues in some of the smaller communities as well. These communities are headed by locally trained rabbis.

✦CULTURE AND EDUCATION✦

The first officially sanctioned Hebrew courses in the Soviet Union were offered in Baku in 1987. Today Hebrew can be studied at two high schools in Baku and at the university. There is a total of five Jewish schools in Baku and Quba (including a day school) with a total enrollment of 1,450 students. A community newspaper appears in Baku.

✦ISRAEL✦

Israel and Azerbaijan have enjoyed diplomatic relations since 1992.

Aliya: Since 1989, 27,650 Azeri Jews have emigrated to Israel.

Embassy
Stroiteley Prospect 1, Baku
Tel. 99 412 385 282, Fax 99 412 989 283

✦

Tat Jews were captivated by Zionism, and one of the leaders of the Caucasian Zionists proposed the establishment of a crack 5,000-strong Tat cavalry brigade to join the Jewish Legion. While this never came to pass, Tats valiantly served in the Soviet army in World War II, and Tat olim played their part in the Israel Defense Forces.

BELARUS

GP 10,350,000 ◆ JP 45,000

◆DEMOGRAPHY◆

The Jewish community in Belarus is the third-largest in the former Soviet Union (following Russia and Ukraine). The largest center is in Minsk, home to some 20,000 Jews. There are several thousand Jews living in many of the country's smaller cities and towns, including Bobruysk (6,000), Mogilev (6,000), Gomel (5,500), and Vitebsk (5,000), and about 500 each in Baranowicz, Borisov, Brest, Grodno, Orsha, Pinsk, and Polotosk.

◆HISTORY◆

Belarus as a territory with a distinct identity is of relatively recent origin. Consequently, the term "Belarus Jewry" has little historic significance. The Ashkenazi Jews living in the territory of present-day Belarus share the history of the Jews of neighboring Lithuania, Poland, Ukraine, and Russia. A part of Belarus was ruled by Poland until 1939 (including such cities as Brest, Grodno, and Pinsk—the population of the latter was about 90% Jewish). However, from a cultural standpoint, most Jews living in Belarus identified themselves as "Litvaks." Most of the Jewish population of the area was wiped out in the Shoah. Although some of the older generation still speak Yiddish, the great majority of Jews in Belarus (like most other urban dwellers in Belarus) are native Russian speakers.

Man and the Village
by Vitebsk-born Marc Chagall, 1914

◆COMMUNITY◆

The Belarus Union of Jewish Organizations and Communities is the major umbrella organization. For the most part, Jewish life is very decentralized, and there are a great number of local organizations that are fully independent. Although anti-Semitism is not as great a problem as in Ukraine or in Russia, there have been a number of incidents that have given cause for concern. Much of the anti-Jewish activity has been orchestrated by elements of the country's large Russian minority, which has been influenced by Vladimir Zhirinovskii. Manifestations of anti-Semitism have been restricted to vandalism of Jewish sites, particularly cemeteries, and the appearance of anti-Jewish articles in certain newspapers and journals. There are fears that the situation could worsen if the economy does not improve. The government has expressed little eagerness to openly discuss the role of local residents in the Shoah.

◆RELIGIOUS LIFE◆

There are synagogues in most of the towns with a large Jewish population, and these generally have Sunday schools for children. Several rabbis, mainly foreign, serve the needs of the community. Kosher food is available, and matzot are produced locally.

◆

The synagogue in Slonim, 1991

✦CULTURE AND EDUCATION✦

About 1,000 students go to any one of about 50 Jewish schools in a number of different cities, among them two day schools (Gomel and Minsk). Minsk has a Jewish People's University, which functions as an evening school and is affiliated with the Belarus State University. In 1994 a Center for Jewish National Culture was opened in Minsk, as was a Center for the History of the Jews of Belarus in Vitebsk. There are about 100 cultural groups, but most of these are small and lead a precarious existence. A lively Jewish press exists, Minsk alone boasting three Jewish newspapers.

> *In a 1926 census, 90.7% of the Jews in Belarus claimed Yiddish as their mother tongue. Belarus was the only former Soviet republic that, at least briefly, included the Communist motto "Workers of the World Unite" in Yiddish on its coat of arms.*

✦ISRAEL✦

Belarus and Israel established full diplomatic relations in 1992.

Aliya: Since 1989, 57,000 Jews from Belarus have emigrated to Israel.

✦SITES✦

In many towns, ruins of synagogues, yeshivot, and burial grounds can be found. Many Jewish buildings are intact but have been put to other uses. Vitebsk was the birthplace of Marc Chagall, and the town was the backdrop for many of his most famous works. There are presently plans under way to convert the Chagall house into a museum of the artist's life.

Belarus Union of Jewish Organizations and Communities
Skorina Prospekt 137-6, Minsk
Tel. 375 172 643 083

Embassy
Partizanski Prospekt 6A
Minsk 220002
Tel. 375 172 303 479, Fax 375 172 105 270

✦

♦ DEMOGRAPHY ♦

The community is divided equally between "native" Georgian Jews and Russian-speaking Ashkenazim who began migrating there at the beginning of the 19th century, and especially during World War II. The largest center is in the capital Tbilisi (11,000). There are also communities in Kutaisi (1,000), Gory (800), Batumi (300), Oni (250), Akhaltsikhe, and several other places.

♦ HISTORY ♦

Georgian-speaking Jewry is one of the oldest of the Diaspora communities. Among the travelers who noted the presence of Jews in Georgia were Benjamin of Tudela in the 12th century and Marco Polo in the 13th. Archeological sites prove the presence of Jews in Georgia since the 2nd century B.C.E. The 5th-century *History of Armenia*, by Moses Chorene, speaks of a family descended from Judean noblemen exiled by Nebuchadnezzar, which later provided kings of Georgia.

Over the years, Georgian Jewry acquired many local habits, especially in its day-to-day culture and language. Georgia was known as a country where there was little anti-Semitism. Still its Jews underwent many difficult periods, and some were even reduced to slavery. Despite this Georgian Jewry remained true to Jewish religious tradition and was exempted from much of the Soviet repression of religion. In 1979 nearly half of the 90 synagogues in the Soviet Union were situated in Georgia.

♦ COMMUNITY ♦

There is no roof organization in Georgia, but some 30 separate Jewish organizations function. These include such diverse groups as the Georgian Jewish Society for Natural Science and Technology and the Religious Society of Ashkenazi Jews.

♦ RELIGIOUS LIFE ♦

Georgian Jewry succeeded in maintaining Jewish tradition to a greater extent than most other Soviet Jews. Intermarriage was and remains low, and the level of Jewish religious knowledge is considerably higher than that of other republics. There are synagogues in

---

It was a letter by 18 heads of Georgian Jewish families in August 1969 to Israeli Prime Minister Golda Meir that sparked the international movement to free Soviet Jewry. That document expressed a fervent love for the Land of Israel and for the Jewish people and the desire to be granted permission to make aliya.
"There are 18 of us who signed this letter. But he errs who thinks that there are only 18 of us. There could have been many more signatures. They say that there is a total of 12,000,000 Jews in the world. But he errs who believes there is a total of 12,000,000 of us. For with those who pray for Israel are hundreds of millions who did not live to this day, who were tortured to death, who are no longer here. They march shoulder to shoulder with us, unconquered and immortal, those who handed down to us the traditions of struggle and faith...We will wait months and years, we will wait all our lives if necessary, but we will not renounce our faith or our hopes. We believe our prayers have reached God. We know our appeals will reach people. For we are asking—let us go to the land of our forefathers."

A Jewish merchant from Akhaltsikhe *A Jewish woman from Akhaltsikhe*
Both paintings by Shalom Koboshvily

Tbilisi, Kutasisi, Batumi, Gori, Oni, and several other communities, including those in which only a negligible number of Jews remains. Kosher food is available.

◆CULTURE AND EDUCATION◆

There is a day school in Tbilisi and six supplementary schools in three other cities. The office of the JDC in Tbilisi organizes Hebrew-language and other Jewish classes, as well as special activities for youth and for the elderly. Several Jewish publications appear, including *Alia Sakhartvelodan, Shalom,* and *Menorah.*

◆ISRAEL◆

Israel and Georgia have enjoyed full diplomatic relations since 1992.

Aliya: Georgian Jews began to settle in Eretz Israel in the 1860s, and by 1914 there were 500 in Jerusalem. Since 1989, 17,000 Georgian Jews have emigrated to Israel.

◆SITES◆

The traditions of Georgian Jewry can be observed in the richly decorated old Georgian Synagogue in Tbilisi and in those of the smaller towns.

Embassy
Achmashenabeli Ave. 61 , Tbilisi 380002
Tel. 995 8832 964 457/951 709
Fax 995 8832 754 469

KAZAKHSTAN

GP 17,027,000 ♦ JP 12,000

♦HISTORY AND DEMOGRAPHY♦

Most of the Jews are concentrated in the capital, Alma Ata, but there are also communities in Karaganda (1,500), Chimken (1,500), Semiplatinsk, Uralsk, Kokchetav, Dzhambul, and several other towns. The great majority of Jews in Kazakhstan are Ashkenazim who settled there during and after World War II. They are predominantly Russian-speaking and identify with Russian culture. There are also about 2,000 Bukharan and Tat Jews, approximately half of whom live in the capital.

♦COMMUNAL LIFE♦

The Mitzvah Association is an umbrella organization that unites more than 20 different local groups, both secular and religious, including an Association of Ghetto Survivors. Mitzvah also has a chair in the All-Peoples Assembly of Kazakhstan. Welfare organizations affiliated with the association, and aided by the JDC, look after the elderly members of the community, many of whose families have emigrated to Israel.

♦EDUCATION AND RELIGIOUS LIFE♦

Synagogues exist in Alma Ata and in Chimkent. There are more than 11 schools with some 650 students in 11 different communities, as well as a Jewish library in Alma Ata.

♦ISRAEL♦

Israel and Kazakhstan have maintained full diplomatic relations since 1992.

Aliya: Since 1989, 8,000 Jews from Kazakhstan have emigrated to Israel.

Embassy
Dgeltoxan Street 87, Alma Ata
Tel. 7 3272 507 215/8
Fax 7 3272 506 283

♦

KYRGYZSTAN

GP 4,669,000 ♦ JP 3,500

♦HISTORY AND DEMOGRAPHY♦

Most Jews are concentrated in Bishkek (Frunze), the capital. The Jews of Kyrgyzstan represent a relatively new community— nearly all of them migrated to the country after the Russian Revolution or came as evacuees or deportees from European Russia during World War II. About 80% of the community is Ashkenazi and 20% Bukharan. The Ashkenazim are nearly all Russian speakers and are almost completely assimilated with the Russian minority, which accounts for about 20% of the population of the country.

♦COMMUNAL LIFE♦

The Menorah Society of Jewish Culture is the major focus of Jewish activity. There was no Jewish community to speak of before the collapse of Communism. Most of the Ashkenazi Jews of Kyrgyzstan are Jewish primarily in the ethnic sense. Consequently, religious activity

♦

is negligible. There is an Ashkenazi synagogue in Bishkek, and also several small Bukharan prayer houses there and in some of the towns of the Ferghana Valley. The capital also has a Jewish library and a Jewish dance and theater troupe. There is a Jewish day school in Bishkek, and also a Sunday school. Maccabi organizes sporting activities for youth. An

Aish HaTorah learning center is in operation, and the Israeli Open University is very active.

✦ ISRAEL ✦

Israel and Kyrgyzstan maintain full diplomatic relations. Israel is represented by its ambassador in Alma Ata, Kazakhstan.

Aliya: Since 1989, 5,000 Kyrgyz Jews have emigrated to Israel.

M O L D O V A

GP 4,450,000 ✦ JP 18,000

✦ DEMOGRAPHY ✦

The largest community is in Kishinev, the capital, where some 15,000 Jews reside. There are other communities in Tiraspol (2,500) and Beltsy (1,000). Smaller numbers live in Bendery, Rybnitza, Soroky, and elsewhere.

✦ HISTORY ✦

Jews have lived in Bessarabia—the territory that constitutes the bulk of what is present-day Moldova—since the 15th and 16th centuries. At that time it was an important transit stop for Jewish merchants from Constantinople and from Poland. By the early 1700s, several permanent communities had been established. In 1812 the territory came under Russian rule and was included in the so-called Pale of Settlement. The Jewish population steadily increased and by 1897 was more than 200,000. In time Bessarabia (and

Ukraine) became the most important venue of Jewish agriculture outside the Land of Israel. Bessarabia was also a stronghold of Chassidism. However, in 1903 and 1905, in the wake of bloody pogroms, Jewish emigration accelerated.

Under Romanian rule, which lasted from 1918 until 1940, Jewish life continued unabated, despite the hostile attitude of the Romanian authorities, who pauperized much of the community. During the year of Soviet rule (1940–1941), Jewish institutions were closed, and many communal activists were arrested. On the eve of the German–Romanian invasion, there were more than 250,000 Jews in Bessarabia. Many of these were deported to camps in Transnistria, where tens of thousands perished at the hands of German and Romanian forces.

In the old synagogue near Armyaskaya Street, Kishinev

When Soviet authority was restored, a large number of the survivors elected to leave for Romania proper, from where many went on to Israel and other countries. The present community is made up of the remaining survivors, their descendants, and Jews from other parts of the Soviet Union who settled in the area after the war.

In 1992 Moldova was torn apart by a civil war that resulted in a division of the country into two separate parts: the Republic of Moldova to the west of the Dniester, and the self-styled Moldovan Soviet Socialist Republic of Transnistria to the east of the river. The civilian population in Bendery in Transnistria, which included many Jews, suffered greatly from fighting in the city. In response, the Federation of Jewish Organizations and Communities (Va'ad) in Moscow and Israeli organizations arranged for the evacuation of the Jewish population.

Kishinev has been seared into Jewish consciousness as the place in which two of the worst pogroms took place. In the first, in 1903, 49 Jews lost their lives and 500 were injured. About 700 houses were looted and destroyed, as were 600 shops and businesses. In the second outrage, in 1905, 19 Jews were killed and 56 injured. These events prompted Chaim Nachman Bialik to write his famous poem Be-Ir ha-Haregah *(In the City of Slaughter), one of the classics of Hebrew literature.*

✦COMMUNITY✦

The Republican Society for Jewish Culture is the umbrella organization for both parts of the divided country. The organization embraces 12 different communities and also has representatives in about 20 other towns in which small numbers of Jews live. A Jewish home for the aged has been established in Kishinev and the community also sponsors soup kitchens and a meals-on-wheels program. Among the communal organizations are a veterans group, a survivors group, and an organization devoted to fostering *aliya*.

Moldovan Jewry, for the most part Russian-speaking, is particularly concerned about new laws that require the use of the Moldovan language. Yiddish is still spoken in many families, especially among the older generation. There are several anti-Jewish groups and publications, and anti-Semitism in Moldova is characterized by accusations on the part of the dominant Romanian population that the Jews are pro-Russian. The Russian population, on the other hand, accuses the Jews of being anti-Russian. Anti-Jewish sentiment is more evident in the Russian-speaking breakaway province of Transnistria. Moldovan Jewry monitors anti-Semitism and has taken energetic action through the courts and the government to quash it.

✦CULTURE AND RELIGIOUS LIFE✦

There are synagogues in all the important towns. The Chabad movement plays a significant role in the religious life of Moldovan Jews.

There are three Jewish day schools in Kishinev and Sunday schools in Beltsy, Bendery, and Tiraspol. Jewish themes are a frequent topic of conferences organized by the Kishinev University together with the Republican Society for Jewish Culture, and some are attended by visitors from abroad. The proceedings are often published in book form, and several other Jewish books have also appeared. A Jewish music group is active, and plans are under way to organize a Jewish theater. There is a a Jewish newspaper called *Yistoky*.

✦ISRAEL✦

Israel and Moldova have enjoyed diplomatic relations since 1992. Israel is represented by its ambassador in Kiev.

Aliya: Since 1989, 42,000 Moldovan Jews have emigrated to Israel.

✦

Poster issued in Moscow by Ozet, the Society for the Promotion of Jewish Settlement, 1928

R U S S I A

GP 148,126,000 ✦ JP 450,000

✦ D E M O G R A P H Y ✦

With the collapse of the Soviet Union and the rise of numerous successor states, "Russian Jewry" no longer embraces many of the communities that were once subsumed under the Communist and even pre-Communist rubric. Even so, Russia still accounts for one of the largest Jewish communities in the world. In addition to the two main cities, Moscow (200,000) and St. Petersburg (100,000), there are several dozen communities with more than 1,000 Jews. In recent years, Russian Jewry has been shrinking, primarily due to emigration and the ageing process. Estimates of the Jewish population of Birobidzhan, the so-called Jewish Autonomous Region, do not exceed 7,000.

✦ H I S T O R Y ✦

Jews were denied the right of permanent residence in Muscovy—the heart of what would evolve into the Russian empire. Some Jews, nevertheless, penetrated the area. Ivan the Terrible (1533–1584) was the first to order the complete expulsion of Jews. Under Czar Fyodor (1676–1682), Jewish traders were excluded from Muscovy. Those who remained in Moscow were forced to the baptismal font, yet some continued to practice Judaism clandestinely. In 1727 Catherine I issued a decree banning Jews from Russian cities. In 1735 her successor Anna expelled 35,000 Jews from Russia.

It was only with the first partition of Poland, in 1772, that sizable numbers of Jews came under Russian jurisdiction. With the two successive partitions, Russia acquired a tremendous Jewish population. In successive years, these Jews were subjected to great repression, including deportations, onerous taxation, and long military service, during which there was intense pressure on them to convert to Christianity. In 1791 Catherine II restricted the Jewish presence in the Moscow and Smolensk provinces. The precedent was thus set for the creation of the so-called Pale of Jewish Settlement, the borders of which varied according to the perceived interests of the Russian rulers.

Russian-speaking Jews played an outstanding role in the Haskala and in the development of Zionism and Jewish Socialism. Outstanding figures included Ahad Ha'am, Leon Pinsker, Vladimir Jabotinsky, and Chaim Weizmann. They also played an enormous role in the development of Hebrew and Yiddish literature.

Until the Russian Revolution, the Russian Empire (which at that time also included much of Poland) had the largest Jewish population in the world. Some 6,000,000 Jews lived under the Czars accounting for 4% of the total population of the empire. However, between 1881 and 1914, two million Jews left the Russian Empire. Most went to the United States, and today their descendants account for the great majority of American Jews.

The Jewish community living in the territory of Russia proper is of relatively recent origin. Until the middle of the 19th century, very few Jews lived in Russian cities. The bulk of "Russian Jewry" was confined to the pale— the territory consisting of present-day Ukraine, Belarus, Moldova, Lithuania, and Poland. The only part of the pale in present-day Russia is the Bryansk oblast. In 1855 Czar Alexander II allowed Jews to live in Moscow, albeit temporarily. A few years later, he allowed military veterans the right of permanent residence, and that category was later expanded. Consequently the Jewish population of the city rose from 500 in 1858 to 35,000 in 1890. However, in 1891 more than 30,000 Jews were expelled from Moscow. Only in 1905 did the community begin to recover.

Many Jews from Belarus and Ukraine settled in what is now Russia during the Soviet period. They were largely drawn to the major cities and towns that offered the greatest opportunities for educational and professional advancement. The Soviet authorities officially recognized the Jews as a national group that was entitled to its own cultural institutions. However, the practice of Judaism was strongly discouraged, and those who continued to do so against all odds were subjected to harsh repression. Moreover, any manifestation of Zionism was strictly outlawed,

Hebrew lesson, Moscow, 1990

including the study of Hebrew. Yiddish books and newspapers were published, and schools were opened in which Yiddish was the language of instruction. Moreover, in the Soviet Far East, Jews were granted their own "national territory," the so-called Jewish Autonomous Oblast, more commonly known as Birobidzhan. Several thousand Jews initially heeded the call to settle that virgin land.

As Stalin tightened his grip in the 1930s, the country was racked by purges that destroyed many of the leading Communist cadres and a great part of the intelligentsia. Soviet policy was always guided by one ultimate aim: the disappearance of the Jews as a national and religious community and their assimilation into other national groups of the Soviet state. Consequently, among Stalin's victims were many of Russia's greatest Jewish writers. Jews were gradually weeded out of the state apparatus. The Jewish commander of the Red Air Force, for example, was arrested and killed. Most expressions of Jewish life that existed in Birobidzhan were gradually whittled down, and the territory became little more than a quixotic Yiddish Potemkin village.

During World War II, this campaign was relaxed, and Jews played an important role in the Soviet war effort, both at the front (in which they served in greater numbers proportionally than many other national groups) and in military production. Although much of Soviet Jewry was decimated in the Shoah, many of those living in Russia proper (notably in Moscow and Leningrad) were spared. Generally speaking the Jews living in territories incorporated into the Soviet Union only immediately before or just after the war were more traditionally inclined than those of other parts of the Soviet Union. The ancient Oriental communities of Soviet central Asia, which clung to Jewish tradition with remarkable fervor, were a notable exception.

Immediately after the war, the campaign to suppress Soviet Jewry was renewed. Among the many casualties was the great Yiddish actor Solomon Mikhoels. The terror against "Cosmopolitanism" (a code word for Jews) culminated in the "Doctors Plot," in which many Jewish physicians were accused of plotting to kill Stalin. Only Stalin's death in 1953 spared Soviet Jewry from facing even greater oppression. Shortly thereafter many of the prisoners in the vast gulag, including tens of thousands of Jews, were released.

Although the situation improved somewhat, Jewish culture continued to be, for the most part, ruthlessly suppressed. Jewish religious articles and books were smuggled into the country, and clandestine study and worship groups were established, but the great majority of Soviet Jews had access to neither. Many of the Jews who did engage in such activity, the so-called refuseniks, were imprisoned and denied the right to leave the country. In the west they were called "Prisoners of Zion." In the late 1960s and early 1970s, under the guise of family reunification, limited emigration was permitted. The efforts of Israel and world Jewry on behalf of Soviet Jews intensified in the early 1970s. Under the slogan Let My People Go, demonstrations were mounted, and governments and parliaments were lobbied in order to bring pressure to bear on the Soviet authorities. In the 1980s, emigration was again restricted. With the rise to power of Mikhail Gorbachev and the policy of *glasnost*, the situation for Jews improved, and by the end of the decade, as the Soviet Union began to crumble, most restrictions on Jews had been lifted.

◆COMMUNITY◆

There are two umbrella organizations of Russian Jewry: the Federation of Jewish Organizations and Communities of Russia (Va'ad) and the Russian–Jewish Congress. Since the collapse of Communism, Jewish organizational life has emerged from "the communal kitchen" (underground). In addition to Jewish associations of a purely local character, major international Jewish organizations have local affiliates.

Anti-Semitism has been a great cause of concern. Although the post-Soviet leadership has officially condemned the phenomenon, it has taken almost no concrete action to crack down on anti-Semitic organizations or publications. The popularity of radical nationalists (often hardline ex-Communists), such as the notorious Vladimir Zhirinovskii, has led to feelings of uncertainty about the future of Russian Jewry.

◆RELIGIOUS LIFE◆

The Union of Jewish Religious Communities is responsible for maintaining and propagating Orthodox religious life. There are now synagogues in all the major cities and towns

---

Throughout the long years of struggle on behalf of Soviet Jewry, the Jews of Russia were often called the "Jews of Silence," as Elie Wiesel first referred to them after a visit to the Soviet Union. However, this was a misnomer. Russian Jewry's thirst for the knowledge that it was denied found expression in numerous Samizdat *(underground) publications, which were smuggled from hand to hand, house to house, and city to city at great personal risk. Through such underground literature, particularly a Russian translation of Leon Uris' novel* Exodus, *a whole generation of Soviet Jewish activists educated themselves and their colleagues. As one of them wrote,* Samizdat *"legitimized for the Soviet Jew the very concept of Jewishness."*

which have a Jewish population, as well as a number of rabbis, many recruited from abroad. In certain localities, the Chabad movement is also active. The Reform and Conservative movements have introduced these denominations of Judaism to the Russian scene. In recent years, over ten Reform congregations have been established, and the first native Russian Reform rabbis have recently taken up their pulpits.

Kosher food is available, including meat, wine, and matzot, and religiously observant Jews have all the facilities they need to practice Judaism. The majority of Russian Jewry, however, is not observant and sees its Jewish identity in terms of ethno-national status.

✦ CULTURE AND EDUCATION ✦
In the fields of education and culture, Russian Jewry has taken dramatic strides. Under the Communist regime, all fields of Jewish learning were strictly repressed, and Jews who sought to learn about Jewish history and tradition, or to study the Hebrew language, were forced to do so in a clandestine fashion. Consequently, only a handful of people received any Jewish education, and this was only at great personal risk. Today, in large part due to the efforts of foreign Jewish organizations, an impressive network of Jewish educational institutions has been established. These include four Jewish universities (in Moscow and St. Petersburg) where a broad range of Jewish topics can be studied.

There are over 100 Jewish schools in about 60 cities, among them 16 Jewish day schools (including those in Birobidzhan, Moscow, Nalchik, Samara, and St. Petersburg). Moreover, the Jewish Agency has organized Hebrew and other classes for those planning or contemplating *aliya*. Various vocational training classes are also available.

Jewish newspapers in the Russian language appear in Moscow, St. Petersburg, Samara, Omsk, Yekaterinburg, Nalchik, and Perm. The Yiddish daily *Birbodizhaner Stern* has passed out of existence and the monthly *Sovietish Heimland* has been succeeded by *Yiddishe Gass*. A large number of Jewish books are published in the Russian language, and others are imported from Israel and elsewhere. There is an active Jewish theater in Moscow.

✦

Entrance to the St. Petersburg Jewish cemetery, 1984

✦ISRAEL✦

The Soviet Union immediately recognized Israel upon its establishment in 1948. Relations were severed in 1967 and were only reestablished in 1992.

Aliya: Between 1948 and 1989, before the collapse of the Soviet Union, 218,170 Soviet Jews emigrated to Israel. Of that number, 137,134 arrived during the period of superpower detente, between 1972 and 1979. Since 1989, 230,000 Russian Jews have emigrated to Israel for a total of 700,000 from the former Soviet Union.

✦SITES✦

The most important Jewish site in Moscow is the Choral Synagogue on Arkhipova Street, which dates back to 1891. In Soviet times, on important holidays, Jews gathered in front of the building to express their identity. Today the synagogue is the focus of Jewish religious life in the capital. St. Petersburg's Moorish-style choral synagogue dates back to 1893. The State Russian Museum has an impressive collection of works by Chagall and other Jewish artists. In the Historical Museum of Birobidzhan, one of the permanent exhibits is called "To Be or Not To Be: Repressed Jewish Culture in the Jewish Autonomous Oblast." In the same city, there is also a museum devoted to themes from the Bible. Many of the works display a mixture of scriptural themes and contemporary political imagery.

Va'ad
71 Varshavskoye Shosse, 113556 Moscow
Tel. 7 095 230 6700, Fax 7 095 238 1346

Embassy
Bolshaya Ordinka 56 , Moscow
Tel. 7 095 230 6700, Fax 7 095 238 1346

✦

The Great Synagogue of Moscow (Arkhipova Street)
on the occasion of the late Prime Minister Rabin's visit

TAJIKISTAN

GP 5,935,000 ♦ JP 1,800

Tajik barber shop with entirely Jewish staff, 1989

♦HISTORY AND COMMUNITY♦

Jewish life is centered in Dushanbe, the capital, but there is a smaller community in Shakhrisabz. In Dushanbe Jews mainly live in the area near the synagogue, which is the center of the *mahalla* (the Jewish quarter). In recent years, however, many have moved to more modern parts of the city. About 40% of Tajik Jews are of Bukharan origin, and the rest are Asheknazim who came from other parts of the Soviet Union during World War II. The history of the Bukharan Jews in Tajikistan parallels that of the Bukharan community in Uzbekistan. There are synagogues in both Shakhrisabz and Dushanbe, where there is also a Jewish library.

♦ISRAEL♦

Israel and Tajikistan have full diplomatic relations. Israel is represented by its ambassador in Tashkent (Uzbekistan).

Aliya: Since 1989, 10,000 Tajik Jews have emigrated to Israel.

TURKMENISTAN

GP 4,155,000 ♦ JP 700

♦HISTORY AND COMMUNITY♦

The majority of the Jews are Ashkenazim who arrived in the area during the Soviet period. Some 20% are Iranian Jews with deeper roots in Turkmenistan. The largest community is in Askhabad with 800 Jews. The other Jews are divided between Chardzhou and Mary. The political situation is unstable, and there is a marked trend toward Islamization. The Jewish community has no formal status. There are no synagogues or rabbis and no other communal life. The JAFI has been active in promoting Jewish identity and in assisting those Jews who wish to leave for Israel.

♦ISRAEL♦

Israel and Turkmenistan have full diplomatic relations. Israel is represented by its ambassador in Moscow.

Aliya: Since 1989, 1,050 Turkmeni Jews have emigrated to Israel.

UKRAINE

GP 51,608,000 ✦ JP 310,000

✦ DEMOGRAPHY ✦

The Jews of Ukraine constitute the third largest Jewish community in Europe and the fifth largest in the world. Jews are mainly concentrated in Kiev (110,000), Dnepropetrovsk (60,000), Kharkov (45,000), and Odessa (45,000). Jews also live in many of the smaller towns. Western Ukraine, however, has only a small remnant of its former Jewish population, with Lvov and Chernovtsy each having only about 6,000 Jews. The majority of Jews in present-day Ukraine are native Russian/ Ukrainian speakers, and only some of the elderly speak Yiddish as their mother tongue (in 1926, 76.1% claimed Yiddish as their mother tongue). The average age is close to 45.

✦ HISTORY ✦

The idea of a distinct Ukrainian Jewry has been revived. In former times, Jews living in various parts of the territory of present-day Ukraine had identified themselves as Russian, Polish, Galician, Romanian, Bessarabian, Hungarian, or even Austrian Jews—and more recently, as Soviet Jews.

Jewish–Khazarian settlement in Kiev can be traced to the 10th century—preceding the unification of the region and the crystallization of Ukrainian national identity. The first

Gathering at the monument to the victims of Babi Yar, 1992

authentic document from this part of the world is written in Hebrew, the so-called Kievan letter (930 C.E.). Later this Russian-speaking community was absorbed by the Yiddish-speaking immigrants who came to Ukraine from central Europe. Large numbers of Jews came from Poland after it colonized much of the area in the 16th and 17th centuries. At that time, Jews played an important role in the economic life of the country, especially as managers, agents, and in the export-import trade. Later, in 1648, the Jews of Ukraine bore the brunt of the Chmielnicki uprising against the Polish gentry, in which tens of thousands of Jews lost their lives.

In the 19th century, Ukraine, as a part of the Pale of Settlement, was densely populated by Jews. Despite restrictions, Jews played a prominent role in the development of commerce and industry in the region, and especially in the growth of its major cities, such as Kiev, Odessa, and Kharkov. Many of the most important Jewish thinkers of the modern age were born there.

Ukraine was the

Torah crown, Lvov, inscribed with dates 1764/1765 and 1773.
Cast, repousse, engraved, parcel-gilt silver with semiprecious stones and glass stones

venue of some of the worst of the pogroms perpetrated under Czarist Russian rule. Later, in the Civil War and during the struggle for an independent Ukraine, about 100,000 Jews were slaughtered in 1919 and 1920. Jews also suffered grievous losses from the White Army. In 1920, with the collapse of the independent Ukrainian state, attempts at organizing Jewish national autonomy under Ukrainian nationalist auspices were stifled.

During the early Soviet period, Ukraine (together with Belarus) became a center of Yiddish culture, albeit devoid of any religious content. Yiddish schools, theaters, newspapers, and publishing houses were established, as was the Institute of Jewish Proletarian Culture in the Ukraine, attached to the Ukrainian Academy of Sciences. Toward the end of the 1930s, during the Stalinist purges, nearly all of these institutions were liquidated. Throughout this time, religious and Zionist activity was forced underground. By the late 1930s, after a thorough crackdown, most of those involved in propagating religious observance or Zionism had been arrested.

The Soviet authorities established four Jewish autonomous districts in the southern part of the republic and in Crimea. These settlements lasted until World War II, when they were overrun by the Germans and their inhabitants murdered. More than half the Jews living in Ukraine were wiped out. The Jews of Ukraine account for a great proportion of the Soviet victims of the Holocaust, with the worst slaughter taking place at Babi Yar outside Kiev. Many Ukrainians played an active role in the murder and despoliation of their Jewish neighbors. After the war, returning Jews were often met with hostility, and the repression of Jewish cultural and spiritual life was especially severe in Soviet Ukraine. Moreover, Kiev became a center for anti-Semitic publicistic activity.

The collapse of Communism and the re-creation of an independent Ukraine set the stage for the revitalization of Jewish life. The Ukrainian government has been sensitive to the needs of Ukrainian Jewry. Still, the precarious economic situation has been a decisive factor in the *aliya* of Ukrainian Jews.

✦ C O M M U N I T Y ✦

The leading umbrella organizations are the Association of Jewish Organizations and Communities of Ukraine and the Jewish Council of Ukraine. The community is made up of many different Jewish religious and cultural groups, including various Zionist organizations. Leading international Jewish organizations have established branches in Ukraine.

The Jewish population is in decline, largely due to emigration and to the aging process. The community, together with international Jewish welfare groups, is striving to alleviate the poverty of the many destitute Jews in the country, a large portion of whom are elderly. Among the community's priorities is securing the return of nationalized Jewish property.

Anti-Semitism has been manifested by sections of both the Ukrainian and Russian populations. The problem is especially acute in the western part of the country, including the city of Lvov, which has been a traditional center of Ukrainian nationalist extremism. There, glorification of the deeds of Germany's Ukrainian collaborators is proceeding apace. Several extremist organizations exist, yet their activities are tolerated. Some publications preach a distinctly anti-Jewish message, others are more subtle. Manifestations of anti-Semitism also include the occasional daubing of anti-Semitic graffiti and sporadic attacks on Jewish property. On a state visit to Israel, Leonid Kravchuk, then president, publicly apologized for his compatriots' role in the bestial murder of Jews during the German occupation.

✦ R E L I G I O U S   L I F E ✦

Since the collapse of the Soviet Union, religious life has undergone a revival, and Jewish communities in many cities and towns have been reconstituted. Synagogues and *mikvaot* are now functioning in all cities and towns with a significant Jewish population. Religious leadership is provided by a number of foreign rabbis. The Ukrainian government recognizes the authority of the Ukrainian Chief Rabbinate, which is located in Kiev. A network of Jewish religious schools has been opened, and Jewish education is available to all who seek it. Kosher meat is produced locally, and other items are imported. The JDC and other Jewish and Israeli organizations have been active in sponsoring Jewish activities. Generally speaking, Jewish religious life is stronger in Ukraine than in Russia.

✦ C U L T U R E   A N D   E D U C A T I O N ✦

Ukraine has about 75 Jewish schools in some 45 cities, among them some 10 day schools (in Chernovtsy, Dnepropetrovsk, Kharkov, Kiev, Lvov, Odessa, Vinnitsa, and Zapozoshye) and 65 Sunday schools. Courses in Hebrew are offered in many places, and there are many outlets for those who wish to express their artistic creativity. Much of the Israel-oriented activity is directed by the JAFI offices. The International Solomon University in Kiev has an enrollment of some 800 students. Among its departments are those of Jewish culture and history.

Several newspapers and journals are published, including the Kiev-based *Hadashot*. There is also a weekly TV program called "Yahad" on state television.

✦

✦ISRAEL✦

Ukraine and Israel have enjoyed full diplomatic relations since 1991.

Aliya: Since 1989, 200,000 Ukrainian Jews have emigrated to Israel.

✦SITES✦

Among the sites which attract large numbers of Jewish visitors is Uman, the burial place of Rebbe Nachman of Bratslav, and Gadyach, the tomb of Rabbi Shneur Zalman, the Alter Rebbe—the founder of the Lubavitch Chassidic movement. Every year thousands of Bratslav Chassidim converge on Uman to pray at the Rebbe's tomb, and the town reacquires some of its former ambience. Other places of interest include synagogues and burial grounds scattered throughout the country (most in a poor state of repair) and the site of the massacre at Babi Yar, on which an imposing monument has been erected.

Association of Jewish Organizations
and Communities of Ukraine
Kurskaya Str. 6, 252049 Kiev
Tel. 7 044 276 3431, Fax 7 044 271 7144

Jewish Council of Ukraine
Nimosnkaya St. 7 , 252103 Kiev 103
Tel. 296 3961, Fax 295 9604

Embassy
G.P.E.—S. Lesi Ukrainki 34
252195 Kiev
Tel. 380 44 294 9753, Fax 380 44 294 9748

The horrible slaughter at Babi Yar inspired the great Russian writer, Yevgeny Yevtushenko, to pen a powerful ode to the victims. It later became the theme of composer Dimitri Shostakovitch's 13th Symphony. *In 1963 both the poet and the composer were denounced by the Soviet authorities.*
"No gravestone stands on Babi Yar,
Only coarse earth heaped roughly on the gash.
Such dread comes over me; I feel so old,
Old as the Jews. Today I am a Jew...
Now I go wandering, as an Egyptian slave;
And now I perish, splayed upon the cross...
I am that little boy in Bialystok
Whose blood flows, spreading darkly on the floor.
The rowdy lords of the saloon make sport,
Reeking alike of vodka and of leek...
On Babi Yar weeds rustle; the tall trees
Like judges loom and threaten...
All scream in silence; I take off my cap
And I feel that I am slowly turning gray.
And I too have become a soundless cry
Over the thousands that lie buried here.
I am each old man slaughtered, each child shot.
None of me will forget..."

♦ DEMOGRAPHY ♦

The three major Jewish centers are Tashkent (13,000), Samarkand (3,000), and Bukhara (2,000). The Jews of Uzbekistan can be divided into two categories: the Ashkenazim who came to the region from other parts of the Soviet Union during Soviet rule and sometimes earlier, and the indigenous Bukharan community, which has its own Tajik–Jewish dialect, and which traces its roots back many centuries. Bukharans account for almost the entire community in Samarkand. Nearly all the Ashkenazim live in the capital, Tashkent, as do some 2,000 Bukharan Jews. In recent years, many Jews left Uzbekistan due to economic impoverishment and fear of the nationalistic "Uzbekization" trend of the government. Most Bukharan Jews have settled in Queens, New York, where they have established a well-organized community. The Ashkenazim have largely settled in Israel, Russia, and Germany. Jewish quarters, traditionally called *mahalla*, still exist in Samarkand, Bukhara, and smaller cities of the Ferghana Valley. There Jews continue to follow a traditional way of life.

Legend has it that in the 14th century, Tamerlane, who made Samarkand the capital of his great kingdom, brought Jewish weavers and dyers to the city. These trades were the major vocation of Jews in the area until the Russian conquest in the middle of the 19th century. It is said that Jews could always be distinguished from other locals by their blue hands, a sign of their work with indigo dye.

♦ HISTORY ♦

Bukharan Jewry is an ancient community that claims descent from 5th-century exiles from Persia. Bukharan Jews believe that Bukhara is actually Habor (II Kings 17:6), to which the ten tribes were exiled. Under Tatar–Mongolian rule, Jews were subject to harsh restrictions. These continued under Muslim rule, which commenced in the first half of the 8th century. Still, in the early years of Muslim rule, a group of local Jewish merchants called the Radanites (believed to be Persian for "those who know the way") was active in commerce between Europe and China.

Genghis Khan's conquest of the region brought misery and destruction, and Samarkand was sacked and leveled. More than 100 years later, however, Tamerlane rebuilt the capital and invited Jewish weavers and dyers from abroad to help develop the textile industry there. Later, in the 1500s, under the Shaybanid dynasty, the capital was moved to Bukhara, which had become an important center of Jewish life. During this time, Islamic law was strictly enforced and the rights of Jews restricted.

The situation improved somewhat when the country was conquered by Russia in 1868. With the construction of the railway to Samarkand, many Russian Jews migrated to the territory. However, the import of manufactured cloth from Russia drove many of the Jewish cloth dyers into other professions, such as peddling, shoemaking, and haircutting.

Although Soviet authority was imposed on the country, Jews were allowed greater freedoms than those afforded their co-religionists in other parts of the Soviet Union, and they clung to their Judaism tenaciously. Still, the number of synagogues in Samarkand plummeted from 30 in 1917 to 1 in 1935. At this time, many Jews became factory workers or collective farmers. There was also a Jewish influx into the new capital, Tashkent. During World War II, Jews from European Russia were evacuated to Uzbekistan, and many remained there.

◆ COMMUNITY ◆

There is no Jewish roof organization in Uzbekistan. The Ashkenazim and Bukharans are organized into numerous separate groups. The major bodies operating on the Jewish scene in Uzbekistan are the JAFI, the JDC, and the Lishkat HaKesher. Youth groups include B'nai Akiva. Anti-Semitism has not been a great problem for Jews in Uzbekistan, but there have been isolated cases of vandalism.

◆ RELIGIOUS LIFE ◆

Bukharan Jews have made valiant efforts to preserve Jewish life, even in the face of pressure from the Soviet authorities, and intermarriage was almost unknown. The community in Samarkand has a synagogue and enjoys the benefits of a Bukharan rabbi who is affiliated with the Chabad movement. He is also qualified as a *mohel* and a *shochet*. There is a Talmud Torah, in which some 200 students are enrolled. Bukhara also has a Talmud Torah and a Sunday school. In Tashkent, where the Ashkenazi element is predominant, religious life is much weaker, and many of the Jews have intermarried. There are four synagogues, a Talmud Torah, and a Sunday school.

◆ CULTURE AND EDUCATION ◆

Several Jewish schools are to be found, among them three day schools, one in Bukhara, one

Grandfather and grandson in a sukkah. *Marghelan, Ferghana Valley, 1986*

in Samarkand and another in Tashkent. Both Tashkent and Bukhara have Jewish cultural centers. Jewish musicians play a leading role in the local musical scene, performing both Uzbek folk music and classical central Asian music called *shash makom*. A Jewish monthly called *Shofar* is published in Russian.

◆ ISRAEL ◆

Israel and Uzbekistan have maintained full diplomatic relations since 1992.

Since the middle of the last century, in the Land of Israel, there has been an important Bukharan community that has retained its distinct identity and customs up to the present day.

Aliya: Since 1989, 66,100 Uzbek Jews have iemigrated to Israel.

◆ SITES ◆

Samarkand's *mahalla*, still home to a large number of Bukharan Jews, contains many sites from the Jewish past and present. There is only one functioning synagogue in the quarter, dating back to 1888. Its plain exterior conceals a magnificent, domed sanctuary. A number of other synagogue buildings still stand but are used for other purposes. The regional museum, located in what was once a Jewish-owned mansion, still contains the ornate room which served as the family's private synagogue. The *mahalla* in Bukhara also contains a number of Jewish relics.

Embassy
16A Lachuti Street, 5th Floor
545 Tashkent
Tel. 7 3712 567 823, Fax 7 3712 543 907

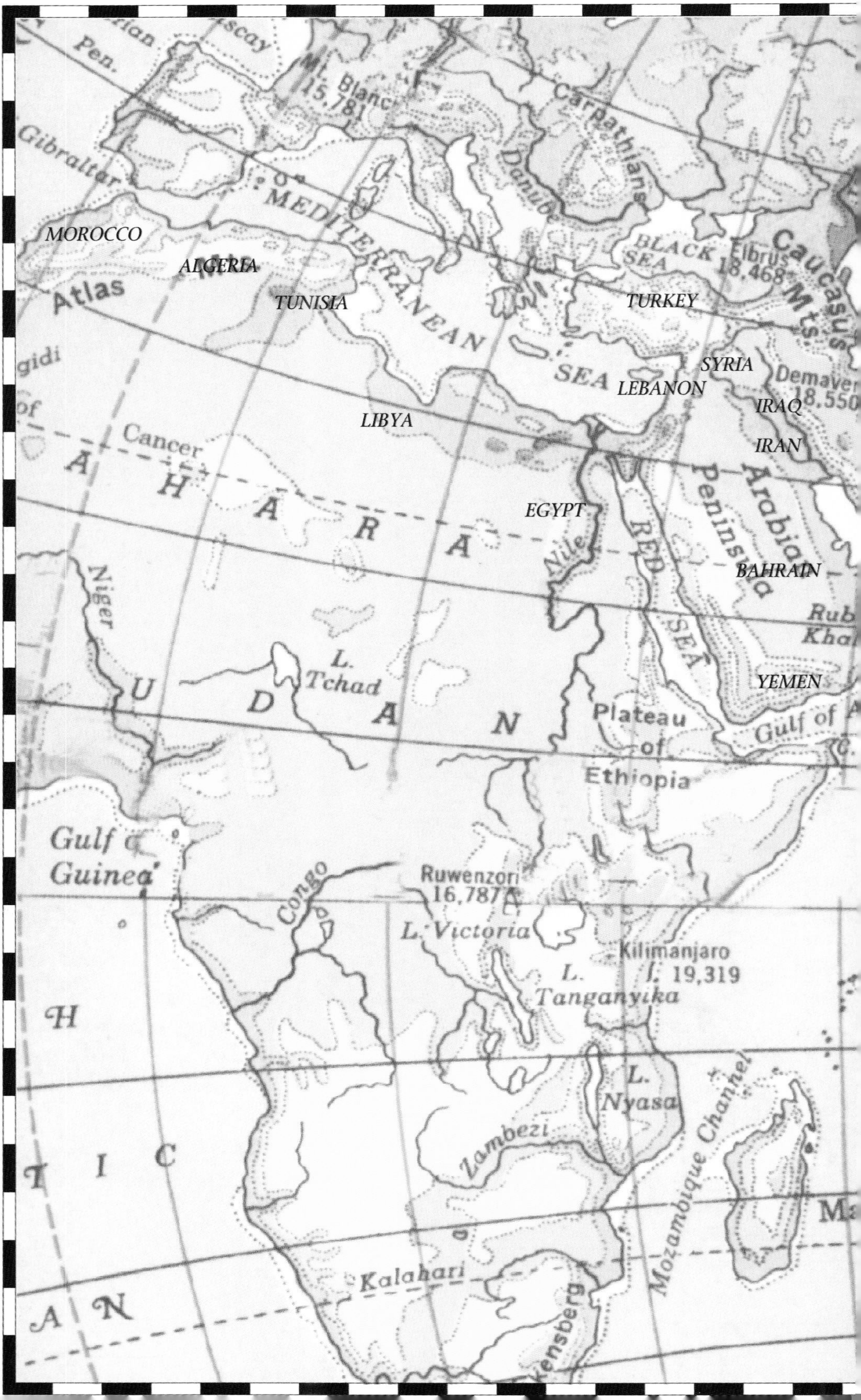
Pen.
Mt. Blanc
15,781
Carpathians
Gibraltar
MEDITERRANEAN
Danube
MOROCCO
ALGERIA
Atlas
TUNISIA
BLACK SEA
Elbrus
18,468
Caucasus Mts.
TURKEY
SEA
SYRIA
LEBANON
Demaven
IRAQ
IRAN
LIBYA
Cancer
S A H A R A
EGYPT
Nile
RED SEA
Arabian Peninsula
BAHRAIN
Niger
L. Tchad
S U D A N
YEMEN
Plateau of Ethiopia
Gulf of Guinea
Congo
Ruwenzori
16,787
L. Victoria
Kilimanjaro
19,319
L. Tanganyika
L. Nyasa
Zambezi
Mozambique Channel
Kalahari
A T L A N T I C

THE MIDDLE EAST
AND THE MAGHREB

Rimonim, Morocco, ca. 18th century.
Repousse and engraved silver

ALGERIA
BAHRAIN
EGYPT
IRAN
IRAQ
LEBANON
LIBYA
MOROCCO
SYRIA
TUNISIA
TURKEY
YEMEN

ALGERIA

GP 28,784,000 ✦ JP 50

✦HISTORY AND COMMUNITY✦
Jewish settlement in present-day Algeria can be traced back to the first centuries of the Common Era. Arab rule, which commenced in the 7th century, was for the most part tolerant, and Jews fleeing Visigothic Spain found sanctuary there. However, during the Almohade dynasty, which lasted from 1130 to 1269, many Jews were compelled to adopt Islam. In the 14th century, with the deterioration of conditions in Spain, many Spanish Jews moved to Algeria. Among them were a number of outstanding scholars, including the Ribash and the Rashbatz. These Jews brought great prosperity to remote communities. They exported ostrich feathers from Mzab and African gold from Tuat, as well as burnooses, cereals, wool, rugs, and pelts.

Algerian Jewish book merchant, ca. 19th century

After the French occupation of the country in 1830, Jews gradually adopted French culture and were granted French citizenship.

In the early part of the 20th century, Algeria became a hotbed of French anti-Semitism, and later in 1934, under the influence of events in Germany, the Muslim population massacred many Jews. Jews played an outstanding role in the resistance against Vichy rule. During that time, the Jews suffered greatly, and their plight was only alleviated by the Allied landings in 1942. Even then it was some time before all discriminatory restrictions were lifted.

On the eve of the civil war that gripped the country in the late 1950s, there were some 130,000 Jews in Algeria, approximately 30,000 of whom lived in the capital. Nearly all Algerian Jews fled the country shortly after it gained independence from France in 1962. Most of them eventually settled in France, where they did much to rejuvenate the French Jewish community.

Most of the remaining Jews live in Algiers, but there are individual Jews in Oran and

✦

In the 7th century the Judeo-Berber tribe of Jarawa in the Aures Mountains was led by a dahia-al-kahnina (warrior-queen) who ruled over a vast area. She achieved brilliant victories over the Arab invaders led by the Caliph Abdalmelek, but with her death in battle at the end of the 7th century, Berber independence collapsed and the territory was overrun.

Blida. A single synagogue functions in Algiers, although there is no resident rabbi. All other synagogues have been taken over for use as mosques.

✦ISRAEL✦

There are no diplomatic relations between Israel and Algeria, and the country has refused to have any part in the ongoing peace process between Israel and the Arab world.

Aliya: Since 1948, 25,681 Algerian Jews have emigrated to Israel.

Consistoriale Israelite d'Alger
6 rue Hassana Ahmed, Alger
Tel. 213 262 85 72

BAHRAIN

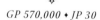

GP 570,000 ✦ JP 30

✦HISTORY AND COMMUNITY✦

Jews from Iraq, Iran and India settled in Bahrain in the late 19th century and became active in commerce and handicrafts. In 1947 there were anti-Semitic disturbances in which one Jew was killed and several injured. At that time, the synagogue was gutted. Over the years, most of the Jews emigrated, and today only a tiny remnant remains.

On holidays religious services are conducted in a private home, and the Jewish community maintains its own burial ground. Most of the Jews are prosperous, and their relations with their Muslim neighbors are good.

✦ISRAEL✦

There are no formal ties between Israel and Bahrain.

♦ HISTORY ♦

Jews have lived in Egypt since Biblical times, and the conditions of the community have constantly fluctuated with the political situation of the land. Until the modern age, Egypt was the leading center of Jewish culture and learning in the region.

Israelite tribes first moved to the Land of Goshen (the northeastern edge of the Nile Delta) during the reign of the Egyptian pharaoh Amenhotep IV (1375–1358 B.C.E.). During the reign of Ramses II (1298–1232 B.C.E.), they were enslaved for the Pharaoh's building projects. His successor, Merneptah, continued the same anti-Jewish policies, and around the year 1220 B.C.E., the Jews revolted and escaped across the Sinai to Canaan. This is the biblical Exodus commemorated in the holiday of Passover.

Over the years, many Jews in Eretz Israel who were not deported to Babylon sought shelter in Egypt, among them the prophet Jeremiah. Large-scale immigration began in 332 B.C.E., at the time of Alexander the Great, when Egypt was ruled by the Greeks. For a time, Jews accounted for one-eighth of the population. The Jewish community adopted the Greek language and developed a Hellenized culture that produced great thinkers such as Philo (20 B.C.E.–40 C.E.). At this time, a Greek translation of the Bible, the

The Ben Ezra Synagogue, Cairo

Septuagint, was produced. Synagogues were founded as early as the 3rd century B.C.E. The port city of Alexandria was at that time the greatest city in the Jewish world, and its synagogue was famous for its grandeur. However, during this period, anti-Jewish feeling among the local Greeks produced civil unrest that culminated in the great Jewish revolt of 115 C.E., when the Jewish community was destroyed.

Jewish life continued under Christian rule, but in a depressed state. By the time of the Muslim conquest of Egypt in 640, only a negligible number of Jews remained. A Jewish community, centered in Cairo, soon emerged and attracted many newcomers from other parts of the Middle East and from Spain. Jews prospered during this period and produced a number of religious and cultural figures. The most prominent of these was Moses Maimonides, the Rambam (1135–1204), who spent much of his life in Cairo as a Jewish scholar and as chief physician to the sultan. With the arrival of Maimonides, the Karaites, who composed the majority of the community, lost their leadership role among the Jews. Maimonides served as *nagid* of the Egyptian Jewish community, a position that was created two centuries earlier. The Maimonides family maintained this appointment until the 14th century.

♦

Over the years, the community was augmented by Spanish Jews seeking refuge from the Inquisition and by settlers from other parts of North Africa. By the 17th century, there were three distinct communities: the Mustaravim (native Arabic-speaking Jews), the Spanish immigrants, and the Maghrebim (primarily from Morocco and Algeria). Under the Turks, the Jewish community stagnated culturally due to economic hardship and authoritative rule. Yet, in 1768, with the independence of Egypt and the growing prosperity of the country, the community was once more rejuvenated. By 1897 there were more than 25,000 Jews in Egypt, concentrated in Cairo and Alexandria. In 1937 the population reached a peak of 63,500.

In 1945, with the rise of Egyptian nationalism and the cultivation of anti-Western and anti-Jewish sentiment, riots erupted. In the violence, 10 Jews were killed, 350 injured, and a synagogue, a Jewish hospital, and an old-age home were burned down. The establishment of the State of Israel led to still further anti-Jewish feeling: 2,000 Jews were arrested and many had their property confiscated. Rioting over the next few months resulted in many more Jewish deaths. Under these circumstances, most Egyptian Jews fled the country, and the majority settled in Israel. In the wake of the Sinai Campaign, a war that again resulted in rioting and the arrest of Jews, the community declined considerably. By 1957 it had fallen to 15,000. In 1967, after the Six-Day War, there was a renewed wave of persecution, and the community dropped to 2,500.

By the 1970s, after the remaining Jews were given permission to leave the country, the community dwindled to a few families.

Jewish rights were finally restored in 1979 after President Anwar Sadat signed the Camp David Accords with Israel. Only then was the community allowed to establish ties with Israel and with world Jewry. The majority of Jews reside in Cairo, but there are still a handful in Alexandria. In addition there are about 15 Karaites in the community. Nearly all the Jews are elderly, and the community is on the verge of extinction.

✦COMMUNAL AND RELIGIOUS LIFE✦

Shaar Hashamayim is the only functioning synagogue in Cairo. Of the many synagogues in Alexandria only the Eliahu Hanabi is open for worship.

✦ISRAEL✦

Since the signing of the peace treaty in 1979, Israel and Egypt have maintained diplomatic relations with an Israeli embassy in Cairo and a consulate general in Alexandria. Israel also has a government tourist office and an academic mission in Cairo.

Aliya: Since 1948, 37,518 Egyptian Jews have emigrated to Israel.

✦SITES✦

The 800-year-old Ben Ezra Synagogue in Cairo, the site of the famous Cairo Gnizah, has been restored to its former grandeur.

Embassy
6 Sharia Ibn-El Maleck, Giza, Cairo
Tel. 20 2 361 0528/361 0380
Fax 20 2 361 0414

In 1980, after the Israeli embassy was opened in Cairo, a hall was sought in which the forthcoming Passover holiday could be celebrated and a seder held. Ironically the only place that met the proper requirements was the Pharaoh Hotel.

❖DEMOGRAPHY❖

The Jewish community of Persia, modern-day Iran, is one of the oldest in the Diaspora, and its historical roots reach back to the 6th century B.C.E., the time of the First Temple. Their history in the pre-Islamic period is intertwined with that of the Jews of neighboring Babylon. Cyrus, the first Achaemid emperor, conquered Babylon in 539 B.C.E. and permitted by special decree the return of the Jewish exiles to the Land of Israel; this brought the First Exile to an end. The Jewish colonies were scattered from centers in Babylon to Persian

A man's headgear, Persian Jewish craftsmanship, 19th or 20th century

provinces and cities such as Hamadan and Susa. The books of Esther, Ezra, Nehemiah, and Daniel give a favorable description of the relationship of the Jews to the court of the Achaemids at Susa.

Under the Sassanid dynasty (226–642 C.E.), the Jewish population in Persia grew considerably and spread throughout the region, yet Jews nevertheless suffered intermittent oppression and persecution. The invasion by Arab Muslims in 642 C.E. terminated the independence of Persia, installed Islam as the state religion, and made a deep impact on the Jews by changing their sociopolitical status. Jews were considered inferior to Muslims and received the status of *dhimmi*. Still a wealthy class of Jewish merchants emerged, and from the 10th century, some became financial experts and served as court financiers to the caliphs.

Under the Il-Khan dynasty (1258–1336), the *dhimmi* status was abolished, and Persian Jews were able to rise in power and influence in affairs of state. The Safawid dynasty (1502–1736) introduced Shi'ism as the state religion, and subsequently the Jews, as "nonbelievers," suffered persecution and intense hatred. The latter half of the 17th century was a period of forced conversions to Islam and of the closure of synagogues—a situation that produced the "New Muslims" who secretly continued to be practicing Jews. The Jews of Isfahan assumed the leadership of all Persian Jewry, which was very traditional. At this time, the tradition of pilgrimages to Jewish holy places was widespread, in particular to the legendary mausoleum of Mordechai and Esther in Hamadan and to the tomb of Daniel in Shushan (Susa). Under the Kajar dynasty and until 1925, the Persian Shi'ite attitude to non-Muslim minorities, including the Jews, remained unchanged.

Throughout the 19th century, Jews were persecuted and discriminated against. Sometimes whole communities were forced to convert. Word of the plight of the Jews reached European Jewry, and the British Board of Deputies and the Alliance Israelite Universelle took action on behalf of their unfortunate coreligionists. These organizations petitioned Shah Nasr-ed-Din, on tour in Europe, and he, impressed by their strength and unity,

✦

promised to protect the Jews and allow them to open schools. In 1898 the first Alliance School was opened in Teheran. During the 19th century, there was considerable emigration to the Land of Israel, and the Zionist movement spread throughout the community.

Under the Phalevi Dynasty, established in 1925, the country was secularized and oriented towards the West. This greatly benefited the Jews who were emancipated and played an important role in the economy and in cultural life. On the eve of the Islamic Revolution in 1979, there were 80,000 Jews in Iran, concentrated in Teheran (60,000), Shiraz (8,000), Kermanshah (4,000), Isfahan (3,000), and in the cities of Kuzistahn. In the wake of the upheaval, tens of thousands of Jews, especially the wealthy, left the country, leaving behind vast amounts of property. Most of the Iranian Jews emigrated to the United States (particularly California and New York), Israel, Britain, Italy, France, and Germany. Iranian Jews in exile have established distinctive communities in which many of their unique customs are preserved.

During his voyage to Europe in 1873, Shah Nasr-ed-Din met with British Jewish leaders, including Sir Moses Montefiore. At that time, the Persian statesman suggested that the Jews buy land and establish a state for the Jewish people. This occurred some 20 years before Theodor Herzl wrote Der Judenstaat.

✦COMMUNITY✦

The Council of the Jewish Community, which was established after World War II, is the representative body of the community, which also has in parliament a representative who is obligated by law to support Iranian foreign policy and its anti-Zionist position.

Despite the official distinction between "Jews," "Zionists," and "Israel," the most common accusation the Jews encounter is that of maintaining contacts with Zionists. The Jewish community does enjoy a measure of religious freedom but is faced with constant suspicion of cooperating with the Zionist state and with "imperialistic America"—both such activities being punishable by death. Jews who apply for a passport to travel abroad must do so in a special bureau and are immediately put under surveillance. The Jews again live under the status of *dhimmi*, with the restrictions imposed on religious minorities.

Anti-Jewish sentiments abound, and official publications make regular use of anti-Semitic propaganda such as *The Protocols of the Elders of Zion* and Holocaust denial. Since the establishment of the Khomeini Regime in 1979, some 13 Jews have been executed, the latest victim being Faisallah Mechubad in February 1994. Those who have remained live in a sensitive and unpredictable situation that requires constant vigilance.

✦RELIGIOUS LIFE✦

There are three synagogues in Teheran, but since 1994, there has been no rabbi in Iran, and the *bet din* does not function. There has been a rise in the number of Jews going to the synagogues, which serve as meeting places and offer an atmosphere of security. Kosher food has become expensive and is difficult to obtain. The Jewish cemetery, south of Teheran, is to be demolished for a housing project.

✦CULTURE AND EDUCATION✦

The Islamization of the country has brought about strict control over Jewish educational institutions. Before the revolution, there were some 20 schools functioning throughout the country. In recent years, most of these have been closed down. In the remaining schools, Jewish principals have been replaced by Muslims. In Teheran there are still three schools in which Jewish pupils constitute a majority. The curriculum is Islamic, and the Bible is taught in Persian, not Hebrew. Special

Hebrew lessons are conducted on Fridays by the Orthodox Otzar ha-Torah organization, which is responsible for Jewish religious education. Saturday is no longer officially recognized as the Jewish sabbath, and Jewish pupils are compelled to attend school on that day.

✦ ISRAEL ✦

Iran severed relations with Israel in 1979 and has subsequently supported many of the Islamic terrorist organizations which target Jews and Israelis.

Aliya: Since 1948, 76,244 Iranian Jews have emigrated to Israel.

✦ SITES ✦

According to local Jewish tradition, the tombs of Queen Esther and Mordechai are located in Hamadan. The tomb of Daniel in Shushan is venerated by both Jews and Muslims.

Orchestra of the Alliance School in Hamadan, 1947

♦HISTORY♦

The Iraqi Jewish community is one of the oldest in the world and has a great history of learning and scholarship. Abraham, the first Jew and the father of the Jewish people, was born in Ur of the Chaldees, in southern Iraq, around 2,000 B.C.E. The community traces its history back to 6th century B.C.E., when Nebuchadnezzar conquered Judea and sent most of the population into exile in Babylonia. Fifty years later they were permitted to return home, yet many chose to remain. Jews lived under favorable conditions through the 1st century C.E. In 20 C.E., two brothers, Anilai and Asinai, even established on the upper Euphrates an independent Jewish kingdom that survived for 20 years.

In the beginning of the 2nd century C.E., the community rose in revolt against the Romans and succeeded in temporarily capturing the town of Mahoza, although it suffered many losses. Yet overall a peaceful atmosphere prevailed under the leadership of the Jewish exilarchs, who claimed descent from the house of David. The community was granted a significant amount of internal autonomy under both the Persians and the Arabs, who conquered the area in 634.

The community also maintained strong ties with the Land of Israel and, with the aid of rabbis from Israel, succeeded in establishing many prominent rabbinical academies. By the 3rd century, Babylonia became the center of Jewish scholarship, as is attested to by the community's most influential creation, the Babylonian Talmud. The prestige of these academies continued through the 11th century, and famous *gaonim*, such as Abbaye (278–338), Saadiah Gaon (882–942), and Sherira (906–1006), attracted students from many different countries.

Under Muslim rule, beginning in the 7th century, the situation of the community fluctuated. Many Jews held high positions in government or prospered in commerce and trade. At the same time, Jews were subjected to special taxes, restrictions on their professional activity, and anti-Jewish incitement among the masses. Still the Jewish community continued to expand, and by the 8th century, there was a trend towards urbanization, with much of the population moving to the new capital city of Baghdad and to other towns. Iraq came under Persian and then Turkish rule beginning in the 16th century. Once again the situation of the community was dependent on the whims of the ruler. Jews remained fairly prosperous, continuing to engage in trade, commerce, and the professions.

Under British rule, which began in 1917, Jews fared well economically, and many were elected to government posts. This traditionally observant community was also allowed to found Zionist organizations and to pursue Hebrew studies. All of this progress ended when Iraq gained independence in 1932. Discriminatory laws were instituted, and persecution peaked in 1941, when 170 Jews were killed and hundreds injured in a pogrom during the German-backed revolt against the British. There were further riots in 1946.

Although emigration was prohibited, many Jews made their way to Israel during this period with the aid of an underground movement. In 1950 the Iraqi parliament finally legalized emigration to Israel, and between May 1950 and August 1951, the Jewish Agency and the Israeli government succeeded

Brass Chanukah lamp, Baghdad, 18th century

in airlifting approximately 110,000 Jews to Israel in Operations Ezra and Nehemiah. This figure includes 18,000 Kurdish Jews, who have many distinct traditions. Thus a community that had reached a peak of 150,000 in 1947 dwindled to a mere 6,000 after 1951.

Persecutions continued, especially after the Six-Day War in 1967, when many of the remaining 3,000 Jews were arrested and dismissed from their jobs. In 1969 eleven Jews accused of spying for Israel were publicly hanged, but due to the public outcry that followed, those Jews who wished were given the opportunity to emigrate.

✦COMMUNAL AND RELIGIOUS LIFE✦

One synagogue still functions in Baghdad. The synagogue committee is the only organization serving the community. Contacts with Jews in other countries are sporadic.

✦ISRAEL✦

Iraq is officially in a state of war with Israel. During the Persian Gulf War of 1991, Israel came under repeated Iraqi Scud missile attack.

Aliya: Since 1948, 129,539 Jews from Iraq have emigrated to Israel; 123,371 of these between 1948 and 1951.

✦

The Jews of Kurdistan can claim a unique scholar and religious leader: Asenath Barazani, who lived in the late 16th and early 17th centuries. The daughter of a rabbi, Barazani studied alongside her father from an early age. Her husband inherited her father's position as the community rabbi and head of the yeshiva. Upon his death, Barazani took over these positions. Sages from around the country wrote to the female rabbi and rosh yeshiva for advice concerning religious matters, and she herself wrote an interpretation of the Book of Proverbs. Unfortunately, that work has been lost to history.

LEBANON

GP 3,084,000 ✦ JP 20

✦HISTORY✦

Jews have lived in Lebanon since ancient times. According to tradition, in the 1st century C.E., King Herod the Great had a temple constructed in the city of Tyre for his Jewish subjects living there and also supported the Jewish community in Beirut. The community grew, and by the 6th century, synagogues had been built in both Beirut and Tripoli. In the late 18th and 19th centuries, Jews mainly settled in villages in Lebanon, and most Jewish communities were interspersed with those of the Druze; the two groups generally maintained cordial relations. During this period, Jews sometimes suffered under Maronite rule from persecution and blood libels.

During the first half of the current century, the community expanded tremendously due

Entrance to the Magen Avraham Synagogue, Beirut, 1982

to immigration from Greece and Turkey, and later from Syria and Iraq. Members of the community held important positions in banking and finance. In 1944 the community numbered more than 6,000, and with the subsequent wave of immigration from Syria, the population continued to increase. By 1952 the population reached more than 10,000, making Lebanon the only Arab country in which the Jewish community increased after 1948. This continued immigration resulted from Lebanon's fairly tolerant attitude, as was evidenced when Lebanon granted residency permits and sometimes even Lebanese citizenship to Jews fleeing persecution in Syria.

Nevertheless, there were incidents of rioting and incitement around the time of the establishment of the State of Israel. This culminated in January 1950, when the Alliance School in Beirut was bombed. For the most part, however, the government protected the community. Only after the Six-Day War and the outbreak of the civil war of 1976 did Jews feel compelled to emigrate en masse. In contrast to their co-religionists in other Arab countries, Lebanese Jews were almost always free to emigrate, and some were permitted to liquidate their property prior to emigration and to expatriate the proceeds.

In the past two decades, the political climate has radicalized, and the remaining Jews are left in a tenuous and vulnerable position. More than 15 years of civil war have seen the establishment of numerous militant Islamic movements that target Jews and Israelis.

◆ COMMUNAL AND RELIGIOUS LIFE ◆

Nearly all of the remaining Jews are in Beirut. Because of the current political situation, Jews are unable to openly practice Judaism. In Beirut there is a committee that represents the community. Prior to 1976, there had been two schools and two synagogues in Beirut, and a school in Sidon.

◆ ISRAEL ◆

Between 1976 and 1982, the PLO occupied an area in southern Lebanon and periodically launched attacks from this location. The Lebanon War was fought by Israel in 1982 in order to destroy this terrorist base. Israel supports the southern Lebanese army, which is mainly composed of local Christians, and continues to maintain a presence in southern Lebanon; skirmishes between the IDF and the radical Islamic movement Hizbollah are frequent occurrences.

Aliya: Since 1948, 4,062 Lebanese Jews have emigrated to Israel.

◆

LIBYA

GP 5,593,000 ♦ JP 5

The first Jewish National Fund Committee, Tripoli, 1915

♦ HISTORY ♦

The Jewish community of Libya traces its origin back to the 3rd century B.C.E. Under Roman rule, Jews prospered. In 73 C.E., a zealot from Israel, Jonathan the Weaver, incited the poor of the community in Cyrene to revolt. The Romans reacted with swift vengeance, murdering him and his followers and executing other wealthy Jews in the community. This revolt foreshadowed that of 115 C.E., which broke out not only in Cyrene, but in Egypt and Cyprus as well. The Jews wreaked tremendous destruction in Cyrene, even demolishing Roman temples. Eventually the Jews were defeated, and the survivors were compelled to flee the country.

Jewish communities slowly re-emerged in various towns around the time of the Arab conquest. The population of Libyan Jewry was also bolstered by refugees from Spain after 1492. Under Turkish rule, the situation of the Jews remained good. Most Jews lived in special Jewish quarters called the *hara*, while members of two villages, Jebel Gharyan and Tigrinna, lived in underground caves. Most of the community worked as craftsmen and peddlers. At the turn of the 20th century, the Jews of Tripoli had four *dayanim* and eight synagogues.

With the Italian occupation of Libya in 1911, the situation remained good and the Jews made great strides in education. At that time, there were about 21,000 Jews in the country, the majority in Tripoli. In the late 1930s, Fascist anti-Jewish laws were gradually enforced, and Jews were subject to terrible repression. Still, by 1941, the Jews accounted for a quarter of the population of Tripoli and maintained 44 synagogues. In 1942 the Germans occupied the Jewish quarter of Benghazi, plundered shops, and deported more than 2,000 Jews across the desert, where more than one-fifth of them perished. Many Jews from Tripoli were also sent to forced labor camps.

Conditions did not greatly improve following the liberation. During the British occupation, there was a series of pogroms, the worst of which, in 1945, resulted in the deaths of more than 100 Jews in Tripoli and other towns and the destruction of five synagogues. Following this tragedy, a Jewish defense organization was established. Thus, in 1948, when Muslims attacked the Jewish quarters in Tripoli and Benghazi, Jews were able to defend themselves. Nevertheless, more than 10 Jews were killed and almost 300 Jewish houses destroyed.

A growing sense of insecurity, coupled with the establishment of the State of Israel, led many Jews to leave the country. Although emigration was illegal, more than 3,000 Jews succeeded in leaving, and many went to Israel. When the British legalized emigration in 1949, more than 30,000 Jews fled Libya. Although Jews were granted civil rights under the independent Libyan regime established in 1952, the atmosphere remained tense. Many Jews left for Italy and elsewhere. Following the anti-Jewish riots that erupted after the Six-Day War, most of the remaining Jews departed.

At the time of Colonel Qaddafi's coup in 1969, some 500 Jews remained in Libya. Qaddafi subsequently confiscated all Jewish property and cancelled all debts owed to Jews. By 1974 there were no more than 20 Jews, and it is believed that the Jewish presence has passed out of existence.

✦ISRAEL✦

Libya vociferously rejects the peace process with Israel.

Aliya: Since 1948, 36,730 Libyan Jews have emigrated to Israel, 30,972 between 1948 and 1951.

✦

In 1948 a group of new olim from Libya arrived in Jaffa and sought a room in which to hold religious services. They came upon a Franciscan monk who led them to an abandoned building, told them that it was a synagogue, and handed them the keys. Inside they found a prayer room and a mikva. Later they learned that the building had been opened in 1740 by the "Constantinople Administrative Committee for Jews in Eretz Israel" as the first Jewish khan (hostel) in Jaffa and had provided lodgings and a place of worship for Jewish pilgrims. In the 19th century, it was abandoned and forgotten. Located on a characteristically narrow, winding street, the restored synagogue continues to serve the Libyan Jewish community in Israel and is a favorite venue for weddings in Old Jaffa.

MOROCCO

GP 27,021,000 ♦ JP 6,500

♦DEMOGRAPHY♦

The Jews of Morocco represent a remnant of an ancient, thriving community that numbered more than a quarter of a million in 1956. Today the largest community is in Casablanca, home to 5,000 Jews. There are small Jewish communities in Rabat (400), Marrakesh (250), Meknes (250), Tangier (150), Fez (150), and Tetuan (100). The Jews are generally descended from three different groups: Sephardim, Berber Jews, and Ashkenazim.

♦HISTORY♦

The Jewish community of present-day Morocco dates back more than 2,000 years. There were Jewish colonies in the country before it became a Roman province. Under the Romans, the Jews enjoyed civic equality. In 429

the Vandal King Genserich conquered North Africa. In the 7th century, many Jews fled Visigothic Spain and introduced modern culture, industry, and commerce. Several Berber tribes adopted Judaism and controlled a vast area, but they were eventually subdued by Arab invaders. The Jews lived in peace until the 11th century.

In a 1033 pogrom in Fez, thousands of Jews were murdered and the women were dragged off into slavery. When the liberal Almoravids came to power in 1062, conditions for Jews improved, but when the Almohades took over in the middle of the 12th century, Jews were forced to embrace Islam or to emigrate. It was during that time that Jews were forced to wear a particular costume—a precursor of the Jewish badge. After the ouster of the Almohades in

Interior of the Sa'adon Synagogue, Fez

the 14th century, the situation of Jews stabilized.

In 1391 a wave of Jewish refugees expelled from Spain brought new life to the community, as did new arrivals from Spain and Portugal in 1492 and 1497. From 1438, the Jews of Fez were forced to live in special quarters called *mellahs*, a name derived from the Arabic word for salt because the Jews in Morocco were forced to carry out the job of salting the heads of executed prisoners prior to their public display. Under Muslim rule, Jews had the status of *dhimmi*, protected vassals.

The condition of the Jews did not improve until the establishment of the French Protectorate in 1912, when they were given equality and religious autonomy. However, during World War II, when France was ruled by the anti-Semitic Vichy government, King Muhammed V prevented the deportation of Jews from Morocco. By 1948 there were some 270,000 Jews in Morocco. In an atmosphere of uncertainty and grinding poverty, many Jews elected to leave for Israel, France, the United States, and Canada. When Morocco gained independence in 1956, Jews became Moroccan citizens and were given equal rights and freedom of movement. However, legislation restricted their right to emigrate. Largely thanks to intervention by the WJC, the government allowed Moroccan Jews to leave. In the aftermath of the Six-Day War, the conditions worsened, and many middle-class Jews left the country.

✦ C O M M U N I T Y ✦

The major Jewish organization representing the community is the Conseil des Communautes Israelites in Casablanca. Its functions include external relations, general communal affairs, communal heritage, finance, maintenance of holy places, youth activities, and cultural and religious life. There are also regional committees that deal with the religious and social welfare needs of the community. The welfare organization in Casablanca is responsible for medical aid to the needy and for hot meals for underprivileged Jewish pupils.

Today most members of the community belong to the upper middle class and enjoy a comfortable economic status. Some have served as special advisors to the king or as ministers. In the 1993 elections, four Jews were included in the list of 2,042 candidates for the 330 seats of the Moroccan parliament. The existence in Israel of a vibrant Jewish community that maintains its Moroccan heritage forms a living bridge between the two countries.

Generally there are few expressions of anti-Semitism in the government and in the media, but anti-Semitic motives have been used to express anti-Israel sentiment on specific events. The rise of Islamic fundamentalist elements has initiated some anti-Jewish activity in Morocco.

The Jews no longer reside in the traditional Jewish *mellahs*, but intermarriage is almost unknown. The community has always been religious and tolerant, and religious extremism of any form never developed. The younger generation prefers to continue its higher education abroad and tends not to return to Morocco. Thus the community is in a process of aging.

✦ R E L I G I O U S   L I F E ✦

There are synagogues, *mikvaot*, old-age homes, and kosher restaurants in Casablanca,

> *According to Jewish tradition, a beautiful 16-year-old girl named Solika was coveted by the Muslim ruler. She refused to marry him or to convert to Islam, and he had her stoned to death. Her martyrdom is venerated by the community, and the mausoleum of Solika the Righteous at the Jewish cemetery of Fez is a place of pilgrimage.*

Visitors to the tomb of Rabbis David and Moshe, Atlas Mountains

Fez, Marrakesh, Mogador, Rabat, Tetuan and Tangier. The Jewish community developed a fascinating tradition of rituals and pilgrimages to the tombs of holy sages. There are 13 such famous sites, centuries old, well kept by Muslims. Every year on special dates, crowds of Moroccan Jews from around the world, including Israel, throng to these graves. A unique Moroccan festival, the Mimunah, is celebrated in Morocco and in Israel.

✦ CULTURE AND EDUCATION ✦

In 1992 most of the Jewish schools were closed down and only those in Casablanca—the Chabad, ORT, Alliance, and Otzar Ha-Torah schools—have remained active. Alongside some 1,700 Jewish pupils, Muslims account for 30% of the student body. The Chabad movement also runs a youth movement called Ufaratzta. Religious education is given in the Lycee Yeshiva, *Kollel* of Casablanca, and in the Lycee Seminaire of Rabat. Since 1963, there has been no Jewish newspaper in Morocco.

✦ ISRAEL ✦

There are close ties between Israel and this Arab country, symbolized by the formal visit of Prime Minister Yitzhak Rabin to Morocco immediately after signing the agreement with the PLO in 1993.

Aliya: Since 1948, 295,833 Moroccan Jews have emigrated to Israel.

✦ SITES ✦

In addition to the Jewish communities, the major sites of pilgrimage for the Jewish traveler are the tombs of the holy sages, scattered around the country. The most popular are Rabbi Yehouda Benatar (Fez), Rabbi Chaim Pinto (Mogador), Rabbi Amram Ben Diwane (Ouezzan), and Rabbi Yahia Lakhdar (Beni-Ahmed).

Conseil des Communautes Israelites du Marcoc
Rue Abou Abdallah—Al Mahassibi
Casablanca
Tel. 212 2 22 28 61, Fax 212 2 26 69 53

Liaison Office
52 Boulevard Mehdi Ben-Barka
Souissi, Rabat
Tel. 212 7 657 680, Fax 212 7 657 683

Page from the Aleppo Codex, illustrated by Avraham Shemi

♦DEMOGRAPHY♦

The last Jews who wanted to leave Syria departed with the chief rabbi in October 1994. Prior to 1947, there were some 30,000 Jews made up of three distinct communities, each with its own traditions: the Kurdish-speaking Jews of Kamishli, the Jews of Aleppo with roots in Spain, and the original eastern Jews of Damascus, called *Must'arab*. Today only a tiny remnant of these communities remains.

♦HISTORY♦

The Jewish presence in Syria dates back to biblical times and is intertwined with the history of Jews in neighboring Eretz Israel. Rabbis were given equal legal status as their peers in Israel. The area was considered to be similar so that Halachic statutes "pertaining to the land" were often applied to Syria.

With the advent of Christianity, restrictions were imposed on the community. The

♦

Arab conquest in 636 C.E., however, greatly improved the lot of the Jews. Unrest in neighboring Iraq in the 10th century resulted in Jewish migration to Syria and brought about a boom in commerce, banking, and crafts. During the reign of the Fatimids, the Jew Menashe Ibrahim El-Kazzaz ran the Syrian administration, and he granted Jews positions in the government. During the 11th century, Jews were concentrated in Damascus, Aleppo, and Tyre, and they produced many scholars, among them Baruch Ben Isaac, and poets who wrote in Hebrew.

The Mamluk period (1260–1516) was a difficult period for the Jews, and many were forced to convert to Islam. When the country was taken over by the Ottomans, the lot of the Jews improved markedly. A large influx of Spanish Jews arrived in Syria, mainly from Italy and Turkey.

The infamous Damascus Blood Libel of 1840 was the first of its kind in the Muslim Arab world: the Jews were accused of killing a Catholic priest who had disappeared and of using his blood for the Passover matzot. Only foreign political intervention, together with international Jewish advocacy, liberated the Jews arrested on the false accusation. During the latter half of the 19th century, the quality of Jewish life greatly improved, and Syrian rulers were quite often dependent on the financial backing of Jewish bankers, such as the Farhi and Sama'ias families.

Syrian Jewry supported the aspirations of the Arab nationalists and Zionism, and Syrian Jews believed that the two parties could be reconciled and that the conflict in Palestine could be resolved. Consequently, they contributed to the dialogue between representatives of JAFI and Syrian nationalists.

The Great Synagogue in Aleppo, rebuilt and enlarged in the 15th century, destroyed by anti-Jewish rioters in 1947. Model in Beth Hatefutsoth

However, following Syrian independence from France in 1946, attacks against Jews and their property increased, culminating in the pogroms of 1947, which left all shops and synagogues in Aleppo in ruins. Thousands of Jews fled the country, and their homes and property were taken over by the local Muslims. After the establishment of the State of Israel, several anti-Jewish laws were passed in Syria that prohibited the sale of Jewish property and that froze Jewish bank accounts. A great deal of the property was confiscated by the Syrian authorities and was thereafter transferred to Palestinian ownership. Jewish movement was greatly curtailed, and Jews were obliged to report to the secret police situated in the Jewish quarter.

In 1954 some Jews were permitted to leave on the condition that they relinquish their property. In 1964 the situation worsened, and Jews were forbidden to move beyond a three-kilometer distance from their city. Following the exposure of the Israeli spy Eli Cohen and the Six-Day War, the situation only deterio-rated. Waves of violence erupted, and Jews were attacked, arrested, and murdered. In 1968 there were an estimated 4,500 Jews living in Syria; 3,700 in Damascus; 700 in Aleppo; and 100 in Kamishli.

For the next decades, Syrian Jews were, in effect, hostages of a hostile regime. They could leave Syria only on the condition that they leave members of their family behind. Thus the community lived under siege, constantly under fearful surveillance of the secret police. This much was allowed due to an international effort to secure the human rights of the Jews, the changing world order, and the Syrian need for Western support; so the conditions of the Jews improved somewhat.

✦ C O M M U N I T Y ✦

Prior to the initiation of the peace process in the Middle East, the Syrian Jewish community was deprived of many basic human and civil rights. All means of communication— mail, telephones, and telegrams—were constantly monitored by the secret police, and Jews were often apprehended without

---

The Aleppo Codex, called in Hebrew Keter Aram Zobah, *is the earliest-known manuscript comprising the full text of the Bible. The text was verified and vocalized by Aaron Ben-Asher. According to tradition, this was the manuscript consulted by Maimonides when he set down the exact rules for writing Torah scrolls. According to recent research, it might very well be that Maimonides sanctified and codified everything he found in the Aleppo Codex. The codex was copied by the scribe Shlomo Ben-Buya'a in the Land of Israel more than 1,000 years ago. Soon after, it was moved to Egypt and was finally deposited with the Aleppo community at the end of the 14th century. The Codex was kept in a vault in the Cave of Elijah, under the Yellow Synagogue of Aleppo, and closely guarded as the talisman of the community for more than 600 years. When the synagogue was put to the torch in 1947, the codex was saved and hidden for ten years. In 1957 it was entrusted to Mordechai Faham, who smuggled the remains out of Syria. In 1958 it was brought to Jerusalem and was presented to President Yitzhak Ben-Zvi. Today the codex is housed in the Ben-Zvi Institute. Of the original 487 leaves of the codex, only about 295 remain. They are a priceless heirloom of the Jewish people.*
The Aleppo Codex is probably the most authoritative, accurate, and sacred source document, both for the biblical text and for its vocalization and cantillation. It has greater religious and scholarly import than any other manuscript of the Bible.

warrants. The major abuse of their human rights was their almost non-existent freedom of movement. They were forbidden to leave the country unless for special business or medical purposes, and then, too, permits were issued only upon submission of huge sums of money. Property and family served as collateral to ensure a swift return. Those who attempted to flee across the borders illegally were usually caught, arrested, and cruelly tortured in the dungeons of the secret police.

The plight of Syrian Jewry became an international human rights issue in the mid-1970s. The United States, Canada, and France played leading roles in the efforts to bring justice to the community. The situation was especially difficult, since the community was almost totally isolated.

At the G'amalia Synagogue, Haleb, 1990

The Madrid Conference in 1992 was the turning point for the Jewish community. American and Israeli pressure succeeded in convincing the Syrian government to declare that Jews could leave freely. At first this was on condition that the Jews would not travel to Israel. Subsequently, in 1992 and 1993, some 2,600 Syrian Jews went to the United States, where there was already a well-organized and supportive Syrian community that welcomed them. Since 1992 nearly all of the Jews have left; 3,565 emigrated to the United States and the rest to Israel.

✦ISRAEL✦

Ever since 1948, Syria has continuously led extreme Arab opposition to the existence of the State of Israel, promoting and supporting hostile and terrorist actions of militant organizations concentrated in Lebanon. Syria is still listed by the U.S. State Department as a terrorist-sponsoring country.

Aliya: Since 1948, 10,250 Syrian Jews have emigrated to Israel.

✦SITES✦

The Joab Ben Zeruiah Synagogue of Aleppo, also known as the Yellow Synagogue, has a history spanning 1,500 years. The synagogue was built on the site of the holy cave of the prophet Elijah, and it is one of the few synagogues that has seven arks and a permanent outdoor *bima* (called a *tevah*) that was used for prayers in the courtyard. Although the synagogue was built by the Musta'arab Jews, when the refugees from Spain joined the community in the 16th century, a separate, adjacent wing was constructed. Over the years, as the two communities integrated, the wings were combined. In the pogrom of 1947, the interior of the synagogue was severely damaged by fire. In the mid-1970s, the Syrian Jewish community in Brooklyn, New York, was permitted to fund its restoration. However, in the mid-1980s, as the community dwindled, the synagogue was closed down, and it remains locked to the present day.

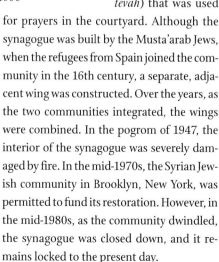

TUNISIA

GP 9,156,000 ♦ JP 1,900

♦ DEMOGRAPHY ♦

The largest communities are in Tunis and on the island of Djerba (Hara Keriba and Hara Sghira). There are also approximately 200 Jews living in the Sousse-Monastir region on the Gulf of Mammamet.

♦ HISTORY ♦

The origins of Tunisian Jewry, like those of the Jewish communities of other Middle Eastern countries, are shrouded in mystery. According to some legends, Jews first settled in the southeast, on the island of Djerba, around King Solomon's time. Others claim that many Jews fleeing Israel after the destruction of the First Temple sought refuge in the land that is now Tunisia. Some Tunisian Jews believe that in 70 C.E., the *kohanim* carried one of the Temple doors to Djerba and that it remains there, concealed in the El Ghirba Synagogue.

The first documented evidence of Jews in this area dates back to 200 C.E. and demonstrates the existence of a community in Latin Carthage under Roman rule. Latin Carthage contained a significant Jewish presence, and several sages mentioned in the Talmud lived in this area from the 2nd to the 4th centuries. Jews fared well under the Romans. Many worked in agriculture, while others were involved in transport and commerce with Rome. The community continued to increase both as a result of immigration and missionary activity.

During the Byzantine period, the condition of the community took a turn for the worse. An edict issued by Justinian in 535 excluded Jews from public office, prohibited Jewish practice, and resulted in the transformation of synagogues into churches. Many fled to the Berber communities in the mountains and in the desert. After the Arab conquest of Tunisia in the 7th century, Jews lived under satisfactory conditions, despite discriminatory measures such as a poll tax. The community particularly benefited from an atmosphere of economic prosperity and intellectual activity. Kairoun, the center of the empire, became the nucleus of Jewish life, with numerous respected *yeshivot*. During Gaonic times, the city became the center of Jewish learning in the West and its leader acquired the title of *nagid*. Jewish merchants played a leading role in trade with neighboring countries. Despite their second-class status as *dhimmis*, many of the Jews prospered and this period is considered the golden age of Tunisian Jewry.

This prosperity came to an end after invasions of Arabs and Christians during the 11th century. Jews were the victims of many repres-

> *Tunisian cuisine is best known for couscous, which is made from semolina. This coarse wheat flour, rich in gluten, was first mentioned in the Bible. In Western countries, semolina is mainly used for puddings and hot cereals. In Tunisia and other parts of North Africa, however, Jews have carried on the tradition of semolina-based cooking for centuries. Couscous and ma'amoul (filled semolina cakes) represent contrasts in the use of this grain. Couscous has traditionally been eaten with mutton, lamb, or fish. Today Tunisian Jews also eat it with beef and chicken, adapting themselves to the diet of the various countries in which they settled.*

sive measures, including a ban that prohibited them from living in Kairouan, which was now considered a Muslim holy city (this ban was removed only at the end of the 19th century). Repression intensified during the reign of the Almohads in the 12th century, and many Jews were forced to convert to Islam. Conditions slightly improved during Hafsid rule (1228–1534), and some Jews were allowed to resume their roles in trade and commerce and were protected from violence. However, they were still subject to special taxes and were required to wear distinguishing garments.

Conditions worsened during the Spanish invasions of 1535–1574, resulting in the flight of Jews from the coastal areas. The situation of the community improved once more under Ottoman rule. During this period, the community also split due to strong cultural differences between the Touransa (native Tunisians) and the Grana (those adhering to Spanish or Italian customs). This latter group was composed of Jews from the port of Leghorn in Italy, Jews of Spanish and Sicilian ori-

gin, and newcomers from Algeria and Morocco. Officially this division lasted only until 1899, although in reality it continued well into the 20th century.

Improvements in the condition of the community occurred during the reign of Ahmed Bey, which began in 1837. He and his successors implemented liberal legislation, and a large number of Jews rose to positions of political power during this reign. The Fundamental Pact of 1857 was thus promulgated, repealing all discriminatory laws. During this period, most Jews lived in tremendous poverty in ghettos, while those in southern Tunisia and Djerba lived more comfortably.

Under French rule, Jews were gradually emancipated. However, beginning in November 1940, when the country was ruled by the Vichy authorities, Jews were subject to anti-Semitic laws. From November 1942 until May 1943, the country was occupied by German forces. During that time, the condition of the Jews deteriorated further, and many were deported to labor camps and had their property seized.

The traditional Lag BaOmer celebration at the El Ghirba Synagogue in Djerba, 1981

Jews suffered once more in 1956, when the country achieved independence. The rabbinical tribunal was abolished in 1957, and a year later, Jewish community councils were dissolved. In addition, the Jewish quarter of Tunis was destroyed by the government. Anti-Jewish rioting followed the outbreak of the Six-Day War; Muslims burned down the Great Synagogue of Tunis. While the community was compensated for the damage, these events increased the steady stream of emigration. The community's sense of security was further shaken in 1985, when a security guard opened fire on Jews leaving the Djerba synagogue, and several were killed. As a result of all these persecutions, the community diminished from 105,000 in 1949 to 8,000 in 1973.

✦ COMMUNAL AND RELIGIOUS LIFE ✦

Each community is headed by a government-appointed committee. The community also has two homes for the aged. There are five officiating rabbis: the chief rabbi in Tunis, a rabbi in Djerba, and four others in Tunis and other communities and there are several kosher restaurants as well. The majority of the community observes the laws of *kashrut*.

✦ CULTURE AND EDUCATION ✦

Djerba has one kindergarten. There are six primary schools (three located in Tunis, two in Djerba, and one in the coastal city of Zarzis) and four secondary schools (two in Tunis and two in Djerba). There are also *yeshivot* in Tunis and in Djerba.

✦ ISRAEL ✦

In comparison to its Arab neighbors, Tunisia has remained fairly moderate in its stance toward Israel. This was true even when the PLO had its headquarters in Tunis. Especially since the Israeli–Palestinian Declaration of Principles in September 1993, relations between the two countries have improved. An Israeli delegation recently visited Tunisia, and representatives of both countries have conducted talks concerning tourism.

Aliya: Since 1948, 53,068 Jews from Tunisia have immigrated to Israel.

✦ SITES ✦

Many tourists come to visit Djerba's El Ghirba Synagogue in the village of Hara Sghira. Although the present structure was built in 1929, it is believed there has been a continuously used synagogue on the site for the past 1,900 years.

Tunisian Jews have many unique and colorful rituals and celebrations, including the annual pilgrimage to Djerba which takes place during Lag BaOmer. The Bardo Museum in Tunis contains an exhibit dealing exclusively with Jewish ritual objects.

✦

TURKEY

GP 61,797,000 ✦ JP 20,000

✦DEMOGRAPHY✦

The great majority of the Jews live in Istanbul. There are also communities in Izmir (2,300) and about 100 Jews in Ankara, Bursa, and Adana. The community is 96% Sephardi. Most members of the Jewish community earn their living as industrialists, artisans, and traders. There are also many in the free professions and in engineering. About 100 Karaites live in Turkey, but for the most part, they do not consider themselves a part of the Jewish community and do not take any part in its activities.

✦HISTORY✦

Relics of Jewish settlement in Anatolia from the 4th century B.C.E. have been unearthed in the Aegean region, making the Jewish community in Turkey one of the old-

Morning services at a synagogue in Ankara

est in the world. The historian Flavius Josephus claimed that Aristotle "met Jewish people, with whom he had an exchange of views during his trip across Asia Minor." Ruins have also been discovered in Sardis, Bursa, and Ankara. In the 4th century C.E., the Roman Empire was divided, and the eastern half, known as the Byzantine Empire, had its capital in Byzantium (later known as Constantinople). The Byzantine Empire attracted many Jews from economically depressed Palestine. It was the first Christian

state, and it set a precedent by enacting legislation to regulate relations between the state and the Jews. The institutionalized inferior position of the Jews notwithstanding, Jewish religious and communal life survived and even flourished. Most of the Jews lived in towns, and the main occupations were in branches of the handicrafts and in commerce. Those Jews who lived along the coast played an important role in international commerce.

In general the Jews welcomed the military successes of the Ottomans in the 14th and 15th centuries. When the Ottomans captured Bursa in 1324, they found a Jewish community that had been persecuted during long centuries of Byzantine rule. Over the next decades, the country became a haven for Jews fleeing repression and expulsion from various parts of Europe, including Hungary, France, Spain, Sicily, Salonika, and Bavaria. Ottomans greatly encouraged Jewish immigration, and the Jews responded with their feet. The reign of Sultan Murad II (1421–1451) marked the beginning of two centuries of Jewish prosperity in Turkey. When Muhammed II finally overran Constantinople in 1453, the Romaniot (Byzantine) Jewish community hailed him as a liberator who freed Jews from the yoke of

✦

Christian rule. The immigration from Spain became a torrent when Spanish and Portuguese Jews were expelled from their homes. These Jews used their international connections and linguistic skills to develop the Ottoman Empire's foreign trade. The sultan is reported to have exclaimed, "I am amazed at the Spanish king's reputation for being astute. By expelling the Jews, he has impoverished his own country and enriched mine."

In the liberal atmosphere of Ottoman rule, Jewish activity flourished and many Jews held important positions. Constantinople was the home of great rabbis and scholars and was a Hebrew book-printing center.

However, the community began to ebb in the 17th century, reflecting the decay of Turkish society and of the country's international position. Moreover, Jews were often scapegoated for the declining fortunes of the empire. In the 19th century, conditions for Jews improved somewhat, but economic hardship compelled many Jews to emigrate. The majority settled in the Americas.

The militantly secular regime that emerged out of Turkey's debacle in World War I was bitterly opposed to religious teaching. As a result, Hebrew was banned until the death of Turkish leader Kemal Ataturk in 1938. Jews were hit hard by various taxes, and

Jewish girls at a costume party in Istanbul, 1925

their economic situation deteriorated. Consequently, many Turkish Jews elected to seek their fortunes elsewhere and joined existing Turkish Jewish communities in North and Latin America and in the Land of Israel. During World War II, pro-Axis sentiment was strong and the position of the Jewish community uncertain. This, however, dissipated after the defeat of the Germans. In 1992 the community celebrated the 500th anniversary of the arrival of the first Sephardim.

⋄COMMUNITY⋄

The Jewish community of Turkey is recognized by the state through its chief rabbinate. At its head is the *haham bashi*, as the chief rabbi is called. The community operates hospitals in Istanbul and in Izmir and also several homes for the aged. There are several youth and family social clubs, and some of these include libraries, sports facilities, and even discotheques.

⋄RELIGIOUS LIFE⋄

There are 17 synagogues in Istanbul, all but one of which are Sephardi. There are ten synagogues in Izmir and one each in the remaining communities. These are served by five rabbis and cantors, all of whom reside in Istanbul or Izmir. Kosher meat is produced in Istanbul and in Izmir. Although the synagogues are Orthodox, most people tend toward Conservative religious observance.

⋄CULTURE AND EDUCATION⋄

Istanbul and Izmir have one Jewish school each. Talmud Torah courses are also provided. A weekly newspaper in Turkish and Ladino called *Shalom* and a monthly journal in Turkish called *Tiryaki* keep the Jews informed.

⋄ISRAEL⋄

Israel and Turkey have full diplomatic relations. In addition to the embassy in Ankara, Israel maintains a consulate in Istanbul.

Aliya: Since 1948, 61,221 Turkish Jews have emigrated to Israel.

⋄SITES⋄

The Ahrida Synagogue in Istanbul dates from the early 15th century. Its most outstanding feature is its *bima*, built to resemble the prow of a ship. Traditions says that its builder was inspired by Noah's ark or by the ships that brought to Turkey Jews fleeing Spain. Nearly destroyed by fire in the late 17th century, an imperial decree called for its immediate reconstruction. Turkey is also the site of synagogue ruins dating back to the 2nd century B.C.E.

Chief Rabbinate of Turkey
Yemenici Sokak 23—Beyoglu, Istanbul
Tel. 90 212 244 8794, Fax 90 212 244 1980

Embassy
Mahatma Gandhi Sok. 85, Ankara
Tel. 90 312 446 3605, Fax 90 312 426 1533

⋄

Gracia Mendes (1510–1569) was one of Jewish history's great women of valor. Born to a Converso family in Portugal and widowed at age 26. Mendes settled first in Antwerp and later in Ferrara, where she headed an "underground railway" that expedited the escape of Conversos from Spain and Portugal and helped them transfer their wealth. Later she moved to Constantinople, where she became one of the city's largest shipowners. Mendes soon became the city's most prominent Jewish personage and greatest patron of Jewish learning, and every day Mendes fed some 80 paupers in her stately residence. When the Jews of Ancona, Italy, were imprisoned and killed by the Inquisition authorities, despite a papal promise to shield them from persecution, Mendes persuaded the sultan to intervene. Supported by Rabbi Joseph Caro, she led an international effort to boycott Ancona. The boycott failed, but Gracia Mendes had set an example for future generations.

YEMEN

GP 15,678,000 ✦ JP 500

✦DEMOGRAPHY✦

The remaining community is concentrated in northern Yemen. It is comprised of the Yahood Al-Maghrib (Western Jews) and the Yahood Al-Mashrag (Eastern Jews). These Jews mostly live in villages in the vicinity of Saada, which is located in Sa'ata Province, close to the Saudi border. The community is extremely insular.

✦HISTORY✦

The Jews of Yemen trace their origins back to biblical times, and the first recorded reference to Yemenite Jews appears in the 3rd century C.E. The community probably arose from the settlement of Jewish traders and merchants and from the arrival of Jewish forces with the Roman troops just

Jewish boy in Saada, northern Yemen, 1983

before the Common Era. Yemen is one of the few countries that has been governed by a Jewish monarch: as King Abu Karib Asad converted to Judaism in the 4th century. Dhu Nuwas, who ruled a century later, also converted, as did many of his subjects.

Jews fared well under Persian rule, but their condition worsened when the country came under Islamic rule. Jewish persecution reached its height during the 10th-century Shi'a reign. These worsening conditions are discussed in Maimonides' *Epistle to Yemen*, written in 1172, in which he tells the Yemenite community to remain faithful despite the persecution. In the following centuries, Jews con-

tinued to suffer from restrictive measures in this war-torn state. Yet some were able to obtain high positions, and thereby also to aid the community. One consequence of this persecution was the rise of numerous false messiahs and messianic movements. Kabbala (Jewish mysticism) also became popular among the Jews, and Shalom Shabbazi, a great Kabbalist poet who wrote in the 17th century, was a product of this environment.

Restrictions continued to be enforced in the 19th century. These included laws forbidding Jews from riding animals, wearing bright colors, or building houses above a certain height. These rules were reinstituted in 1905. In addition, a new law was implemented that required Jewish orphans under 13 years of age to convert to Islam.

On the social ladder, Jews occupied the lowest rung as the only non-Muslims in the country. Yemenite Jewry also suffered from tremendous poverty. Most of the community worked as craftsmen and laborers, earning very little. They were also victims of famines that caused starvation throughout the country.

Due to the worsening conditions, successive waves of Jews began fleeing Yemen in 1882, mainly to the Land of Israel. Despite the fact that the Yemenite ruler, Imam Yahya, forbade emigration to Palestine in 1929, one-third of the Jewish population, or approximately 16,000, made *aliya* between 1919 and 1948. This is the largest percentage of Jews from a single country to emigrate prior to the establishment of the State of Israel. In 1948 Yahya's son and successor eased the ban on emigration and thus allowed for the massive airlift of Jews to Israel. Between May 1949 and September 1950, almost 50,000 Jews were flown to Israel from the Aden Protectorate on more than 400 flights. This airlift was called Operation Magic Carpet and was the model for the later airlift of Ethiopians and of other groups. Almost the entire Yemenite community was thus transferred to Israel.

After intense rioting (100 Jews were killed in 1947) and continued persecution, most of the community of South Yemen also emigrated, many settling in Israel. The remaining members of the South Yemen community were evacuated to Israel and to Britain in June 1967, as a result of rioting that followed the Six-Day War.

The small community that remains in the northern area of Yemen is tolerated and is able to practice Judaism. Its members are still treated as second-class citizens and cannot own land, serve in the army, or be elected to political positions. Most work as artisans and small traders. During the past few years, about 400 Jews have also emigrated to Israel, despite the official ban on emigration.

·COMMUNAL AND RELIGIOUS LIFE·

The Jews are scattered and a communal structure no longer exists. Yemenite Jews have little social interaction with their Muslim neighbors and are largely prevented from communicating with world Jewry.

It is believed that there are two synagogues still functioning in Saiqaya and in Amlah.

Religious life has not changed much in the past few centuries. Jews continue to maintain strict observance of Jewish tradition. To ensure that they adhere to the laws of *kashrut*, Jews are not allowed to eat meals with Muslims. Also, marriage is absolutely forbidden outside of the religion.

·ISRAEL·

Israel and Yemen have no formal ties.

Aliya: Since 1948, 52,000 Jews have emigrated to Israel from Yemen (including Aden), 48,315 of them between 1948 and 1951.

Historians have focused on the first modern immigrants to Eretz Israel who arrived from eastern Europe in 1882, but some have overlooked the immigrants from Yemen who began to arrive a few months earlier. By 1884 there were 450 Yemenite Jews in the country, and that flow of immigration continued in successive decades. Most of the Yemenites settled in Jerusalem, in the vicinity of the Old City, where they reestablished the village of Silwan (Siloam). Unlike the new European immigrants, who were motivated by a desire to reclaim the land and to develop Jewish agriculture, the early Yemenite settlers dominated the building trades, working in quarries as stonecutters, masons, construction laborers, and plasterers. They became independent and financially secure, and by the turn of the century, they were one of the largest Jewish communities in the country.

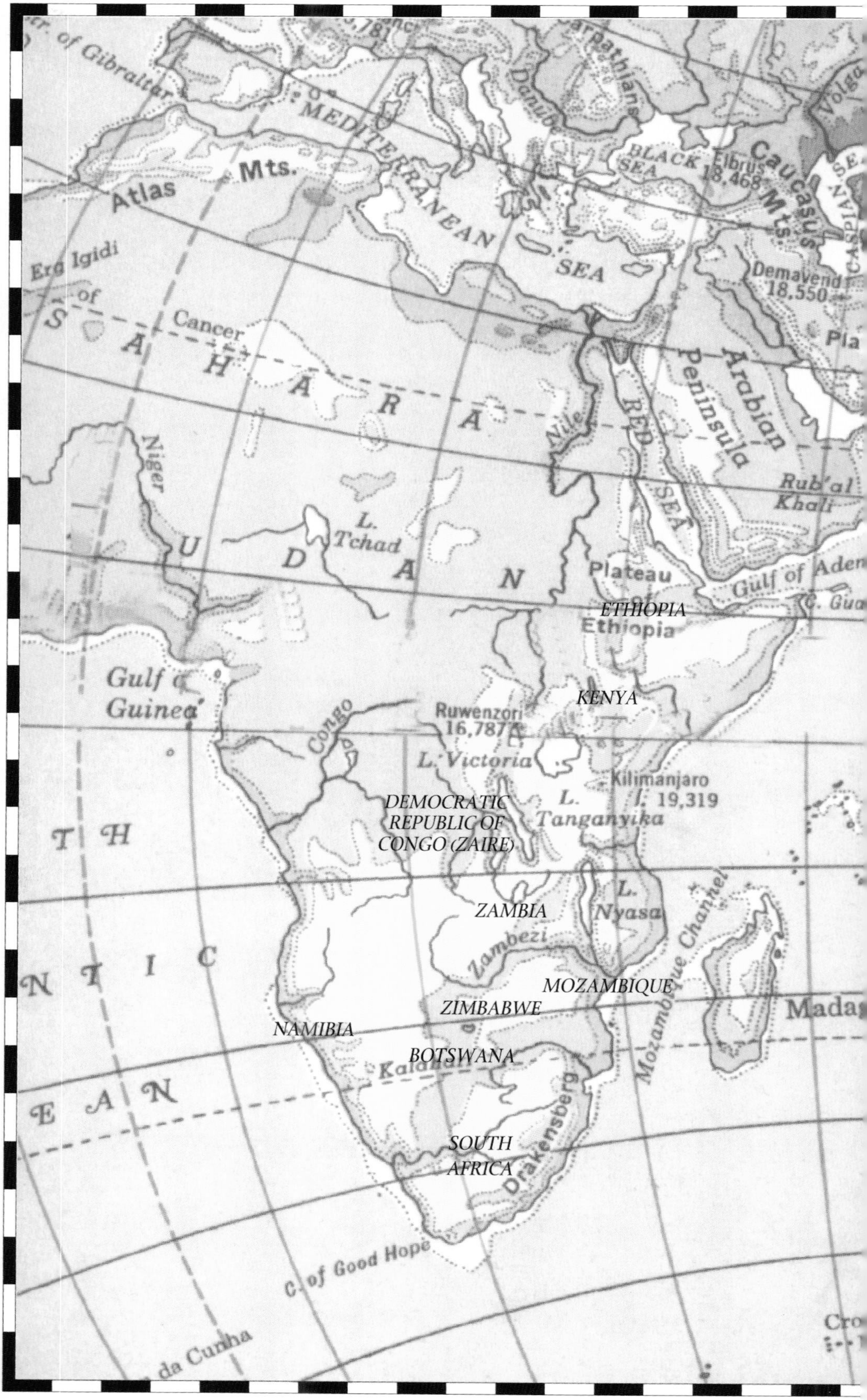

Str. of Gibraltar
Carpathians
Danube
Volga
MEDITERRANEAN SEA
BLACK SEA
Elbrus 18,468
Caucasus Mts.
CASPIAN SEA
Atlas Mts.
Erg Igidi
Demavend 18,550
Tropic of Cancer
SAHARA
Arabian Peninsula
Nile
RED SEA
Niger
Rub' al Khali
L. Tchad
SUDAN
Plateau of Ethiopia
Gulf of Aden
ETHIOPIA
Gulf of Guinea
KENYA
Congo
Ruwenzori 16,787
L. Victoria
Kilimanjaro 19,319
DEMOCRATIC REPUBLIC OF CONGO (ZAIRE)
L. Tanganyika
ATLANTIC OCEAN
L. Nyasa
ZAMBIA
Zambezi
Mozambique Channel
MOZAMBIQUE
ZIMBABWE
Madag
NAMIBIA
BOTSWANA
Kalahari
Drakensberg
SOUTH AFRICA
C. of Good Hope
da Cunha

Sub-Saharan Africa

Amulet, Ethiopia, early 20th century.
Ink on parchment

South Africa
Ethiopia
Botswana
Mozambique
Namibia
Kenya
Democratic Republic of Congo (Zaire)
Zambia
Zimbabwe

SOUTH AFRICA

GP 42,393,000 ♦ JP 92,000

A Lithuanian Jewish family takes leave of their father upon his departure for South Africa in 1925. The family joined him the following year.

♦DEMOGRAPHY♦

The great majority of South African Jews trace their origins back to Lithuanian immigrants who arrived between the end of the 19th century and 1930.

The two largest centers are Johannesburg (55,000) and Cape Town (15,000). There are many smaller communities, including Durban (5,000), Pretoria (3,000), and Port Elizabeth (1,200). Since 1970 some 50,000 Jews have left the country, but approximately 10,000 Israelis have moved to South Africa. In recent years, many of the Israelis have begun to return home. The level of intermarriage and assimilation remains low compared to that of other Western communities but is on the increase. South African Jewry is an aging community, and virtually every family has been affected by the emigration of its younger members.

♦HISTORY♦

Only at the beginning of the 19th century, when freedom of religion was introduced, were Jews able to come to South Africa legally. At that time, small numbers of Jews arrived from Britain and Germany, and the first Hebrew congregation was established in Cape Town in 1841. Jews were later among the pioneers in the Transvaal when diamonds and gold were discovered there in 1866. Soon after the establishment of Johannesburg, a Jewish community was organized, and Jews played an active role in the development of trade and industry.

In the 1880s, large numbers of Jews began to arrive from Lithuania, and their contributions changed the character of the community. By 1910 there were around 40,000 Jews in the country. The Quota Act of 1930

♦

restricted immigration, and in 1937 the entry of German Jews was explicitly prohibited. This was coupled with growing anti-Semitic sentiment among militant Afrikaners, who mounted demonstrations against the arrival of steamers carrying refugees. Still some 8,000 Jews, mainly from central Europe, found sanctuary in the country.

◆ C O M M U N I T Y ◆

The community is overwhelmingly Ashkenazi, with a small Sephardi population in Cape Town. It is affluent, well-educated, and has a strong traditional and Zionist bent. Individual Jews were among the most vocal opponents of Apartheid, but Jews could be found across the political spectrum with the exception of the extreme right. The community did not involve itself in national politics, but the vast majority of its members voted for majority rule so as to end Apartheid. After his election in 1994, President Nelson Mandela expressed sympathy and understanding for Jewish concerns and called on the community to stay and help reconstruct South Africa.

The central body of the Jewish community is the South African Jewish Board of Deputies. The board represents all major Jewish organizations and congregations and is recognized by the government as the official representative of South African Jewry. The board was instrumental in establishing the African Jewish Congress, which provides sub-Saharan Jewish communities with assistance and support. In 1985 the board passed a resolution explicitly rejecting Apartheid. The community is active in welfare work and runs homes for the aged, who constitute an ever-increasing proportion of the Jewish population of South Africa.

South African Jewry has a long record of Zionist activity, and the movement remains strong. There are local chapters of most of the major international Jewish and Zionist organizations. The four main youth movements are Habonim, Betar, B'nai Akiva, and Maginim (Progressive).

◆ R E L I G I O U S   L I F E ◆

Most of the community is religiously traditional, and some 80% are affiliated with Orthodox synagogues, of which there are 65 in the country. About 10% are affiliated with the Progressive movement and a smaller number with the Masorati (Conservative) movement. The chief rabbi of the Orthodox Federation is the country's most widely recognized Jewish religious authority. Kosher food is widely available, and there are several kosher restaurants and hotels.

◆ C U L T U R E   A N D   E D U C A T I O N ◆

There are Jewish museums in Johannesburg and Cape Town (the latter housed in the beautiful Gardens Synagogue, built in 1849) and several Jewish libraries. A number of weekly, monthly, and quarterly publications appear, notably the quarterly *Jewish Affairs* published by the Board of Deputies.

The Jewish day school system is comprehensive, embracing about 60% of all Jewish youngsters. Most of the schools are Orthodox in orientation, and some are ultra-Orthodox. The community trains many of its own Hebrew teachers and rabbis in Johannesburg, where there is also a Lubavitch Torah Academy. Some universities, notably that of Cape Town, offer courses in Jewish studies.

◆ I S R A E L ◆

In the United Nations and in other forums, Israel was often singled out for special

Among old-timers, the town of Oudtshoorn in the semi-arid Little Karoo is known as the "Jerusalem of Africa." Lithuanian Jews were pioneers in the ostrich feather trade and developed it into an important export business. Jews from Chelm were among the most active in the trade, and they strove valiantly to recreate the atmosphere of their beloved hometown synagogue and graft it on to the veldt. Many years later, when the synagogue fell into disuse, the magnificent onion-domed ark was preserved in Oudtshoorn's C.P. Nei Museum, which has a special Jewish section.

condemnation on account of Jerusalem's commercial and military ties with Pretoria, despite the fact that, compared to the level of trade with other states, the scale of Israel's ties was negligible. Relations with the new majority government are good.

Aliya: Since 1948, 16,300 South African Jews have emigrated to Israel.

⋆ S I T E S ⋆

The Mooi Street Synagogue in Johannesburg, founded by Lithuanian immigrants from the *shtetl* of Poswohl, has been declared a national landmark. In Johannesburg there is an impressive Holocaust memorial at the West Park Cemetery. South Africa's wine country outside Cape Town is also home to the Zaandwijk Winery, the country's only kosher vintner.

South African Jewish Board of Deputies
P.O. Box 87557
Houghton, Johannesburg 2041
Tel. 27 11 486 1434, Fax 27 11 646 4940

Embassy
Dashing Center, 339 Hilda Street, Hatfield
P.O. Box 3726, Pretoria
Tel. 27 12 34 22 693, Fax 27 12 34 21 442
(From January to June, the embassy is
    in Cape Town.)
Church Square, P.O. Box 180, Cape Town 800
Tel. 27 21 34 22 698, Fax 27 21 32 41 442

Tree planting at the Herzlia Jewish Day School, Cape Town, 1981

ETHIOPIA

GP 58,243,000 ✦ JP 1,000

✦DEMOGRAPHY✦

Although nearly all the Jews of Ethiopia were brought to Israel (about 50,000), thousands of Ethiopians who claim Jewish ancestry were left behind. Historians argue whether these people represent descendants of converts to Christianity, or whether they simply left the Jewish fold without adopting another religion. The motivation for conversion is a matter of dispute: some claim that the conversions were undertaken by people who wanted to improve their socioeconomic status, while others claim that they were made under duress. Many of these so-called Falash Mura have family ties with those who emigrated to Israel and are returning to Judaism. It is estimated that there may be as many as 30,000 people who fit this category. A number of these have relatives in Israel, and their requests to emigrate are treated as matters of family reunification.

Ethiopian Jews on their way to Israel, 1991

✦HISTORY✦

Ethiopian Jewry represents one of the oldest Diaspora communities. Little is known about the early origins of the community, but it is believed that they adopted Jewish beliefs around the 2nd and 3rd centuries C.E. The community calls itself Beta Israel, but Ethiopian Jews are also often referred to as Falashas, which means "strangers" or "immigrants" in the Ge'ez tongue (the classical literary and ecclesiastical language of the country). In the 10th century, the Zague dynasty arose. Some of its rulers adopted Jewish beliefs and were considered Jewish kings. That kingdom was crushed by King Susenyos in 1617, and the lot of Ethiopian Jews deteriorated. Over the centuries, many Jews came under the influence of Christianity (which was the religion of most Ethiopians) and left Judaism. Others, however, persisted in observing their Judaism, despite the fact that they had no contact with the outside Jewish world. Ethiopian Judaism was based on the Torah but did not include later Rabbinic laws and commentaries, which never reached Ethiopia. Still, in the 16th century, Radbaz, an Egyptian rabbi, recognized the Jewishness of Ethiopian Jewry.

Traditionally Jewish settlement was concentrated in the mountainous Gondar Province around Lake Tana and in the Tigre Province. In 1867 Joseph Halevy was dispatched by the Alliance Israelite Universelle to investigate the conditions of Jews in the "Land of Kush," as some Jews called the country. In 1904 his student Jacques (Jacob) Faitlovitch went to Ethiopia and devoted the rest of his life to the needs of Ethiopian Jewry. Faitlovich established Jewish schools in Ethiopia and brought some of the best and brightest of the

✦

Ethiopian youth to Europe and to the Land of Israel to be trained as teachers. In 1934 it was estimated that there were some 50,000 Ethiopian Jews (18th-century Christian missionaries estimated their numbers at between 200,000 and 500,000).

During the Italian occupation, which lasted from 1935 until 1941, the small Jewish communities of Addis Ababa and Diredawa, which were made up of European and Yemenite Jews, were disbanded. Members of Beta Israel took part in the struggle against the Italian occupation, and several students of Faitlovitch lost their lives.

Throughout the succeeding decades, Israeli, and Jewish organizations provided help in education and welfare and later lobbied for Ethiopian Jews' right of emigration. In 1975 the Israeli rabbinate recognized the status of Ethiopian Jews, thus paving the way for mass immigration. It was only in 1984 and 1985, during the Ethiopian Civil War, that the Mengistu government agreed to allow Israel to airlift the community to Israel via Sudan. Some 10,000 Jews went to Israel at that time. Media leaks led the Sudanese government to withdraw its cooperation, ending "Operation Moses" and stranding some 15,000 Jews. Only in 1991, when the Ethiopian government was on the verge of collapse, did Israel mount "Operation Solomon," which succeeded in airlifting most of the remaining Jews to Israel.

⋆COMMUNITY AND RELIGIOUS LIFE⋆

Religious life is concentrated in Addis Ababa, where most of those awaiting eventual repatriation to Israel live. Within a central compound are located a synagogue, a vocational training center, and other facilities. There are also several dozen Adenite Jews residing in the capital. They have their own synagogue and burial ground, which is also used by the Falash Mura. There are still several hundred Jews living in rural villages in Gondar.

⋆ISRAEL⋆

Israel and Ethiopia enjoy full diplomatic relations.

Aliya: Since 1948, 50,700 Ethiopian Jews have emigrated to Israel.

Embassy
Higher 16 Kebele 22, House 22, P.O.Box 1266
Addis Ababa
Tel. 251 1 610 999, Fax 251 1 612 456

Ethiopian Jews in Israel have preserved their unique culinary traditions. Injira, *a flat pancake that is the staple of the Ethiopian diet, is prepared from a mixture of flour and water. The mixture is allowed to ferment for several days in a pottery vessel. It is then combined with more water to create a batter, which is cooked on a circular pan and then baked over an open fire.* Injira *is eaten with a piquant stew called* wat, *which is made of lentils or meat mixed with many spices. This delicious combination is generally washed down with a beer called* talla, *brewed from water, hops, and barley. In recent years, a number of Ethiopian restaurants have opened in Israel, and they have introduced non-Ethiopian Israelis to the delicacies of Ethiopian cookery.*

BOTSWANA

GP 1,484,000 ✦ JP 50

✦HISTORY AND COMMUNITY✦

Nearly all the Jews live in Gaborone. The largest segment of the community consists of Israelis working in industry, agriculture, and business. Occasional religious services are held on Friday nights. On high holidays, a rabbi is provided by the South African Jewish Board of Deputies, and services are conducted either at a private house or at a communal center. There is a Jewish cemetery.

✦ISRAEL✦

Israel and Botswana renewed diplomatic relations in 1993. Israel is represented by its ambassador in Zimbabwe.

Contact:
Tel. 267 352 990, Fax 267 314 413

MOZAMBIQUE

GP 17,796,000 ✦ JP 40

✦HISTORY AND COMMUNITY✦

Most of the Jews live in Lourenco Marques. Jewish settlement was initiated at the turn of the century by South African Jewish refugees exiled by President Kruger's government for their pro-British activities. In 1926 a synagogue was consecrated in Lourenco Marques. There is a cemetery in Alto Maha.

✦ISRAEL✦

Israel and Mozambique established relations in 1993. Israel is represented by its ambassador in Zimbabwe.

Contact:
ONUMOZ, P.O. Box 1915, Maputo
Tel. 1 42 32 17, Fax 1 42 33 82

NAMIBIA

GP 1,575,000 JP 60

✦HISTORY AND COMMUNITY✦

Most of Namibia's Jews are residents of Windhoek. The Windhoek Hebrew Congregation has maintained a synagogue since 1924, in which regular *shabbat* and holiday services are conducted. The South African Jewish Board of Deputies provides a *chazan* for the festivals. The children receive religious education from their mothers, who are assisted by Cape Board of Jewish Education in South Africa. There have been manifestations of anti-Semitism on the part of certain elements of the country's large German minority.

✦ISRAEL✦

Israel and Namibia established diplomatic relations in 1994. Israel is represented by its ambassador in Zimbabwe.

Windhoek Hebrew Congregation
P.O. Box 140, Windhoek
Tel. 2761 221990, Fax 2761 226444

A Jew in an isolated area of Namibia left instructions that some Hebrew words be inscribed on his tombstone. His survivors only found one object with Hebrew letters, and therefore the inscription on his tombstone reads, "Here lies Peter Cohen, Kosher-le-Pesach (kosher for Passover)."

KENYA

GP 27,799,000 ♦ JP 400

♦HISTORY♦

Most of Kenya's Jews live in Nairobi. Jews have lived in what is present-day Kenya since the turn of the century. The community was later bolstered by the arrival of Holocaust survivors. Among the members of the community are Israelis who come to work on a short-term basis in Kenya.

♦COMMUNITY AND RELIGIOUS LIFE♦

Communal life centers around the Nairobi Hebrew Congregation. Regular *shabbat* and holiday services are held in the synagogue in Nairobi, the only one in the country. Kosher products, including wine and matzot, are imported. A broad range of educational, social, and sport activities are offered at the community center in Vermont Hall.

♦ISRAEL♦

Israel and Kenya renewed relations in 1988.

Jewish Community
P.O. Box 30354, Nairobi
Tel. 254 2 722 182, Fax 254 2 715 996

Embassy
Bishop Road, P.O. Box 30354, Nairobi
Tel. 254 2 722 182, Fax 254 2 715 966
♦

The Uganda Scheme, a proposal from the British government to settle Jews in present-day Kenya, was discussed at the Sixth Zionist Congress in August 1903. It caused sharp controversy and was rejected by the Seventh Congress in July 1905.

Aerial view of the Nairobi Synagogue, built in 1954, and the adjacent Vermont Memorial Hall

DEMOCRATIC REPUBLIC
OF CONGO (ZAIRE)

GP 46,812,000 ♦ JP 320

♦HISTORY AND COMMUNITY♦

Most Jews live in Lubumbashi but there is also a community in Kinshasa. Jews have lived in Congo since the beginning of the century, when the first immigrants arrived from eastern Europe, the Land of Israel, and South Africa. A few years later, they were joined by Sephardim from the island of Rhodes. With the departure of the Belgians in 1960, many of the Jews left the country. Since that time, however, a large number of Israelis have worked on development projects there. During the strife in 1997, many of the remaining Jews were evacuated, and the community is now dormant.

The Communaute Israelite du Shaba represents the Jews of Congo. There is a synagogue in Lubumbashi.

♦ISRAEL♦

Zaire was one of the first African countries to reestablish diplomatic relations with Israel in 1983, following the severing of relations by African states in 1973.

Embassy
12 Avenue des Aviateurs
P.O. Box 8343—KIN 1, Kinshasa
Tel. 243 12 21955, Fax 243 88 45055

ZAMBIA

GP 8,275,000 ♦ JP 50

♦HISTORY AND COMMUNITY♦

Nearly all the Jews in Zambia live in Lusaka. The community is composed of a core of settlers with roots in the country going back to the turn of the century and of a number of Israelis and other foreigners presently working in Zambia. The early Jewish pioneers actively developed the cattle and ranching trade, as well as the country's first iron foundries. Today there are Jewish farmers, traders, and professionals in Zambia.

The Lusaka-based Council for Zambian Jewry, founded in 1978, is the central body. It has given medical, educational, and financial assistance to needy members of the community and to political refugees. There are synagogues (with communal halls) in Lusaka and in Ndola. Very few Jews remain in the Copperbelt, and the Ndola synagogue has been closed.

♦ISRAEL♦

Israel and Zambia enjoy full diplomatic relations. Israel is represented by its ambassador in Harare, Zimbabwe.

Council for Zambian Jewry
P.O. Box 30089, Lusaka 10101
Tel. 260 1 229 556, Fax 260 1 223 798

Zimbabwe

GP 11,439,000   JP 900

+History and Community+

Jewish settlement dates back to the turn of the century and, in some respects, parallels that of South Africa. Jews began to leave the country in large numbers during the civil strife that gripped Zimbabwe (Rhodesia) in the 1970s. Today more than two-thirds of the community's members are 65 or older.

The first synagogue in the country was established in a tent in Bulawayo in 1894.

Most of the young people have left for South Africa, Israel, or elsewhere. The communities in the midlands no longer exist.

+Community and Religious Life+

The Zimbabwe Jewish Board of Deputies is the leading communal organization. There are two synagogues in Harare (Ashkenazi and Sephardi) and another in Bulawayo (Ashkenazi Orthodox). The Central African Zionist Organization is the Zionist umbrella body and was established in 1898 in Bulawayo. Communal centers exist in both Harare and Bulawayo. Despite the small number of youth, several Zionist youth organizations are active. The two Jewish schools, Carmel in Bulawayo and Sharon in Harare, have a large enrollment of African and Indian pupils. Bulawayo has a home for the elderly and various benevolent and welfare committees. The Central African Zionist Organization publishes a bulletin.

+Israel+

Israel and Zimbabwe established relations in 1993.

Aliya: Since 1948, 714 Jews from Zimbabwe and the former Rhodesia have emigrated to Israel.

Zimbabwe Jewish Board of Deputies
P.O. Box 342, Harare
Tel. 263 4 723 647

Embassy
Three Anchor House
54 Jason Moyo Ave, Harare
Tel. 263 4 756 808, Fax 263 4 756 801

Belvedere Jewish boxing team, Harare (Salisbury), 1939

Asia and Oceania

Afghanistan
Australia
China
Fiji
Hawaii, U.S.A.
Hong Kong
India
Indonesia
Reunion
Japan
Myanmar (Burma)
New Caledonia
New Zealand
South Korea
The Philippines
Singapore
Tahiti
Taiwan
Thailand

*Israeli youth prepare for a Chabad-sponsored
seder in Katmandu, Nepal, in 1991.*

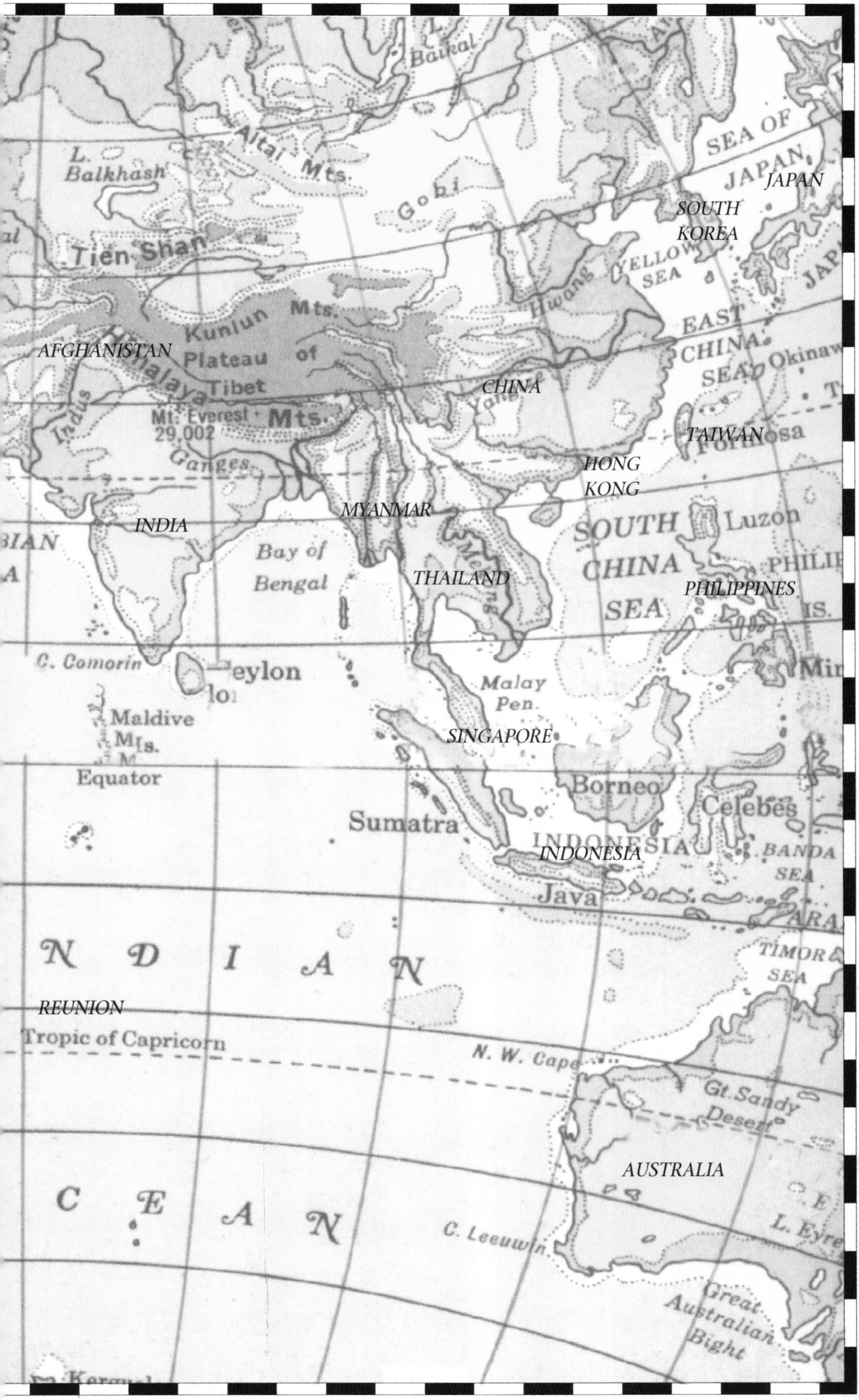

L. Baikal
Altai Mts.
L. Balkhash
Gobi
SEA OF JAPAN
JAPAN
SOUTH KOREA
Tien Shan
YELLOW SEA
Hwang
Kunlun Mts.
EAST CHINA SEA
AFGHANISTAN
Himalaya
Plateau of Tibet
Okinawa
CHINA
Indus
Mt. Everest 29,002
Mts.
TAIWAN
Formosa
Ganges
HONG KONG
MYANMAR
SOUTH CHINA SEA
Luzon
INDIA
Bay of Bengal
THAILAND
PHILIPPINES
C. Comorin
Ceylon
Malay Pen.
Maldive Is.
SINGAPORE
Equator
Borneo
Celebes
Sumatra
INDONESIA
BANDA SEA
Java
INDIAN OCEAN
TIMOR SEA
REUNION
Tropic of Capricorn
N. W. Cape
Gt. Sandy Desert
AUSTRALIA
C. Leeuwin
L. Eyre
Great Australian Bight

Ketuba from Herat, paper, 5573 (1813)

♦COMMUNITY♦

The Jewish community of Afghanistan can be traced back at least 800 years. In the 12th century, Benjamin of Tudela claimed that there were 80,000 Jews in the Ghazni on the River Gozan. The community was isolated and had little contact with the outside world. In the first half of the 19th century, many Persian Jews came to Afghanistan fleeing the forced conversion in Meshad, and 40,000 Jews were living there in the second part of the 19th century. In 1948 there were some 5,000 Jews in the country, but the vast majority left the country for Israel in the early 1950s. Today nearly all the remaining Jews live in Kabul. There is a synagogue on Charshi Torabazein Street.

♦ISRAEL♦

Israel and Afghanistan have no formal ties.
Aliya: Since 1948, 4,123 Afghan Jews have emigrated to Israel.

Afghan Jews, like their neighbors, would go to great pains to ward off the evil eye. In isolated areas, there were no physicians, and folk medicine was practiced until recent times. For example, a pan of burning coals would be brought into the sick room. The mullah *(religious teacher) would take an ember in a pair of tongs and encircle the patient's head with it while reciting psalms and verses from the Bible containing the names of angels who have the power to cure the sick. He would then hurl the ember into a bowl of water to extinguish it quickly. This would be repeated seven times. Afghan Jews believed that the sickness would be extinguished just like the embers.*

AUSTRALIA

GP 18,057,000 ♦ JP 95,000

♦DEMOGRAPHY♦

The Australian Jewish community is the largest in the Asian region. The bulk of Australian Jewry is divided between the two cities of Melbourne (45,000) and Sydney (35,000), but smaller communities can be found scattered throughout the country in places such as Adelaide, Brisbane, Canberra, the Gold Coast, Perth, and even in Hobart on the island of Tasmania, in which the oldest-standing synagogue in the country, built in 1845, is situated. About 5% of the Jewish community are Israeli expatriates.

♦HISTORY♦

Jews were among the first convicts deported from the United Kingdom to Australia in the 18th century. By the 19th century, there was an established Jewish community, overwhelmingly made up of free settlers. Jews arrived in several successive waves of immigration, primarily from Britain and eastern Europe. The gold rushes of the 19th century were one source of attraction for Jewish migrants to Australia, and synagogues were built in gold rush cities such as Ballarat.

In the late 1930s, about 7,000 Jewish refugees, mainly from Germany and Austria, found sanctuary in the country. After the war,

Sculptural relief of Jewish convicts on their way to Australia

Australia admitted tens of thousands of Holocaust survivors, and today Australia has the highest percentage of Holocaust survivors of any Jewish community in the world. These post-war immigrants rejuvenated a community that was threatened by assimilation, and they have largely set the tone for contemporary communal life.

In the 1970s, Jews arrived from the Soviet Union, and the country has also become a favorite destination for Jewish emigrants from South Africa. In addition there is a small community of Asian and North African Jews. Generally speaking the Melbourne community, in which Jews of Polish origin are dominant, is more traditional than that of Sydney. The majority of Jews in Sydney are of German, Hungarian, and English stock.

♦COMMUNITY♦

The leading communal organization is the Executive Council of Australian Jewry.

Zionism is strong in Australia and Australian Jews have emigrated to Israel in larger numbers than any other English-speaking Jewish community. All the main Zionist organizations and youth movements are represented. These groups are affiliated with the

Sir John Monash (1865–1931), an engineer by profession, commanded Australian and New Zealand (ANZAC) forces in Europe during World War I. British statesman Lloyd George described him as the only soldier of World War I with the necessary qualities of leadership. The scion of several generations of Viennese Hebrew printers, Monash was a practicing Jew and an active Zionist. Today one of Australia's largest universities, as well as a village in Israel, bear his name.

Zionist Federation of Australia. There are also local chapters of other international organizations, such as B'nai B'rith.

Anti-Semitism is not a serious problem in Australia's multicultural society, but there are a number of hate groups, which are carefully monitored.

◆ CULTURE AND EDUCATION ◆

The Australian Jewish community is characterized by a number of phenomena that distinguish it from other English-speaking Jewish communities. These include a high rate of enrollment in Jewish day schools (75% of all primary school pupils and 55% of all high school pupils) and a low rate of inter-marriage, currently around 10%. Melbourne and Sydney each boast Jewish day schools, including Melbourne's Mount Scopus, the largest Jewish day school in the world. Some of the universities also offer courses on Jewish themes, including Hebrew language. Two of Sydney's major universities have Jewish halls of residence for students and academics—Shalom College and Mandelbaum House. The Australian Union of Jewish students has an active campus presence.

There are two Jewish weeklies (the Melbourne and Sydney editions of the Australian Jewish News) and several other periodicals, including the *Australia–Israel Review* and *Generation*. Each week Australia's ethnic radio stations feature several hours of programming of Jewish interest in English, Hebrew, and Yiddish. The community also maintains several Jewish museums, including two devoted to the commemoration of the Holocaust. Jewish film festivals have become cultural fixtures for the general community in Sydney and in Melbourne. Melbourne's

The Shalom Aleichem School in Melbourne, 1984. In this school, belonging to the Bundist movement, all pupils learn Yiddish.

tradition of Jewish (often Yiddish) theater continues to this day. Thousands of people of all ages participate in Maccabi athletic events, which culminate in a major carnival each year.

◆ RELIGIOUS LIFE ◆

There are dozens of synagogues affiliated with all major religious movements, from Reform to ultra-Orthodox. In Melbourne, Sydney, and several other places, there are *mikvaot* and kosher butchers, bakers, and restaurants. There are also two kosher hotels in Melbourne. It is estimated that about one-quarter of the Jewish community observes *kashrut. Batei din* are located in Melbourne and Sydney.

◆ ISRAEL ◆

Israel and Australia have full diplomatic relations. In addition to the Israeli embassy in Canberra, there is a consulate in Sydney.

Aliya: Since 1948, 3,539 Australian Jews have emigrated to Israel.

◆ SITES ◆

The oldest synagogue in the country, in Hobart, is often visited. The late Victorian Great Synagogue of Sydney is an especially impressive example of Jewish sacral architecture. There are new Jewish museums in both Sydney and Melbourne. Jewish travelers will especially appreciate Sydney's Hakoah Club, where it is possible to make the acquaintance of local Jews.

Executive Council of Australian Jewry
146 Darlinghurst Road
Darlinghurst NSW 2010
Tel. 61 2 360 5415, Fax 61 2 360 5416

Embassy
6 Turrana Street
Yarralumla, Canberra ACT 2600
Tel. 61 6 273 1309, Fax 61 6 273 4273

CHINA

GP 1,320,083,000 ◆ JP 50

Model at Beth Hatefutsoth of the Synagogue of Kaifeng, constructed in 1163.
After the community had disintegrated through assimilation, the building fell into decay.

◆HISTORY◆

An ancient trading nation, the Chinese have had contacts with traveling Jewish merchants since the 8th century. By the 12th century, a considerable number of Jews had made their homes in the city of Kaifeng, in a far western region of the country. At least one synagogue was constructed, and the community was active for about eight centuries. As recently as the 19th century, some Chinese Jews were practicing Jewish rituals, including Torah reading.

In the late 19th century, Russian Jewish communities were founded in Harbin, Tientsin, and elsewhere. The project to construct a Russian railway to eastern Asia was centered in Harbin. Anxious to populate the city, the Russian government provided incen-

tives to minorities, including Jews and Karaites, to settle there. In the early years of the 20th century, Jews fleeing pogroms in the Pale of Settlement and demobilized soldiers from the Russo-Japanese War joined them, raising the Jewish population of Harbin to approximately 8,000 by 1908. The Russian Revolution of 1917 practically doubled the size of the community and served as a stimulus to Zionist activism. Japanese annexation in 1931 brought increased restrictions on many facets of life, and many Jews left for free countries. Most of the Russian Jews remaining at the end of World War II emigrated to the West. Some were repatriated, both voluntarily and involuntarily, to the Soviet Union.

The development of the port city of Shanghai as a Jewish center parallels that of Hong

◆

The charismatic Chinese nationalist leader Sun Yat-Sen drew together a diverse band of supporters and advisers from many parts of the world in his efforts to rid China of its oppressive warlords. Within this group, two of Sun's key assistants benefited from a special link of their own—the chief bodyguard "Two-Gun" Cohen and the Russian interpreter Moishe Schwarzberg spoke to each other in Yiddish.

Kong. Sephardi families from Baghdad, Bombay, and Cairo, including the Kadoories, Sassons, and Hardoons, established a communal structure in Shanghai in the 19th century. By 1903 there were three synagogues in the city. The rise of Nazism brought 25,000 Jewish refugees to Shanghai, where a thriving, if transient, community took shape. After Shanghai fell to the Japanese, many Jews were held in semi-internment in Hongkew. Almost the entire community subsequently migrated to the United States, Britain, Israel, Australia, and other countries.

Today there are no Jewish communal structures in China, and the Jews who live there are thought to be extremely few. In the past decade, Chinese–Jewish links have been cultivated on an intellectual level through academic exchange programs with Jews in Israel and elsewhere. There is a small Jewish museum in Kaifang. Relics of the Jewish presence in China can be seen elsewhere, particularly in Shanghai.

✦ISRAEL✦

Israel and China have had formal relations since 1992.

Aliya: Since 1948, 1,070 Jews from China have emigrated to Israel, 504 between 1948 and 1951.

Embassy
West Wing Offices (CWTC)
1 Jianguo Menwai Da Jie, Beijing 100004
Tel. 86 10 6505 2970, Fax 86 10 6505 0328

FIJI

GP 797,000 ✦ JP 40

✦HISTORY AND COMMUNITY✦

Nearly all Jews in Fiji live in Suva, the capital. Jewish settlement in Fiji can be traced back to the arrival from Australia of 20-year-old Henry Marks in 1881. Marks laid the foundation of what became one of the most extensive commercial enterprises in the Western Pacific. Marks was later joined by Jews from India and elsewhere in the Middle East and the Orient. Until very recently, there was no organized Jewish life. However, this changed with the creation of a communal organization called the Fiji Jewish Association. Religious life has been confined to a communal seder organized by the Israeli embassy and attended by 50 to 60 people.

✦ISRAEL✦

Israel and Fiji enjoy full diplomatic relations. The Israeli ambassador in Canberra, Australia, represents Israeli interests in Fiji.

Fiji Jewish Association
Carpenter Street, P.O. Box 882 G.P.O., Suva
Tel. 679 387 980, Fax 679 387 946

HAWAII, U.S.A.

GP 1,172,000 ✦ JP 7,000

✦HISTORY AND COMMUNITY✦

The first mention of Jews in connection with the islands which ultimately became the 50th U.S. state was in 1798, when a sailor on the whaler *Neptune* recorded in the ship's log that the Hawaiian king had come aboard and brought "a Jew cook with him." It is believed that Jewish traders from Britain and Germany arrived in the islands in the 1840s. They were later joined by Jews from California at the end of the 19th century. However, it was not until 1901 that the Hebrew Benevolent Society and a cemetery were established. In 1938 the Honolulu Jewish community was formed, and this was followed in 1951 by the consecration of a Reform synagogue. Over the years, Chabad and Conservative congregations were established. There is also a Jewish chapel called "Aloha" at Pearl Harbor. Although Jewish life is centered around Honolulu, there are also congregations in Hilo, Maui, and Kauai. Kosher food is available, and some of the synagogues have Sunday schools and other educational facilities. There are local chapters of B'nai B'rith and Hadassah. The Jewish community has been bolstered by the constant influx of new arrivals from the American mainland.

Jewish Federation of Hawaii
2550 Pali Highway
Honolulu, HI 96817
Tel. 808 595 5218, Fax 808 595 5220

✦HISTORY AND DEMOGRAPHY✦

Jewish merchants have had commercial ties with traders in Hong Kong for many centuries. A modern community, however, was only established in the first half of the 19th century with the immigration of a number of families from Baghdad. The community's establishment was encouraged by the arrival of the British as sovereign powers in Hong Kong.

The Sephardi settlers, among whom were the Sassoon and Kadoorie families, centered community activities around their homes until the Ohel Leah Synagogue was consecrated in 1900.

Jewish children at Sunday school

Prior to World War II, the community numbered only a few hundred. Jews made enormous contributions to the development of Hong Kong, particularly in the field of transportation. Jews developed the Star Ferry, the Harbor Tunnel, and the Peak Tramway—leading components of the city's infrastructure. Moreover, Kowloon's primary avenue, perhaps the foremost commercial thoroughfare in Asia, Nathan Road, was named for the Jewish engineer who laid it out and later served as governor of the colony.

Hong Kong's development as a strategic trade and finance center has attracted tens of thousands of foreigners from the 1960s onward, among whom were many Jews. These Jews, primarily from the United States, Israel, the United Kingdom, Australia, and Canada, revitalized the community. Today two-thirds of the Jewish community are Americans and Israelis. In July 1997 Chinese sovereignty over Hong Kong was restored.

✦COMMUNAL LIFE✦

There are four synagogues, three served by rabbis. They range from the Sephardi Ohel Leah to the Chabad House. The leading venue of Jewish communal activities is the large Jewish community center which contains a library and recreational facilities, including a swimming pool and a kosher restaurant. The Conservative United Jewish congregation holds services in its auditorium. The Carmel School includes children up to eight years old, and after-school learning for older students is provided by the Ezekiel Abraham School.

The Jewish Community Center
One Robinson Place
70 Robinson Road, Mid-Levels, Hong Kong
Tel. 852 2801 5440, Fax 852 2877 0917

Consulate General
Tower 2
701 Admiralty Center, Hong Kong
Tel. 852 2529 6091, Fax 852 2865 0220

Among the many institutions in the colony founded by the Kadoorie family is the Kadoorie Experimental and Extension Farm in the New Territories. The farm has conducted extensive research in animal husbandry and has succeeded in eliminating the traditional swayback of the Hong Kong pig. Following this development, Lord Kadoorie was heard to remark, "We Kadoories know everything about pigs but the taste."

The interior of Bombay's most famous synagogue, on Cruzon Street at Wellington Circle

♦ DEMOGRAPHY ♦

Today most Indian Jews live in and around Bombay, particularly in Thane, a suburb 35 kilometers from the city. The community is composed of three distinct groups: the dominant Bene Israel, who believe themselves to be the descendants of the original settlers who came to India as early as 2,000 years ago; the Jews of Malabar, centered in Cochin, whose forefathers arrived in India from Europe and the Middle East as early as 1,000 years ago; and the Iraqi Jews, called "Baghdadis," who began settling in India at the end of the 18th century.

The Indian Jewish community has shrunk considerably in recent years, primarily due to emigration. Consequently, the remnants of Indian Jewry have come together to forge a united community. There is very little assimilation or intermarriage, as few Jews interact socially with Hindus or Muslims. The Hindu caste system has also served to isolate the Jewish communities and to prevent assimilation. All of these different communities lived in an environment of tolerance and pluralism, with almost no anti-Semitism or discrimination of any kind.

♦ HISTORY ♦

Myths surround the origins of the Jews of India, particularly the Bene Israel and the Jews of Cochin. The Bene Israel claim to have arrived in India in the 2nd century B.C.E.

The first documented evidence of this community dates from the 17th century. Isolated from the rest of Jewry, the Bene Israel adopted many Muslim and Hindu customs. Although they had no synagogues, the Bene Israel retained many Jewish practices, such as circumcision, observance of the dietary laws, and sabbath observance. However, they were

Although Vasco da Gama is credited as being the first European to explore the Indian coast, a Polish Jew from Poznan whose original name is unknown was already there to greet the Portuguese mariner upon his arrival. When da Gama's ship approached the coast, this bearded, turban-clad, sword-wielding Jew sailed out to meet him. Da Gama was suspicious of his guest, who claimed to be a Christian convert to Islam who had come to offer the local Muslim ruler's hospitality to the visitors from Portugal. However, the truth soon emerged. As a young man he had left his native Poland and headed east, ultimately winding up in Goa. There he was hired by the local ruler to lead a band of pirates to attack the Portuguese. Da Gama arrested the man and took him to Portugal, forcibly converting him to Christianity en route. The Polish Jew's linguistic skills and knowledge of India made him an invaluable asset to the king of Portugal and to da Gama, whom he accompanied on later voyages under his new name—Gaspar da Gama.

unfamiliar with the Bible (except for the Shema, which was their only prayer) or later Jewish texts. Many members of the Bene Israel worked as oil pressers and were termed the *Shanwar Telis*, or "Saturday oil pressers," because they refrained from working on the sabbath. In the early 17th century, the Bene Israel came in contact with Jews from Cochin, who brought them into the mainstream of modern Judaism.

The Bene Israel began to move to Bombay in the late 18th century and built their first synagogue, Shaare Rahamim (Gates of Mercy), in 1796. In time the Bene Israel in Bombay became a strong community. Many of its members were employed in government service, and a considerable number of others distinguished themselves as officers in the Indian army. In the 1950s and 1960s, when the majority of Indian Jews emigrated to Israel, a significant number of the Bene Israel remained in India. This was partly because they initially had encountered difficulty gaining recognition as Jews. This situation, however, was later rectified. In the early 19th century, the Bene Israel numbered approximately 6,000 and peaked at 20,000 in 1948.

The Cochin community was divided into three distinct groups, *Paradesi* or "White Jews," "Black Jews," and *Meshuhrarim* or "Freedmen." These divisions were maintained until recent times by a rigid caste system. The *Paradesi* are descended from a mixture of Jewish exiles from Cranganore and (later) Spain, the Netherlands, Aleppo, and Germany. Firm evidence of their presence dates back to around 1000 C.E., when the local Hindu leader granted certain privileges to Joseph Rabban, the leader of the community. The *Paradesi* in Cochin still have the copper tablets on which these privileges are inscribed. The Black Jews, whose origins are less clear but are believed to precede those of the *Paradesi* (and may date back to antiquity), closely resemble their Indian neighbors and often bear biblical names. The *Meshuhrarim* were manumitted slaves, whose offspring were affiliated with either the *Paradesi* or the Black Jews. In the 1950s and 1960s, almost all of the Jews of Cochin emigrated to Israel, and only about 90 *Paradesi*, the vast majority of them elderly, remain in India.

The Baghdadi Jews first arrived from Iraq, Syria, and Iran around 1796, fleeing persecution in their native lands. The most prominent Baghdadi Jew was David Sassoon, who established the Indian House of Sassoon in 1832 and paved the way for the arrival of many other Iraqi Jews in India. They mainly settled in Bombay and Calcutta. This community was the least assimilated into the native Indian culture and tended to identify with the

British rulers of India. In the 1950s and 1960s many of the Baghdadis left for Israel and other countries.

✦COMMUNITY✦

The central communal organization is the Council of Indian Jewry, which was established in 1978 in Bombay. It replaced the Central Jewish Board, founded during World War II. The council consists of representatives from the various synagogues and Jewish organizations. There are a variety of other organizations, including the Zionist Association, B'nai B'rith, a Jewish Club in Bombay, *Bikur Cholim,* and two women's associations.

✦RELIGIOUS LIFE✦

At its height, the community maintained 35 synagogues and prayer halls, but that number has declined to 18, the majority of which is in Bombay. While at different periods, rabbis served these congregations, there are currently no rabbis officiating at these synagogues. A committee deals with important religious rituals such as marriage and conversion. Kosher food is available and *shechita* is performed locally.

✦CULTURE AND EDUCATION✦

There are three Jewish schools in Bombay, but over the years, the percentage of Jews in their student bodies has dwindled. In the ORT school, for example, fewer than half the students are Jewish. There are also two small Jewish schools in Calcutta.

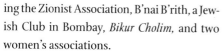

The tzedaka box embedded in the outside wall of a Cochin synagogue

✦ISRAEL✦

Since 1992 Israel and India have enjoyed full diplomatic relations. In addition to its embassy in New Delhi, Israel maintains in Bombay a consulate that has functioned since before the initiation of formal ties between the two countries.

Aliya: Since 1948, 26,641 Jews from India have emigrated to Israel.

✦SITES✦

India has many sites of Jewish interest, including numerous historic synagogues. Among the most magnificent is the Paradesi Synagogue in Cochin, which houses the copper plates on which the community charter of independence is kept. The synagogue, built in 1568 and reconstructed in 1662, has a clock tower featuring numerals in Roman, Hebrew, and Malayalam characters. Another place steeped in history is the Bene Israel cemetery in Navgaon, where it is thought that the original members of Bene Israel were shipwrecked.

Council of Indian Jewry
c/o The Jewish Club
Jerro Bldg., 2nd floor
137 Mahatma Gandhi Road
Bombay 400 023
Tel. 91 22 270 461, Fax 91 22 274 129

Embassy
3 Aurngzeb Road, New Delhi—110001
Tel. 91 11 3013 238, Fax 91 11 3014 298

✦

INDONESIA

GP 200,453,000 ♦ JP 20

The interior of the synagogue in Surabaya, 1992

♦HISTORY AND DEMOGRAPHY♦

Dutch Jews played an active role in the development of the so-called Spice Islands. In the 1850s, there were at least 20 Jewish families of Dutch and German origin living in Jakarta and in other parts of the country. However, most Jews had tenuous ties to Judaism, and attempts to organize a community came to naught. In successive years, Jews from the Netherlands, Baghdad, and Aden settled in Indonesia. By the 1920s, there were several thousand Jews in the country, and communi-

ties were established in Jakarta, Surabaya, Bandung, and elsewhere. In the 1930s, Jews fleeing the rise of Nazism also found sanctuary in Indonesia. Jews, particularly those with Dutch citizenship, suffered greatly during the Japanese occupation. After the war, and later upon the country's independence, nearly all Jews left the country. A few Jewish families, all of Iraqi origin, live in Surabaya. They continue to maintain a small synagogue, but there is neither a rabbi nor a teacher. There are also individual Jews living in Jakarta.

♦

REUNION

GP 640,000 ♦ JP 50

♦COMMUNITY♦

Nearly all the Jews on the island (an overseas department of France east of Madagascar), are Sephardim and are concentrated in St. Denis. There is a synagogue and a kosher hotel.

Communaute Juive de la Reunion
8 Rue de l'Est, St. Denis 97400
Tel. 262 23 78 33

♦

♦HISTORY AND DEMOGRAPHY♦

About half of Japan's community lives in Tokyo, while the remainder is spread among a number of other cities.

Japan's modern opening to the Western world in the 19th century attracted many Jews to the country. The first Jewish settlers arrived in the 1850s on the eve of the Meiji Restoration, which set Japan's course towards the status of a major world power.

Small numbers of Jews from the United Kingdom, the United States, and central and eastern Europe made their homes in Japan (especially in Yokohama and Nagasaki). Persecution in the Czarist Pale of Settlement encouraged many Russian Jews to migrate to China, and some continued on to Japan. After World War I, several thousand Jews were living in Japan, with the largest community in Kobe.

Japan's affiliation with Nazi Germany in the 1930s resulted in the importation of anti-Semitic ideas from Europe. However, due to the small size of the community, Japanese Jews remained largely unnoticed and thus escaped active hostility. Some refugees fleeing Nazi persecution in Europe found their way to Japan, often receiving assistance from the Kobe community and from international Jewish welfare organizations such as the JDC.

In 1941, thanks to the efforts of the Japanese consul-general in Kaunus (Kovno), Lithuania, the entire Mir Yeshiva, together with several thousand other Jews, succeeded in escaping from Europe. Acting against orders, Senpo Sugihara issued some 5,000 Japanese transit visas to Jews who had escaped to Lithuania from Germany and German-occupied Poland. As a result of his actions, Sugihara lost his job. Asked to explain his heroism, he quoted a Samurai maxim from the Bushido code of ethics: "Even a hunter is not allowed to kill a bird who flies to him for refuge." Sugihara is the only Japanese honored with a tree in Yad Vashem's Garden of the Righteous.

The post–World War II occupation of Japan by American forces brought Jewish military personnel to the country for temporary periods. This created the need for Jewish religious services, which were provided primarily by army chaplains. During this period, some of the Russian Jews in China fled the civil unrest in that country and settled in Tokyo, where they founded a synagogue in 1952. By the early 1970s, 1,000 Jews lived in Japan, the majority in Tokyo and Yokohama. In the 1970s and 1980s, there was an influx of *gaijin* (foreign workers), which consequently increased the number of Jews living in Japan.

♦COMMUNAL LIFE♦

The Tokyo synagogue, served by a full-time rabbi, is not aligned to any denomination. It caters to a community of American, Israeli, Australian, British, and French Jews, and has a kosher kitchen which provides takeout food and *shabbat* meals.

The community maintains a Sunday school, attended by 45 students, and holds twice-weekly classes for adolescents. An adult education program attracts 30 participants on a weekly basis. A cultural center operated by the Israeli embassy serves the community and educates members of the general public about Israel and Judaism. The community bulletin, *Tokyo Jewish News,* is produced five times annually.

✦ISRAEL✦

Formal diplomatic ties between Japan and Israel were established in 1952.

Aliya: Since 1948, 169 Jews from Japan have emigrated to Israel.

✦SITES✦

Hiroshima is the site of a Holocaust Memorial.

Jewish Community of Japan
8-8, Hiroo 3-Chome, Shibuya-ku
Tokyo, 150
Tel. 81 3 3400 2559
Fax 81 3 3400 1827

Embassy
3 Niban-Cho, Chiyoda-ku
Tokyo
Tel. 81 3 3264 0911
Fax 81 3 3264 0832

✦

Japanese calligrapher master Kampo Harada, who believes himself to be of the Zevulun tribe, in front of the ark in his Kyoto home

Myanmar (Burma)

GP 45,922,000 ♦ JP 20

♦History and Community♦

Jews from Iraq and from elsewhere in the Middle East first settled in Yangon (Rangoon) early in the 18th century and established a Sephardi community there. In 1896 they erected the Musameah Yeshua Synagogue on land donated by the government. By the outbreak of World War II, there were more than 2,000 Jews in the country. The great majority fled in advance of the Japanese assault and were evacuated to Britain, India, and other countries. Only a small number returned after the country was liberated. Over the years, due to emigration and assimilation, the remaining Jewish population dwindled, and today the community is on the verge of extinction. In northern Myanmar there is a small tribe which claims descent from the tribe of Menashe.

♦Israel♦

Israel and Myanmar have full diplomatic relations.

Aliya: Since 1948, 751 Jews from Burma have emigrated to Israel.

Musmeah Yeshua Synagogue
85, 26th Street, Yangon
Tel. 951 75062

Embassy
49, Pyay, Yangon
Tel. 951 222 290, Fax 951 222 463

A tiny community that claims descent from the tribe of Menashe in its prayer house, 1987

NEW CALEDONIA

GP 184,000 ◆ JP 70

◆COMMUNITY◆

The community, concentrated in Noumea, is composed of recent Jewish immigrants from France, nearly all Sephardi. Most Jews work in commercial ventures or in the state administration. In 1987 a Jewish community was officially established. In Noumea there is a synagogue that is served by a cantor. Kosher food is imported from Australia.

Association Culturelle Israelite de Nouvelle Caledonie
B.P. 4173, Noumea
Tel. 687 285 043, Fax 687 272 101

NEW ZEALAND

GP 3,602,000 ◆ JP 5,000

◆HISTORY◆

The two major centers of New Zealand Jewry are Auckland and Wellington. Jews began to arrive in New Zealand in the early decades of the 19th century. Many were active in commerce with Australia and the United Kingdom. One pioneer, Abraham Hort, Sr., settled in Wellington in 1843, hoping to encourage emigration from poor Jewish neighborhoods in England. As settlement spread across the islands and immigration increased due to the discovery of gold on South Island, synagogues were established in Auckland, Wellington, Dunedin, Christchurch, Hokitika, Timaru, Nelson, and Hastings. Some of these were eventually abandoned. In 1867 the Jewish population stood at 1,262. In the 20th century, the community was bolstered by Jews who joined the flow of immigrants from Britain. However, New Zealand's immigration policies discriminated against central and eastern Europeans. Consequently few Jews found refuge prior to and during World War II. A notable exception was the Austrian-born Jew Karl Popper, who went on to become one of the century's most prominent philosophers.

◆COMMUNAL LIFE◆

The New Zealand Jewish Council represents the Jewish community. At present there are six synagogues in New Zealand, two in Auckland (Orthodox and Liberal), two in Wellington (Orthodox and Liberal), and one each in Christchurch (Orthodox) and Dunedin (Liberal). Both Auckland and Wellington have communal centers that offer educational and cultural facilities. There are also two Jewish old-age homes. Kosher food is available.

Auckland and Wellington each have a Jewish day school, although the school in

Senior minister of the Auckland Hebrew Congregation at prayer, 1981

Wellington offers classes only at the primary level. The Zionist Federation of New Zealand embraces several Zionist groups that are the focus of Israel-oriented activity. WIZO, the Council of Jewish Women, and B'nai B'rith are all active. Youth activity is sponsored by B'nai Akiva and Habonim Dror. The *New Zealand Jewish Chronicle* is produced in Wellington for circulation throughout the country.

✦ISRAEL✦

Israel and New Zealand have full diplomatic relations.

Aliya: Since 1948, 443 Jews from New Zealand have emigrated to Israel.

New Zealand Jewish Council
P.O. Box 27–156, Wellington
Tel./Fax 64 4 475 7622

Embassy
DB Tower 111, The Terrace
P.O. Box 2171, Wellington
Tel. 64 4 472 2362, Fax 64 4 499 0632

During the Victorian period, New Zealand had a Jewish prime minister. The gold rush attracted London-born Julius Vogel (1835–1899) to Australia in 1852. In 1861, after the failure of his mining ventures, he moved to New Zealand. By 1873, in what was certainly one of history's greatest immigrant success stories, Vogel was elected prime minister of the country. In 1875 he was knighted. Because of his striking self-confidence, remarkable oratory skill, ambitious novel-writing, and reputation as a dandy, contemporaries likened Vogel to Benjamin Disraeli. Unlike the British leader, Vogel remained a Jew all his life. Anti-Semitic detractors called him "Jew-lius Caesar."

THE PHILIPPINES

GP 69,282,000 ♦ JP 250

✦ HISTORY ✦

Conversos were present in the Philippines since at least the 16th century, when the country was conquered by Spain. In the second half of the 19th century, Jewish traders arrived from France and other countries. They were followed by American Jews who came in the

many of its members elected to emigrate. Today the Manila community includes a large number of temporary residents, including many Israelis.

✦ COMMUNAL LIFE ✦

The communal organization is the Jewish Association of the Philippines. A community

The entrance to the cemetery in Manila, 1983

wake of the U.S. occupation of the country in 1898 during the Spanish-American War. Shortly thereafter, many Jews arrived from Turkey and elsewhere in the Middle East. A number of Jewish refugees from Russia also found sanctuary in the Philippines after World War I. However, it was not until 1924 that the first synagogue was erected in Manila. In the years leading up to World War II, several thousand Jews who escaped Nazi persecution in Europe were admitted to the Philippines, along with others who fled in advance of the Japanese occupation of Shanghai. When the Japanese overran the Philippines, all Jews who were citizens of Allied countries were interned and subjected to great suffering. The synagogue was destroyed in the fighting to liberate the capital. At the end of the war, the community was reconstituted, but

synagogue, opened in 1983, contains a sanctuary, social hall, and classrooms for the Sunday school. Services in the synagogue follow the Syrian–Sephardi *nusach*. There is a *mikva* on the premises. The rabbi also acts as a *mohel* and *shochet*. Religious services are also conducted on the large U.S. Air Force bases situated on the island.

✦ ISRAEL ✦

Israel and the Philippines maintain full diplomatic relations.

Jewish Association of the Philippines
M.C.P.O. Box 1925, Manila 1259, Makati
Tel. 63 2 818 9988, Fax 63 2 818 9900

Embassy
Philippines Saving Bank Bldg.
6813 Ayala Ave., Rm. 538
Makati, M.M. Philippines, Manila
Tel. 63 2 892 5329, Fax 63 2 894 1027

SINGAPORE

GP 3,384,000 ♦ JP 300

♦HISTORY AND COMMUNITY♦

A Jewish community has existed in Singapore for more than 150 years. The first Jews to settle there were merchants from Baghdad, and this group set the Sephardi tone of Jewish life that continues to this day. The first synagogue was erected in 1878. The early immigrants from Iraq were later joined by Jews from India and Ashkenazim from central Europe. On the eve of World War II, there were 5,000 Jews in Singapore, and they suffered great hardship during the Japanese occupation. Many emigrated after the liberation, but today the city is at least the temporary home to several hundred Israelis and other foreign Jews who have found work on the island. Sephardim account for about 90% of the permanent residents.

The Jewish Welfare Board represents the community. There are two synagogues (both Sephardi), but only one is used on a regular basis. Another congregation, Progressive Ashkenazi, holds services but does not have

A rabbi in the midst of a lecture on the importance of attending shabbat *morning service, Reuben Manasseh Mayer Hall, 1981*

its own building. There is one resident rabbi and a Sunday school for children. Kosher food is available, and there is a *mikva* and a cemetery.

A Jewish Welfare Board newsletter called *L'Chaim* appears monthly, as does the *Singapore Shofar*, published by the Progressive congregation. The community center, where the Hebrew school, an auditorium, and a library are located, is a focus of cultural life. The Jewish Welfare Board also operates an old-age home.

♦ISRAEL♦

Israel and Singapore have full diplomatic relations.

Jewish Welfare Board
Maghain Aboth Synagogue
24 Waterloo Street, Singapore 187950
Tel. 65 337 2189, Fax 65 336 2127

Embassy
58 Dalvey Rd, Singapore 259463
Tel. 65 235 0966, Fax 65 733 7008

♦

When Singapore was granted partial independence in 1955, David Saul Marshall, who had earlier served as president of the Jewish community, was appointed as the country's first chief minister. In 1956 Marshall resigned from his post when Great Britain refused to grant full sovereignty. When Singapore finally did attain independence, Marshall was elected to its legislature and later served in its foreign ministry as ambassador to several European countries.

SOUTH KOREA

GP 45,314,000 ♦ JP 150

♦HISTORY AND COMMUNITY♦

The first significant Jewish presence on the Korean peninsula appeared at the time of the Korean War (1950–1953). Hundreds of Jewish American G.I.s were members of the armed forces that supported the anti-Communist government in resisting the invasion from the North.

The Jewish community of South Korea is essentially a transient group concentrated in Seoul. Many of the Jews are soldiers and officers who serve in the American force that is permanently stationed in South Korea. There is also a handful of Jews who have come to live and work in South Korea as businesspeople or teachers. On *shabbat* and holidays, religious services are led by a U.S. Army chaplain at Yongsan Army Base in Seoul.

♦ISRAEL♦

Israel and South Korea enjoy full diplomatic relations.

Jewish Community of the Republic of Korea
G.P.O. Box 7595, Seoul
Tel. 82 2 544 0834, Fax 82 2 796 3808

Embassy
Dae Kong Building
823–21 Yoksam-Dong, Kangnam-Ku, Seoul
Tel. 822 564 3448, Fax 822 564 3449

> *During the Korean War, author Chaim Potok served as a U.S. Army chaplain. Potok later wrote two books drawing on his experiences in Korea—* The Book of Lights *and* I Am the Clay.

TAIWAN

GP 21,000,000 ♦ JP 75

♦HISTORY AND COMMUNITY♦

In the 1950s, a Jewish community, primarily made up of American military personnel stationed in Taiwan, was established but dwindled with the withdrawal of U.S. forces. The current community was established in the mid-1970s by foreign businesspeople working on the island. Nearly all the Jewish residents live in Taipei, the capital. The majority of them are dispatched by multinational corporations or international organizations for a two- or three-year tour of duty. Others are employed in academia and government service. More than half of the community are American citizens, a quarter are Israelis, and the rest are from various other countries.

♦RELIGIOUS LIFE♦

Regular *shabbat* services are held at a hotel in Taipei. On holidays and on occasional Friday nights, services are conducted at the Jewish community center in suburban Tienmu. The community center also operates a Sunday school for youngsters of pre–bar/bat mitzva age. Kosher food is imported.

♦ISRAEL♦

Israel maintains an economic and trade office in Taipei.

Taiwan Jewish Community
No. 7, Lane 343, Shiphai Road, Section 2
Tienmu, Taipei
Tel. 886 2 874 2763

Israel Economic and Trade Office
Suite 3205
32F INT, L Trade Building No. 333
Keelung Road Section 1, Taipei
Tel. 886 2 757 7221, Fax 886 2 757 7247

TAHITI

GP 215,000 ♦ JP 120

♦HISTORY AND COMMUNITY♦

Most members of this community in French Polynesia are of North African origin. The first Jew to arrive in Tahiti was Alexander Salmon, a banker from France and the son of a London rabbi. Once in Tahiti, he married Arrioehau, a Polynesian princess who led the local Teva clan. Over time other Jews settled on the islands, but most eventually assimilated into the local population and converted to Catholicism. In the 1960s, with the arrival of Algerian Jewish refugees, the first foundations of a permanent Jewish community were laid.

The Association Culturelle des Israelites et Sympathisants de Polynesie (ACISPO), established in 1982, represents the Jewish community. Some of the intermarried members of the community are active in communal life together with their non-Jewish spouses, hence the word "sympathisants." In 1993 a synagogue and community center were consecrated in Papeete, the capital, and in 1994 a *mikva* was opened. Two of the community's Torah scrolls were a gift of the Egyptian Jewish community of Paris, and another was donated by a community in Los Angeles. Services are conducted according to the Sephardi *nusach*. Twice a year, a rabbi from the United States comes for a period of several weeks to conduct Talmud Torah classes for both children and adults. Kosher food is available.

ACISPO
P.O. Box 4821, Papeete
Tel. 689 412 829, Fax 689 435 643

♦

The new synagogue, consecrated in 1993, Papeete

THAILAND

GP 58,703,000 ◆ JP 250

◆ HISTORY ◆

Nearly all the Jews of Thailand live in Bangkok, the capital. The Jewish community is of recent origin. The first permanent Jewish settlers arrived in the 1920s, having fled from Soviet Russia. Their number was bolstered in the 1930s when refugees from central Europe made their way to Thailand. Most of these left the country at the end of World War II. However, in the 1950s and 1960s, a number of Jews settled in Thailand, and in 1966 a synagogue and community center were established. The Jews are a mixture of Sephardim from Syria and Lebanon and Ashkenazim from Europe, the United States, and Shanghai. There is also an Israeli presence. Many Jews are involved in trade and production of jewelry and precious stones.

◆ COMMUNAL AND RELIGIOUS LIFE ◆

In Bangkok there are three synagogues, one Ashkenazi—which also acts as the community center—one Sephardi, and the third and newest, a Chabad House, primarily catering to Jewish backpackers. The Ashkenazi synagogue has a resident rabbi and maintains a Sunday and nursery school. Classes for adults are offered in Hebrew and in English (the latter held after a biweekly barbecue). The Chabad House is noted for its communal seders and other holiday observances which are often attended by hundreds of travelers from all over the world. Kosher food is available, and there are several kosher eateries (including those attached to the synagogues).

◆ ISRAEL ◆

Israel and Thailand enjoy full diplomatic relations.

Jewish Association of Thailand
21 Soichaisamarn, Soi 4 Nana South
Sukhumvit Road, Bangkok
Tel. 66 2 253 1638, Fax 66 2 253 8371

Embassy
31 Soi Lang Suan
Ploenchit Road, Bangkok 10330
Tel. 66 2 2523-131, Fax 66 2 255 5260

◆

Jewish precious stone merchants in their Bangkok office. On the right wall,
a portrait of the Lubavitcher Rebbe; on the left, the King of Thailand

The military cemetery at the River Kwai contains the graves of a number of Jewish P.O.W.'s who lost their lives during the construction of the infamous Death Railway during World War II. The struggle of those hapless Allied soldiers, Jews and Gentiles, became the subject of the famous American film Bridge over the River Kwai.

GLOSSARY

ORGANIZATIONS

Betar	Revisionist Zionist youth movement
B'nai Akiva	Religious-Zionist youth movement
B'nai B'rith	Jewish fraternal and benevolent organization
Chabad	Lubavitch Chassidic movement
Habonim Dror	Labor Zionist youth movement
Hadassah	American women's Zionist organization
Hashomer Hatzair	Kibbutz-oriented Socialist Zionist youth movement
JAFI	Jewish Agency for Israel
JDC	American Jewish Joint Distribution Committee
Lishkat HaKesher	Israeli government's direct connection to Jews in the former Soviet Union
Maccabi	Organization for Jewish sportspeople and groups
Masorati	Conservative Judaism, traditionalists
Na'amat	Israeli women's labor movement
UJA	United Jewish Appeal
WIZO	Women's International Zionist Organization
WJC	World Jewish Congress
WZO	World Zionist Organization

TERMS

Aliya	Jewish emigration to Israel; literally, "to go up"
Bet din	Traditional Jewish law court
Bikur cholim	Society for visiting ill or home bound people
Charedi	Ultra-Orthodox Jew
Chazan	Synagogue prayer leader, also called cantor
Chevra kaddisha	Jewish burial society
Converso	Spanish or Portuguese convert to Christianity who continued to practice Judaism in secret; also called "New Christian" or, derogatorily, "Marrano"
Dhimmi	A non-Muslim in an Islamic society, with a second-class status
GP	A country's general population
Haskala	Jewish enlightenment movement
JP	A country's Jewish population
Karaites	Jewish sect which recognizes only the written Torah
Kollel	Yeshiva for Orthodox married men
Maghreb	North Africa
Mahalla	Jewish quarter in the Maghreb, Middle East, and Asia
Megilla	The Book of Esther
Mikva	Ritual bath
Nusach	Particular tradition of religious rite
Olim	Jewish immigrants to Israel
Shechita	The slaughter of animals according to the Jewish law
Shtiebel	Prayer room
Tzedaka	Charity

PICTURE CREDITS

Beth Hatefutsoth, The Nahum Goldmann Museum of the Jewish Diaspora, Tel Aviv: 32, 33, 34, 52, 57, 59, 61, 62, 69, 71, 72, 74, 75, 77, 89, 91, 99, 103, 108, 111, 114, 116, 117, 120 ph. Mike Ganor (Israel), 122, 124, 126, 132, ph. Doron Bacher (Israel), 156, 158, 165, 174 ph. Doron Bacher, 196, 199 ph. Micha Bar-Am (Israel), 201, 207, 211 ph. Jan Parik (Germany), 213, 214, 216, 220 ph. Yakov Brill, 234, 235, 238, 244, 245, 247, 248, 249, 252. **The Israel Museum, Jerusalem**: on cover (Stieglitz coll.) 87, 98, 143 (Stieglitz coll.), 190, 194, 198, 188 (Stieglitz coll). **The New York Jewish Museum:** 31, 35, 96, 128, 155, 161, 169, 183. **The Tel Aviv Museum of Art:** 24. **The Wolfson Museum, Hechal Shlomo, Jerusalem:** 81. **The Museum of Italian Jewish Art, Jerusalem:** 106. **The Center for Jewish Art, the Hebrew University of Jerusalem:** 170, 203. **The Jewish National and University Library, Jerusalem:** 232. **Israel Government Press Office, Jerusalem:** 37, 56 ph. Roi Boshi, 180. **The Budapest Jewish Museum:** 145. **The State Jewish Museum in Prague:** 130, 139. **The Sydney Jewish Museum:** 233. **The State Museum at Auschwitz-Birkenau:** 154 ph. Adam Bujak (Poland). **The Janashia Georgian State Museum, Tbilisi:** 172. **Levi Strauss & Co., San Francisco**: 36. **The Jabotinsky Institute, Tel Aviv:** 147. **The Central Archives for the History of the Jewish People, Jerusalem:** 54. **The Israel Philharmonic Orchestra, Tel Aviv:** 25. **Faitlovich Collection of the Elias Sourasky Central Library, Tel Aviv University:** 119. **World Center for Aleppo Jews' Traditional Culture, Tel Aviv:** 79, 206, 209. **The Chabad Youth Movement, Tel Aviv:** 230. **Alfred Moldovan Collection, New York:** 151, 176. **Mordechai Arbell, Jerusalem:** 39, 41, 46, 48, 51 ph. Micha Bar-Am (Israel), 110. **Geoffrey Wigoder, Jerusalem:** 84, 104 ph. Andres Lacko (Israel), 140. **Trionfo Collection, Jerusalem:** 112, 166. **Other Private Collections:** 150, 152. **WJC Archives:** 123, 133, 136, 159, 179. **Jewish Communities:** Canadian Jewish Congress 38, Latin American Jewish Congress 65, Jewish Welcome Service, Vienna, 83, European Jewish Congress 94, Cultural Association of Ukraine 182, South African Jewish Board of Deputies 222, Jewish Community of Nairobi 226, Harare Jewish Community 229, Association Culturelle des Israelites et Sympathisants de Polynaisie, Tahiti, 251.

PHOTOGRAPHERS

David Beller (Israel): 17, **Frederic Brenner** (France): 19, 101, 167, 181, 187, 205, **Sophia Busch** (Germany): 100, **Arieh Doobov** (Israel): 141, 223, **Rivka and Ben Zion Dorfman** (Israel): 134, 160, **Daniel Franck** (France): 93, **Baruch Gian** (Israel): 26, **June Jacobs** (England): 242, **Dominique Jarrassé** (France): 92, 95, **Andres Lacko** (Israel): 27, 150, 152, **Paul C. Margolis** (United States): 42, **Colin McPherson** (Scotland): 16, 23, 239, 241, **Richard Pare** (England): 192, **Serge Weinberg** (Belgium): 85.

INDEX OF COUNTRIES